FROM
GI Brides
~ TO THE ~
Modern Family

65 YEARS OF RELATE NI

Jonathan Bardon (signature)

Jonathan Bardon

Relate Northern Ireland (NI) is a registered charity and a company limited by guarantee. The organisation was established in 1947 and provides relationship counselling services annually to over 3,000 people in 9 centres in Belfast, Foyle, Portadown, Newry, Dungannon, Coleraine, Cookstown, Ballymena and Irvinestown.

Relate NI's services are open to anyone seeking help to deal with relationship issues:
- Married, co-habiting, separating, divorced and LGBT couples
- Family groups
- Young People
- Individuals
- Victims/perpetrators with regard to domestic abuse
- People interacting with the health and social care and criminal justice systems
- Couples preparing for a committed relationship
- Sex therapy

Relate NI is funded by the DHSSPS, the Health and Social Care Board, Health and Social Care Trusts, the Big Lottery Fund, and a range of statutory and charitable bodies, companies and individuals to provide relationship counselling services to the community.

Vision Statement
Relate's vision is a future in which healthy relationships form the heart of a thriving society.

Mission Statement
Relate's mission is to enhance emotional wellbeing in individuals, couples, families and communities by delivering professional counselling and therapeutic services.

Values
ACCESS – our services will be accessible and confidential to all who require them regardless of religion, race, gender, age, disability or sexual orientation.
INTEGRITY- we treat people with respect and dignity and demonstrate our commitment to clients' emotional wellbeing.
PARTNERSHIP - we work in partnership with statutory, voluntary and community organisations thereby contributing to health and social care goals of emotional and psychological wellbeing.
QUALITY - we respond to community needs, are committed to professional standards and monitor and measure what we do to ensure continuous improvement of our services.
LEARNING - we reflect on our practice and that of others so that we continue to be flexible and innovative in how we deliver our services.

Published 2014 by Relate Northern Ireland

3 Glengall Street, Belfast. BT12 5AB
Tel. 028 9032 3454
Fax. 028 9031 5298
Email: office@relateni.org
Web: www.relateni.org
Company Registration No: NI 32111
Charity Registration No: XN 47378A

© Relate NI, November 2014
ISBN 978-0-9931146-0-1

Front cover, image of women at the table: "GI Brides and Friends, Kilkeel, April 1946", by Pat Hudson, used with permission.

Designed by Colourpoint Creative Ltd, Colourpoint House, 21 Jubilee Road, Newtownards BT23 4YH. Northern Ireland.

Contents

relate

Northern Ireland

Foreword

Marriages which were the outcome of whirlwind romances blossoming during the tumultuous years of a world war frequently lacked lasting qualities. In 1946 welfare workers from a range of voluntary organisations, together with lawyers, medical practitioners, clergy and other professionals, were alarmed by evidence of a sharp rise in marital breakdown. Led by Professor J L Montrose, Dean of the Faculty of Law at Queen's University, they were convinced that there should be some independent body to which couples could turn for help – friends and in-laws, Montrose observed, 'were not always the best people to consult in such cases'.

The Marriage Guidance Council had been founded in England in 1938 and, though it suspended its activities during the war, it was now back in action attempting to cope with the flood of people seeking its help. The decision that Northern Ireland should have its own branch was duly made by a group meeting in the Lord Mayor's parlour in Belfast City Hall on 4 September 1947.

The launch of the Northern Ireland Marriage Guidance Council (NIMGC) on 20 October was surprisingly stormy. The great and the good did not hesitate to pledge their support but some used the opportunity to emphasise their own strong views. At the opening meeting Dr Charles Irwin, Church of Ireland Bishop of Connor, after complaining that the 'rising generation' had 'grown up undisciplined and pleasure-seeking', declared that a registry office gave a 'shoddy' form of marriage. Lord Chief Justice John McDermott was even more forthright: after warmly welcoming the establishment of the Council, he assured the audience that registry marriages were 'one of the root causes' of the disruption of family life. A furious debate followed in the letters pages of local newspapers. One correspondent feared that members of the new body would 'merely be interfering busybodies'.

The publicity did at least draw attention to the services being offered by the Council. The organisation at first restricted itself to addressing relationship and marriage issues. Naturally the views held by its most active volunteers reflected the times they were living in. One member had a firm view on the duties of a wife and told the *Northern Whig* that her role in 'feeding the brute' was 'of some importance' and that 'bad housekeeping' prepared the way 'for discord that may end in a broken marriage'. This, however, was a period of rapid social change and NIMGC not only moved with the times but could also be regarded as a force for progress.

In retrospect it is remarkable that the Council could do so much with such slender resources. In 1954 Belfast Corporation awarded its first grant of £200 and the government increased its grant from £200 to £250; and when the annual grant from Stormont was raised to £600 in 1960, it was still a paltry sum. A popular view in the early years was that middle-class ladies with time on their hands would drop in to Bryson House to dispense advice to the poor benighted. In fact, right from the start, preparation for training as a volunteer counsellor was very demanding. Selection, beginning with a residential weekend conference, was always rigorous. Those with strong personal prejudices or a powerful urge to run other people's lives were weeded out – 45 per cent of applicants failed to be accepted. Those who succeeded had to travel regularly to Rugby for intensive training. Qualified counsellors at first had only to give a minimum of three interviews a week; most conducted many more and much time had to be devoted to writing up detailed notes and attending review meetings. And for all of this commitment, counsellors received not a penny.

Demand for the Council's services had grown at such a rate that after twenty years the office space in Bryson House in Belfast's Bedford Street was no longer sufficient. In 1967 a new home at 76 Dublin Road was leased less than half a mile away near Shaftesbury Square. 'Marriages may be made in heaven', the *Belfast Newsletter* declared, 'but more than a few of them are serviced, repaired and renovated in the Dublin Road'.

Superficially, Northern Ireland appeared like any other part of the United Kingdom. But, of course, it was different: society in the region was deeply fractured, with the people divided along confessional lines with clashing political aspirations. Many observers at the time, aware of this, thought that 'the situation' was improving. NIMGC was in step with those who sought to create a more open and tolerant society. At the outset, the composition of the Council was entirely Protestant and, indeed, its first secretary, William Long, was elected as a Unionist MP and given a ministerial post in Captain Terence O'Neill's government. By the time of the move to the Dublin Road the organisation had become more all-embracing and was attracting Catholic members as well as Catholic clients. Presiding at the sixteenth annual general meeting in 1964, Sir Robin Kinahan (a former Unionist Lord Mayor) went out of his way to welcome the recently-inaugurated Catholic Marriage Advisory Service. Contact between the two bodies was established and after one conference in Dublin in 1970 Father M Browne, Director of the Service, commented on the willingness of the organisations to work more closely together: 'It might not yet be a marriage between us, but we are doing a very strong line'.

By then a vibrant civil rights movement, inspired by direct action on the streets overseas, dissolved into intercommunal conflict, plunging Northern Ireland into turmoil. Very quickly Northern Ireland moved from a promising period of cooperation to intense and protracted violence. Though its educational work was disrupted for a time, the Council in extremely testing circumstances was able to increase the number of interviews given to clients. It offered its services not only in Belfast, Derry and Portadown but between 1972 and 1975 extended them also to Omagh, Coleraine, Bangor, Ballymena, Antrim and Downpatrick. Magherafelt and Lisburn were added as centres in 1982.

Relationship difficulties could be found in every social class but the Council was finding that the pressures of life in new housing estates had led to a dramatic rise in the number of marriage break ups in specific areas. Nowhere was this more noticeable than in the new city of Craigavon, which was exceptionally bleak and severely lacking in the usual urban facilities. The *Sunday News* observed, 'Ulster's signpost to a new and prosperous future is turning into the headstone on a multiple grave of broken homes'. The demand for the Council's services in its Portadown centre, set up in 1971, was understandably very strong.

The work of NIMGC was widening all the time. Perhaps the most striking indication that times had changed considerably since 1947 was the opening of a Sexual Function Clinic in the Dublin Road offices. The establishment of this service was the outcome of pioneering work and tenacious advocacy by a dynamic clinical psychiatrist, Dr Ethna O'Gorman, who then acted for many years as an external trainer in this area for the Council. In November 1987 the Council established the Family Mediation Service. The Troubles sometimes had the effect of postponing reforms which had been introduced across the Irish Sea. Epoch-making reforms to divorce laws had been put through Westminster in 1969, but they were not extended to Northern Ireland for nearly another decade. When at last the Matrimonial Causes (Northern Ireland) Order 1978 came into force it included provision for a service of voluntary conciliation which had been lobbied for by NIMGC.

In 1988 the Northern Ireland Marriage Guidance Council was renamed Relate Northern Ireland (Relate NI). This was an outward and visible sign that the organisation had been transformed since 1947. The organisation still depended very heavily on people volunteering to give their time to it without pay, but with a full-time Chief Executive since 1975 it had become a thoroughly professional body. Not only did Relate NI ensure that its staff were highly trained, it also provided quality training to other organisations. In this way it won and maintained a deep respect from professionals in other organisations across the region. Indeed Relate National produced a report in 1992 which identified Relate NI as the top centre in the UK in terms of the total number of courses provided. This was a considerable achievement in view of the disruption caused by a bomb detonated close to the organisation's premises in March 1992.

Relate NI also created a pioneering service which was ultimately adopted by the national body across the United Kingdom. This was RelateTeen, launched by Princess Diana in 1991, which was a service specifically for children of parents who were separating. The scope of Relate NI's work continued to be extended during the last years of the millennium. In 1999 the organisation began delivery of 'Preventing Violence in Relationships', a training programme to address issues of domestic violence and abuse. Indeed, domestic violence was by then featuring in 28 per cent of Relate NI's counselling casework.

The 50th Anniversary in 1997 gave the Chief Executive, John Chambers, the opportunity to reflect on half a century of change. When NIMGC was formed 'it was responding to severe marriage problems largely arising from the strain on relationships during World War Two'. Since then, he continued, an ageing population had seen some remarkable changes in attitudes to love and marriage, including a rise in divorce petitions from 196 to about 2,500; a significant fall-off in marriages; and an increase in those who chose to live together rather than to marry. NIMGC dealt with 103 cases in 1947 and Relate NI had over 2,000 in 1997.

Gerald Clark was in post as Chief Executive when the Dublin Road premises were found to be unsafe and when it moved into the Glengall Exchange in 2004. He oversaw a major shake-up designed, amongst other things, to maximise the returns from resources set aside for training and to increase the availability of counsellors in the evenings. By now counsellors were being paid for their work. Some long-serving counsellors found it impossible to meet the new terms of employment and, having no choice but to withdraw, found it a painful time.

Relate NI offered its services 'to all sections of the community, irrespective of social class, religion, gender, disability, colour, creed or ethnicity' and which, by this stage, included sexual orientation. The number of public bodies depending on the services and training provided by Relate was growing. This explains a major development from the start of the new millennium onwards, the creation of partnerships with a range of statutory, voluntary and community organisations. In 2005-2006, for example, Relate began to deliver counselling services to clients of the Probation Board for Northern Ireland and in Maghaberry Prison.

Gerald Clark, the organisation's longest-serving Chief Executive, had overseen the transformation of Relate NI before he retired in 2011. Dave Murphy, his successor in that post, continued, fine-tuned and expanded those developments. Data from client surveys had been gathered for some time but now increasing attention was being paid to the outcomes of the organisation services. During the year 2012-2013 Relate NI piloted the Clinical Outcomes in Routine Evaluation (CORE) system with a sample of Probation Board for Northern Ireland clients. This was to measure the outcomes of the organisation's services with clients and to promote positive mental health and wellbeing for clients, in addition to demonstrating the impact of the services offered to the Probation Board.

NIMGC had been established to address relationship and marriage issues in a postwar environment. As Dave Murphy explained, 'our development over the past 65 years has reflected tumultuous societal changes' and these he outlined as he continued: 'our counselling services have evolved, developed and diversified to reflect increasing rates of breakdown of couple and family relationships, increasing divorce rates, the development of blended families, sexual and intimacy issues, the impact of domestic abuse, services for children and young people, the impact of addiction issues on families, those interacting with the health and social care and criminal justice systems and more recently the current economic difficulties on relationships'.

Relate NI strives to continue to support people in meeting the challenges they face in their relationships. To do this it provides counselling services to support parents, families, individuals, children and young people where there may be a kaleidoscope of issues. These issues include: alcohol and drugs misuse; mental health problems; joblessness; domestic abuse; and family relationship difficulties. Relate NI's counselling and therapeutic services are designed to provide a safe, secure and supportive family environment – particularly important for children and those clients affected by low esteem and who are liable to be poor decision makers. The evidence is that the design is right: client survey feedback in 2012 revealed that 95 per cent of Relate NI's services were either good or excellent and that 86 per cent said that their emotional wellbeing had improved after counselling.

Jonathan Bardon

Acknowledgements

When Gerald Clark first approached the author, and shortly afterwards Patricia Donnelly chaired a meeting between him and the trustees, no one expected the gestation period to be so long. Relate Northern Ireland is extremely fortunate to have Lynn Davidson in its administration team. Lynn was unfailingly helpful and welcoming from the outset, helping the author, for example, to sort the newspaper cuttings files weighing down Gerald as he brought them to the table. The author would like to thank Gerald Clark and those counsellors, trustees and former senior civil servants who like him submitted to lengthy interviews. They are: Patricia Donnelly, Rosemary Dunlop, Dr Alan Elliott, Julia Greer, Marjorie Houston, Bob Jordan, John Kennedy, Elaine McCormick and Derick Woods. On completion of the draft chapters, a publications subcommittee composed of Alan Elliott, Rosemary Dunlop and Julia Greer carefully scrutinised the text with enthusiasm, expertise and great dedication. Thanks also to Claire Archbold for undertaking a final proof of the maunscript. Their corrections, additions and suggestions have substantially improved the draft presented to them, and the author is most grateful for that help. Sadly, Alan Elliott died just as the task of editing was being completed. Alan wanted to stay on as a trustee to help steer this book towards publication and it is deeply to be regretted that he, Relate NI's longest-serving trustee, did not live to see it in print. Finally, the author has had many enjoyable meetings with Dave Murphy. The aura of great good humour, energy and enthusiasm was infectious as we exchanged one idea after another – a great many of them summarily scrapped – over coffee in his busy Chief Executive's office.

Jonathan Bardon

CHAPTER ONE

The Northern Ireland Marriage Guidance Council: The first decade

The 'forgotten Ulster GI wives'

Total war delivers a more destructive impact on the stability of family relationships than anything else. The Second World War was the most terrible human conflict of all time, taking a toll of an estimated fifty million across the globe. Well over twenty million citizens of the Soviet Union lost their lives, for example, not to speak of untold millions in China where the conflict had begun as early as July 1937. For a time the United Kingdom was fighting alone; there, after families had been dislocated by the evacuation of children, the worst of the suffering was brought about by the Blitz between the late summer of 1940 and the beginning of 1943.

German aerial bombardment of Northern Ireland was brief but terrible. Belfast, the most unprotected city in the United Kingdom, lost nearly a thousand of its citizens during the raid of Easter Tuesday 1941. There the casualties were particularly high because few families had taken advantage of a voluntary scheme to evacuate children to the countryside. By the end of May 1941, however, some 220,000 had left Belfast, over half the population of the city. Nevertheless, Northern Ireland suffered less than most other parts of the UK: German attacks all but ceased after the night of 4-5 May; and conscription was never imposed there.

The United States came into the war in December 1941. Actually American servicemen – described then as 'technicians' – had been arriving secretly many months beforehand, helping to make Derry/Londonderry the main anti-submarine base in the north Atlantic and Castle Archdale a great seaplane centre on Lough Erne. On 26 January 1942 the first American troops officially stepped ashore at Belfast's Dufferin Quay. The region became the principal place where Americans prepared for, first, the North Africa landings and then for the invasion of Normandy.

Over four years around 300,000 Americans made Northern Ireland their temporary home and, at times, US service personnel formed one-tenth of the region's population, then less than one and a half million. At times the American presence led to severe friction. In east Belfast servicemen were 'warned off' Dee Street and 'never came near it'. Joseph McCann recalled that 'girls who had gone out with them were likely to get their hair cut off'. In October 1942 a black GI was killed in a fight between local men and American troops. Such incidents were extremely isolated, however. All the evidence is that, almost everywhere, relations between the Americans and the indigenous population were extremely cordial. African American GIs in particular were impressed by the way local girls frequently asked them to dance. One of them, Benjamin Garrison, remembered: 'The Irish people were very friendly, very cordial, very polite, very courteous'.[1]

Friendships struck up could lead to marriage. Army regulations had been relaxed, even before troops had left the United States, so that servicemen could marry without having to seek permission from their commanding officer. The first wedding took place as early as 13 April 1942, in College Square Presbyterian Church in Belfast, between Private H W Cooke of Cleveland, Ohio, and Miss Thelma Smith from Belfast. A remarkable 1,800 marriages between GIs and local girls followed, even though it was made clear that wives would not automatically receive American citizenship and that they would not be taken across the Atlantic at government expense.

Soon after the end of the conflict, the *Belfast Telegraph* embarked on the 'Forgotten Ulster GI Wives' campaign, claiming that Northern Ireland girls were not being treated as well as their English counterparts in being reunited with their American husbands.

On Thursday 24 January 1946, the *Belfast Telegraph* reported:

Styling themselves "the forgotten GI wives", a hundred or so girls today besieged the US Consulate in Donegall Square South, Belfast, demanding transportation to the United States to rejoin their husbands.

They complained that the Ulster wives of American soldiers had received a "raw deal" compared with English and Continental brides, and told a "Belfast Telegraph" reporter that they intend to send a deputation to the US Army Base in England, armed with a memorial signed by 120 wives. They also threatened to stage a demonstration at Stormont in an effort to get the Prime Minister to intervene.

The arrival of the crowd of excited, chattering girls, some of them with babies, almost caused a dislocation of the office routine, and members of the Consulate had to beg again and again for "a little quietness, please." Nevertheless the girls were received with the utmost courtesy, and six of their number were escorted straight away to an inner office for a heart-to-heart talk with the Consul-General, Mr Quincy F Roberts. They were closeted with the Consul for nearly an hour, while the others waited in the main office.

The Consul emerged to address all the women assuring them that he was 'doing everything to expedite transportation to the United States' and that the Army planned to send a ship to Belfast – 'he was constantly pestering them for a date'. 'Please be patient', he urged. The women then held a meeting on the stairs outside the Consulate. They declared that they were not satisfied with the Consul General's reply. One of their leaders, Mrs Jean Daly from Comber, said: 'Our husbands may be sending us money, but it means that they have two homes to keep going'. She had said to the Consul: 'We are not America mad. All we want is to see our husbands again and to settle down without any more delay'. 'Our husbands are keeping writing and writing', Mrs Mary Drake from Belfast declared, and another said about her husband: 'Mine is going mad. Our baby won first prize in the Ulster-American baby show, and he is simply dying to see it, and me too, he says'.[2]

Undoubtedly many of these marriages were the outcome of whirlwind romances and in the US Army headquarters in London's Grosvenor Square there was mounting evidence that, in the United Kingdom as a whole, many of them were on the rocks. On 30 January 1946 the *Belfast Telegraph* reported that a 'Heartbreak File' was being added to 'with sad regularity'. This file contained particulars of GIs instituting divorce proceedings against their English wives. Unwanted brides faced with notice of divorce petitions – in many cases after the period for launching a defence had expired – were appealing to the American authorities, the Army, the US Embassy and the Red Cross. 'Before a GI bride can sail she must have a written request from her husband', a US Army official stated. 'If she cannot get that we are helpless'. A Public Relations Officer added: 'We help all we can but we can't mend broken marriages'.

Back in Northern Ireland the Consul-General kept his promise. Edgar Sutor, of the US Immigration and Naturalisation Service, opened the doors of his office in 40 Academy Street in Belfast on 20 February 1946 to speed up the vetting of wives and children. Then the 12,000-ton transport vessel, *Henry Gibbons,* arrived in Belfast Lough and on 6 March 1946 314 GI wives and 140 children trooped on board. As the ship began its journey from the Herdman Channel, John Cole reported for the *Belfast Telegraph:*

A group of men from the dock sheds and works gathered on the quay and sang "Land of Hope and Glory" and "Come back to Erin". The GI brides, who had crowded along the deck-rail, responded amid smiles and tears with "when Irish eyes are smiling" and "Auld Lang Syne"… Handkerchiefs were whipped from handbags along the length of the deck rail, kiddies were hoisted a little higher, and brides stood on tip-toe and waved briskly.[3]

A second American vessel, the *James Park,* collected another 219 wives a few weeks later.

Three days before the *Henry Gibbons* left Belfast, on 3 March 1946, the *Belfast Telegraph* carried an article with the headline: 'Marriage Guidance Council Proposed'. This was in a regular column, *News of the Churches*. It reported that, at a meeting of the Church of Ireland Moral Welfare Association for Northern Ireland, a proposal had been made to set up a Marriage Guidance Council. This was referred to the Executive Committee. The Bishops of Down and of Dromore and Connor had called a meeting in connection with Home and Family Weeks. The honorary secretary, Bishop Hind, reported that sermons would be preached throughout the dioceses on Home and Family Life and that the Association would confer with the Dean of Belfast to discuss the possibility of holding a central meeting in Belfast.[4]

The Northern Ireland Marriage Guidance Council – an 'independent body to which married couples could turn for help'

The Marriage Guidance Council came into being in Great Britain in 1938 and, after a suspension of activities early in the Second World War, it was reconstituted in 1942 and again in 1946 when it was renamed the National Marriage Guidance Council. It had the task of coordinating the work of local groups in hundreds of towns. The Presidents were the Bishop of London and Lord Horder and among the vice-presidents were the Chancellor of the Exchequer, Sir Stafford Cripps, and the film and cinema entrepreneur, J Arthur Rank. Following preliminary meetings early in August 1947, the Northern Ireland branch, provisionally named the

Marriage Guidance Council for Northern Ireland, was to be launched on Thursday 4 September. All interested were invited to attend in the Lord Mayor's Parlour in Belfast City Hall and those unable to be there were invited to write to F McIlreavy, Belfast Council for Social Welfare, 50 Dublin Road, Belfast. In its account of this meeting the *Belfast News-Letter* recorded that, after a brief discussion, the 'practically unanimous' decision was made to name it the Northern Ireland Marriage Guidance Council (rather than the Belfast Marriage Guidance Council).[5] The *Northern Whig* gave a full report:

A Marriage Guidance Council for Northern Ireland, to be affiliated with the National Council in England, was formed yesterday at which Professor Montrose presided.

The Council is the direct result of much investigation and discussion of social problems by professional men and women, doctors, lawyers and clergymen, and by welfare workers in various organisations. They all felt, Professor Montrose said, that the happiness of all the people was seriously affected by the lack of such a Council.

They had become increasingly aware, he continued, that many of the court cases which occurred because disharmony had broken out between married people were caused by ignorance of certain fundamental facts, and that they could be prevented by educating people in the real character of the married relationship.

There were, unfortunately, many who regarded it simply as a way of obtaining more pleasure for themselves, and had no realization of the responsibilities involved in it towards each other, their relatives and the community as a whole. This had to be rectified.

Moreover, when disharmony did arise, it was necessary that there should be some independent body to which married couples could turn for help. At present they could call only on their own friends or their families and "in-laws", who, Professor Montrose remarked, were not always the best people to consult in such cases.

The alternative, he continued, was the law courts, to seek separation or divorce. It was the general feeling of lawyers that 'the position all round was not very satisfactory'.[6] The National Council had intervened frequently and successfully in England and it was commonly held that conciliatory tribunals should be established everywhere. 'We believe that an informal tribunal should exist to which such people may go', he said. 'A Royal Commission has recommended that conciliation tribunals should be set up, and receive State support'.[7] Professor Montrose outlined the Council's principles. All its work, he said, would be 'dominated by a conviction' that the normal environment in which children should be brought up was a home in which parents, united in happy marriage, contributed to the moral and physical training of their offspring. 'For this reason', he declared, 'the safeguarding of the family unit, based on permanent monogamous marriage, is vital to the welfare of the race'. The report continued:

Such a marriage was not easy of fulfilment, and it was felt that an adequate course of detailed preparation should be made available to all who were about to marry. It was also a public duty to provide sympathetic and expert treatment for the prevention and cure of marital disharmony so that the tragedy of broken homes, and the evils which followed therefrom might be averted.

During early discussions all creeds had been represented and there had been general agreement on these points. However, he reported, there was 'a split' over what attitude the Council ought to adopt in the matter of birth control, 'which they knew was widely practised in Northern Ireland and for a variety of reasons'. The majority felt that, to ensure that the Council proved effective, it must take this into account – the Council could not take the stand that practices which were widespread should be denounced as immoral. 'It was unfortunate', he said, 'that this decision should have necessitated a break with the Roman Catholic Church, with which they had worked happily up to this point but it was decided that the Council would have to work independently of the Roman Catholic Church henceforward'.[8]

In order to achieve 'the greatest possible variety of opinion and assistance', it was decided that, when the Council was formed, the Executive Committee should contain equal numbers of churchmen, doctors, lawyers and social workers. A temporary executive was formed with Professor Montrose as chairman and Mr J McIlreavy as secretary, its principal task being to launch a publicity campaign for membership and support. The other members of the committee were Bishop Hind, the Rev Dr J L Northridge, the Rev J Mulree, Professor Francis Newark, Captain B Watts, Dr Lothian, Dr Charlotte Arnold, Dr W Brennen, Mrs Barcroft and Mrs T L Sinclair. It was eventually agreed that the inaugural meeting would be held in the Grosvenor Hall on 20 October.

The day before, the *Northern Whig* provided welcome publicity. It explained the Council's origins:

Education for marriage is coming to be regarded as essential as education for any of the professions, and the Marriage Guidance Council of Northern Ireland, which was formed at the beginning of August and is planning to hold a big public meeting in Belfast this month, has been considering the type of training that this should involve.

The Council arose here as a result of investigation and discussion on social problems by a group of professional men and women – lawyers, doctors, clergymen – and by welfare workers attached to various organisations. It has been functioning during the past two months through the Belfast Council of Social Welfare, helping young married couples who have been recommended to seek its assistance.

Though only a comparatively small number have so far come under the notice of the Council the members feel both from a consideration of them and from their previous study that much marital discord might be avoided if there were some initial preparation for marriage.

It is not only education on the big subjects like sex, parenthood and child nursing that is required, they say, but also on such domestic matters as shopping and laundering, cooking and housework.

Many young girls leave school without acquiring any knowledge of domestic economy and go straight into factory or office work. In numerous cases these are the girls who have little opportunity of learning how to sew or clean in their own homes, and when they marry and are faced with great difficulties of rationing and probably also of "making do" in rooms in other people's houses they cannot manage efficiently.

The Council recognises that "feeding the brute" may not be the most important factor in ensuring a happy marriage, but it is of some importance. Bad housekeeping leads to bad tempers and prepares the way for discord that may end in a broken marriage.

'It is this tragedy which the Council hopes to prevent', the article continued. There was a mistaken assumption that this organisation only functioned when a rupture occurred. It was the hope of those associated with this work that it would be broadened to help young people get the most out of their lives. Advice would be both expert and sympathetic and given privately and confidentially. This would be given in the first instance by social workers who had attended special classes organised by the National Council. Later, experts 'who have the appropriate technical or scientific knowledge' would be called in. A panel of consultants – 'clergymen, psychiatrists, physicians, lawyers and economists' – was available to the Council and they were already represented on the provisional committee formed two months earlier.[9]

A 'shoddy form of marriage'? A controversial beginning

Miss Edith Major, Art Florist of Bradbury Place, personally supervised the flower arrangement in the Grosvenor Hall. According to the *Belfast News-Letter*, 'leading clergymen, lawyers, doctors and social workers supported the formation of the Council'. Controversy immediately followed the meeting.

The tone set by the principal speakers was rather different from that intended by most members of the provisional committee. Dr Charles Irwin, the Church of Ireland Bishop of Connor, declared:

For years past, fathers and mothers have shown themselves, in the majority of cases, indifferent to the bringing up of their children, and the rising generation has grown up undisciplined and pleasure-seeking.

What the Council should do, he continued, was, 'quite unequivocally', to enforce the Christian view of marriage, and to discourage register office marriages. A registry office gave a 'shoddy' form of marriage and it was 'so regarded by very many people'. There was a 'want of solemnity and ceremony' about such a wedding and there was no attempt to drive home to the 'minds of the couple' what marriage really meant. A registry office marriage was an 'act by the State and what the State could do the State could undo' – it was 'a sort of experiment which those who participated felt they could get out of it if it did not suit them'. The prime cause of the present 'surge of divorce' was not the war. The moral condition of the country lay at the doors of the parents of the rising generation. Young people rushed into marriage without realising what it meant. 'Discipline, obedience and the moral sense highly developed' were essential for a happy marriage. If the new Council failed to discourage registry office marriages then all its activities would be of very little use.

The Lord Chief Justice, after strongly favouring the establishment of the Council, was even more forthright than the Bishop. Registry marriages were 'one of the root causes' of the disruption of family life. The informality of the service – 'if it could be called a service' – made no impression on those who took part in it. It was a 'back door entry' into married life. 'The sooner the law comes to our aid', he said, 'and insists upon those who wish to enter into the bonds of holy matrimony going into the Church of God the better it will be for the community as a whole'. He denounced the recklessness with which many young people rushed into marriage, and the over-addiction of many of them to dancing and films, drinking and gambling. The *Belfast News-Letter* continued in its report of his speech:

It was deplorable that in recent years much of the stigma attaching to divorced persons had been removed, and he believed that the register office ceremony was one of the root causes of the new approach to marriage. It seemed to offer a back-door entrance to matrimony, and the sooner the law was altered to make a church ceremony compulsory the better.

Dr David Mace, general secretary of the National Council in London and the main speaker, 'agreed with the Bishop that, fundamentally, the issue was religious'. 'Sooner or later', he went on, 'the Church would have to come forward, and state frankly its views about sex and its place in human life, about romantic love, parenthood and family life. What they were facing now was nothing more or less than a fight to save the whole basis of community life.' The 'fundamental causes' for the disintegration of married life were present before the war. These included social and economic changes, the 'new status' of women, the 'scientific attitude' to life, decline of religion and international insecurity following two world wars.

The disintegration was world-wide. He told the audience that it was a chastening thought that Britain, which had taken pride in the fact that her divorce figures were not on the same level as America's, was fast approaching equality. He wished that the figures in Britain were more like Northern Ireland. Before the War, the rate of marriage breakdowns had been one in twenty; in 1943 this had doubled, and in 1946 it had been computed at one in five. The 'mediocre and low grade' marriage was a more real menace than separation or divorce. The community must be persuaded to seek help before 'difficulties had vitiated the whole marriage'. The main task of a Marriage Guidance Council should not be curative, but preventive, and should be largely concerned with the preparation and education of young people for marriage. Professor C H G Macafee spoke briefly to recommend pre-marital medical examination.

Professor J L Montrose, who presided, was more measured in his observations than the Bishop and the Lord Chief Justice. The mounting divorce and separation figures he cited as proof that such a Council was necessary. These had risen from 67 in 1941 to 117 in 1942, and to 174 and 217 in 1945 and 1946. For every case that came into court, he pointed out, there were dozens that did not. It was announced that the newly-formed Council had opened an office at 28 Bedford Street, Belfast, with a secretary, Mrs Muriel Nisbet, in daily attendance. Courses of lectures in cooperation with the Central Council for Health had been arranged for the autumn and winter months. As the Council was dependent on public support, an appeal was made for subscriptions and gifts of office furniture and equipment.[10]

A lively correspondence ensued in the press, largely concerned with the observations made by Bishop Irwin and the Lord Chief Justice. On 25 October, 'R A', writing to the *Belfast News-Letter*, thought 'it would be interesting to know whether these opinions are founded on fact or fancy'. 'R A' continued:

The remedy proposed by the two speakers, namely abolition of civil marriages and making Church marriages compulsory by law, does not seem very realistic today and suggests that the new Council is unlikely to be very practical in its approach to this difficult problem. No doubt the Churches have lost ground in recent years, but they will not regain it by demanding the restoration of powers which they possessed in the middle ages. Also, we have not been told how these register office abolitionists would deal with agnostics, who would certainly be conscientious objectors to compulsory Church marriages...

The writer concluded by asking: 'is there any good evidence to suggest that there is a higher percentage of "bad marriages" today than there was when divorce was so difficult as to be practically impossible for the majority of men and women?'[11] Two days later Stephen Gilbert of Gilnahirk wrote to the *Northern Whig* to say that, having read the report on the inaugural meeting, he would be 'glad of the following additional information':

(a) If a Marriage Guidance Council is formed in Northern Ireland will members have to prove that they themselves have been happily married for many years, or will they merely be interfering busybodies?
(b) Do a greater percentage of register office weddings than of church weddings end in the divorce courts?
(c) Would evidence in cases of bigamy which come before the Courts in Belfast tend to prove that more bigamous marriages took place in (say) St Anne's Cathedral or in the register office in Great Victoria Street?
(d) Why is it desirable that divorced people should be made unhappy by having a stigma attached to them? Or the legal point of view? Or both?

I should also like to point out that any effort to make church marriage ceremonies compulsory is an effort to interfere with religious liberty. People who are not Christians are surely just as entitled to marry as those who are, and it may be against the conscience of many of them to take part in a church ceremony.[12]

A letter to the *Belfast Telegraph*, simply signed 'Reader', expressed disagreement with the Lord Chief Justice:

Sir,– The Lord Chief Justice has spoken against registry office marriages. Does there exist statistical or other solid evidence that the degree of marital superiority is higher among those married in church than among those married outside it? To compel people to submit to ceremonies they consider unnecessary would be the negation of liberty.[13]

An anonymous letter in the Belfast News-Letter assured readers that, though he had been married six years ago in the Register Office 'my wife and myself have enjoyed over six very happy years together. What's more, we have a happy home and, thank God, we have Christ in our hearts as well as in our home. If the reverend gentleman has any doubts about this you are free to give him my name and address. One of many who has found a Saviour in Jesus.'[14]

Another letter to the *Belfast Telegraph*, signed 'A "Back-Door" Entrant', took issue with the Bishop of Connor:

Sir, – One might be allowed to ask: Who has a better right to speak about a marriage in church, as contrasted with a marriage in a registry office, than one who has had personal experience of both methods?

The present writer has had such an experience, and wishes to testify against the somewhat dogmatic deliverance of the Bishop of Connor, who condemns the legal and straightforward ceremony in the registry office as "a shoddy form of marriage". Personally, I found it anything but "shoddy". On the contrary it impressed me as decorous, serious, and even solemn, and entirely adequate both legally and morally.

To any law-abiding and conscientious man or woman, the obligations inherent in this ceremony cannot be in any way inferior or less binding than any marriage ceremony in a church. A vow is a vow wherever made, and no ceremony in a church can make it binding if the contracting parties have no proper respect for a vow deliberately taken. We are informed that during the present year some fifty thousand divorces have occurred in the United Kingdom, the vast majority, we may presume, having had a church ceremony. Would the Bishop of Connor declare that a church marriage is a guarantee against either "shoddiness" or moral slackness?

In his enumeration of the causes of unhappy marriages by Dr D Mace, secretary of the National Marriage Guidance Council, London, not a word was said, as reported, about a "shoddy form of marriage" in a registry office.[15]

One contributor to the letter pages expressed this anxiety about the Council. Having attended the inaugural meeting and 'listened with deep interest to the various speakers, who offered wise counsel':

A Concerned Citizen (Name and address enclosed) on entering the hall was appalled to see women workers (presumably under the auspices of the Council) selling books relating to scientific methods of birth control. The question that occurs to me is: Do these books, sold with the approval of the Council, of which some of our prominent clergymen are members, represent the Christian attitude? Surely, it is vitally important that prominent Church leaders should beware of associating themselves with such pagan practices as are described in these books.[16]

The controversial remarks of Bishop Irwin and the Lord Chief Justice, despite the hostile letters to the press, may actually have helped to give wide publicity to the new Council. In the short term however, the chairman, Professor J L Montrose, had no choice but to write a damage-limitation letter to the press. He was careful not to cause offence to ministers of religion whose support for the Council would be vital:

I feel that your report of the meeting of the Northern Ireland Marriage Guidance Council in the Grosvenor Hall on October 20, may give an erroneous impression of the Council's views.

It should be made clear that, while the Council was honoured by the presence of distinguished speakers, and encouraged by their general support, yet some of the opinions they expressed were nevertheless not those of the Council. The Council emphasises the importance of spiritual values in marriage, and recognises that for most people those values are expressed in the religious creeds to which they adhere. We have ministers of religion on our committee, but the Council is not a sectarian body, nor even strictly speaking a religious body. It is our view that the cause of marriage guidance would not be advanced if the Council were to become a strictly religious body.

Nor does the Council condemn persons who have entered upon marriage obligations in register offices. The Council does stress the importance of due solemnity in such ceremonies, and acceptance of the Council's principles does not prevent anyone from advocating what he considers to be the proper ceremony for marriage, but the Council does recognise that many sincerely conscientious men and women prefer the register office marriage. There is no evidence that marriages solemnised in register offices are more likely to break down than those celebrated in churches.[17]

R A Waugh, writing to the *Northern Whig* after reading Montrose's letter, thought that the Professor and Dr Mace were not actually in agreement. He quoted a recent speech by Dr Mace:

People in the modern world are trying to understand this business of sex and love. They know deep down that they will never understand it till they get hold of its inner spiritual meaning. I believe that the Church has the key. Christianity is supremely the religion of divine love which came down into this world and expressed itself in human life...Can anything bring back love again? I want to say that there is a power in true religion which can sometimes do it. I have seen it happen.

Waugh agreed with these observations but added:

What is the use of trying to mend broken marriages, if multitudes of young couples are entering into marriage with a wrong set of values? How can they weather future storms, if they have no spiritual anchorage?[18]

Montrose felt constrained to write again to reply to 'R A' who had criticised the Council 'apparently without having read its published memorandum or attended its meetings'. He continued:

The Council stresses the necessity for the "scientific study of marriage as a social institution", and, while recognising the supreme truth of spiritual values, is fully aware of the importance of statistical information and practical experience. Co-operation with doctors and social workers is fundamental. One of our aims is to spread scientific knowledge about matters where formerly ignorance prevailed.

He reminded readers that Dr Mace had made it clear that 'it is not true that marriages solemnised in register offices are more likely to break down than those celebrated in church'. The breakdown rate for marriages was one in five – 'out of every five marriages one will terminate in nullity, divorce, or separation at some time, not necessarily in the first year after marriage'. In fact it looked as if the breakdown rate was approaching one in four. He went on to argue that A P Herbert's Matrimonial Causes Act of 1937 was irrelevant to the main issue: 'For every unhappy marriage that gets to the courts there are still many which do not'. The proportion may have been greater before the extension of valid causes for divorce, 'but even if we assume that the proportion of unhappy marriages to total marriages is no greater today than one hundred years ago, is this a reason for complacency?' Montrose concluded:

Even if we assume that the breakdown rate reflects the total of unhappy marriages, is it not appalling when translated into terms of human suffering? The Marriage Guidance Council thinks that some of this unhappiness can be prevented. Will "R A" not help us? We would welcome his co-operation, even if it consists only in criticism of our methods. But would he please discover what those methods really are by communicating with us. We have insufficient funds to advertise our principles and the Press has but limited space. Anyone can obtain a copy of our memorandum from 50 Dublin Road. – Yours, etc.[19]

Raising awareness and funds

On 25 November 1947 the Council met in Belfast City Hall. By now there were 76 members and at that meeting the Executive Committee was appointed. They were: Professor Montrose, chairman; the Right Rev Dr John Hind; the Rev Dr W L Northridge; the Rev J L Mulree; Professor F H Newark; Dr Charlotte Arnold, Dr K Sax; Mrs M Grummitt; Mr J Barbour; Mr R Watts; and Mr Wilfred Brennen, FRCS. The chairman made an appeal for financial help, pointing out that the work of the Council was being done by honorary workers and that the need for a paid secretary was great. He issued an invitation to any organisations which would care to have lecturers to talk to them on marriage guidance.[20]

And so the lecture programme got under way. One series, promoted jointly by the Council and the Central Council for Health Education, advertised a 'Lecture Course on Parenthood and Child Care' in Bryson House, 28 Bedford Street, Belfast, starting on 30 September 1948 at 7.30 pm. The fee was 7/6. They were: 'Aims and Possibilities: The Physiology of Sex' by Mr Wilfred Brennen; 'The Psychology of Sex' by Dr K Sax; 'Answering the Child's Questions' by Dr Alexandra Sloan; 'Preparation for Adolescence' by Mr Brennen; 'Guidance for the Young Adult' by Dr Sax; 'The

Difficult Child' by Dr Sax; and, in conclusion, a 'Brains Trust'. The advertisement explained:

Films will be shown following some of the lectures. Demonstrations dealing with clothing and layettes, and information on budgeting and expenses will be included. While this course is primarily for parents and engaged couples it will contain information of value to others, such as factory welfare workers, nurses, and teachers who are responsible for children and adolescents.

In the same year the two organisations also organised lecture courses 'for young adults over the age of 18' and 'for Engaged Couples' which added to the speakers referred to above Mrs A L Irwin, BA, LLB, on 'Social Aspects of Marriage', Rev R R Cunningham on 'Happy Marriage' and Mrs Seth MA on 'Answering the Children's Questions'. Lectures were also arranged for Council members. Some of these were reported in the newspapers. One was by Dr George Seth, Head of the Department of Psychology at Queen's University. 'We have yet to arrive at some solution of the problem of the woman who has to combine an outside job with marriage and home-making', he said.

Despite the fact that the marriage rate for women between the ages of 20 and 45 has risen from 47 per cent to 54 per cent now the child population continued to decrease, he said: the so-called "parents' revolt" and the loss of interest in the home by working women were factors in this tendency towards smaller families.

Many of the difficulties were emotional and neurotic, he said, and if we wanted to maintain the family as the central unit of society we should have to face the problem of the mental health of prospective clients as we faced up to the problem of the mental health of our soldiers during the war.

Another report added that he believed that 'he thought the solution was to find what kind of employment could best be combined with the demands of a home and a family... The problems of psychological adjustment and mental health were likely to lead to the breakdown of individual marriages, and help should be available in their adjustment. There should also be educational preparation for marriage of boys and girls'.[21]

Though all of these lecturers gave their services without payment, the Council desperately needed more funds to continue and extend its work. Professor Montrose made an appeal to the press in October 1949. This letter began with an acknowledgement of a large anonymous donation:

Sir, – I should be obliged for space in which to afford public recognition of a donation of some £400 which has recently been received by the Northern Ireland Marriage Guidance Council. The liberality of the donor is equalled by his modesty (he desires to remain anonymous) but my Committee feels that only a public statement is a sufficient expression of our gratitude.

I must add that this donation has not solved the financial difficulties of the Council. We have paid off some of our debts, but we still have an overdraft. Relying as we do entirely on voluntary contributions, we appeal for further support. The large number of cases that come to us daily from all parts of the Province necessitate us employing a full-time secretary. He is seriously over-worked, and we appeal to the public not only for financial support, but also for assistance in interviewing applicants. We should be very grateful for help from those qualified to interview husbands and wives who are experiencing matrimonial difficulties. A course for those interested in marriage guidance has been organised in conjunction with the Home Office. Particulars can be obtained from our secretary at 28, Bedford Street, Belfast.[22]

Members of the Council helped to give publicity to its work by giving talks elsewhere. One meeting was held in Ballygomartin Presbyterian Church Hall. Here Miss M E G Martin MBE said to the audience that 'although the number of divorces and the illegitimacy figure for Northern Ireland were not as bad as in England, they were nevertheless problems about which they had reason to worry'. Mrs M Nesbit said that it was not until she became secretary that she realised the need for such a Council. Now there was a full-time secretary and Montrose was right in pointing out the problems of finding money for the Council's work. Much of the funding was obtained from 'bring-and-buy' sales, offering, in addition to coffee, fruit, vegetables, cake stalls, grocery stalls, white elephant stalls and 'work'. Among those agreeing to open these events was Lady MacDermott, wife of the Lord Chief Justice, and Mrs J Maynard Sinclair, wife of the Minister of Home Affairs (the minister was later drowned in the *Princess Victoria* disaster on 31 January 1953). The support of prominent citizens was considered vital and the Council's profile was raised further when Lord Denning, chairman of the Denning Commission on Divorce Law, was the principal speaker at the annual general meeting on 7 January 1949. A 'Grand Concert' was held in the Wellington Hall on 19 April 1949, 'Admission Unreserved 2/6; Reserved 3/6. Servicemen and women in Uniform Half-Price'. Artists included George Beggs, May Sterrett, Rhoda Melville, Will Dunn, Doris Randewich, The Monarian Troupe (with Albert Edwards), Alfie Donnelly, The Fowler Brothers, The Rhythm Sisters (with Tony Forte) and Jimmy Gillespie, with Terry O'Dare as compere.[23] Later in the year Professor Montrose made another appeal for funds and for volunteers. As he explained, expenses had increased as a result of an extension of the Council's services:

A recent appeal was sufficiently successful to make it possible for us to have an interviewer present on Monday morning from 10 am to 12-30 pm, and to assure the presence of two interviewers at other times when hitherto owing to their large numbers, inquirers have had long periods of waiting.

The response to the previous appeal was gratifying, but we are still in need of further voluntary interviewers, and we should also be grateful for offers of voluntary clerical assistance.

Even with these voluntary helpers, the increase in our work, which still continues, involves us in further financial expenditure...[24]

The Council's entry in the Charities Year Book of 1949 provided readers with details of its guiding principles and aims. It began:

One of the urgent needs of the present day is the safeguarding and strengthening of the family unit, the basis of our social order. But, though the importance of the family is generally recognised, facilities are inadequate for education in the knowledge required for a happy marriage and for the guidance of those who have encountered difficulties in their marital relations.

The Northern Ireland Marriage Guidance Council provides some of these facilities and strives for their improvement.

The Council's basic principles were:

1. The normal environment in which children may be brought up to become worthy and honourable citizens is a home where two parents, united in happy marriage, both contribute to the physical, moral and spiritual training of their offspring. For this reason the safeguarding of the family unit, based on permanent monogamous marriage, is vital to the welfare of the race.
2. Sustained and disciplined effort, on the part of both partners is required in order to build up such physical, mental and spiritual harmony as can bring the marriage relationship to full maturity.
3. We owe it to the rising generation to provide its members with such guidance and instruction as may safeguard them from wrong attitudes and false judgments and train them in the right approach to marriage.
4. An adequate course of detailed preparation should be made available to all who are about to marry.
5. It is the right basis for personal and social life that sexual intercourse should not take place outside marriage.
6. It is a public duty to provide sympathetic and expert treatment for the prevention and cure of marital disharmony, that the tragedy of the broken home and the evils which necessarily follow from it may be averted.
7. Since parenthood brings to marriage not only the fulfilment of its union but also one of its deepest satisfactions, everything possible should be done to promote fertile unions.
8. Self control is an important element in the proper conduct of sexual relations in marriage. Contraception should not be used to enable people to escape the duties and discipline of marriage and parenthood. If it be used by married couples to regulate the spacing of their children it should be practised only in accordance with the methods advised by the medical profession.
9. Every effort should be put forth to bring about a state of society in which parenthood should labour under no social or economic disabilities, and in which the welfare of the family shall receive the consideration which, by reason of its importance to the nation and race, it deserves.

The aims of the Council were two-fold:

1. Education: *(a) To encourage in the young a right attitude to marriage by impressing upon parents and all concerned with child welfare the importance of sound knowledge in the right atmosphere. (b) To provide, and to encourage others to give instruction to young adults in the principles of marriage. (c) To give advice on the principles of marriage to engaged couples. (d) To keep the general public informed of advances in the scientific study of marriage as a social institution.*
2. Personal Service and Conciliation: *To provide a panel of trained counsellors to give confidential and sympathetic advice and help in cases where difficulties may have occurred, with a view to restoring happy conditions, and, where appropriate, to enable specialist treatment to be obtained.*[25]

The Northern Ireland Council was attracting some attention across the Irish Sea. This, in part, seems to have been due to the efforts of Captain W.J. Long who had been appointed full-time secretary. An Englishman, who went on to become a Unionist MP in 1962 and served as a government minister at Stormont in 1968-69, Long proved a dynamic and resourceful servant of the Council. In June 1949 Long gave an interview to the *Sunday Dispatch*:

THEY MEND BROKEN MARRIAGES

About 100 couples have been reconciled in Northern Ireland by the Marriage Guidance Council in Belfast.

The council was set up only 18 months ago.

All the 200 husbands and wives had been living apart – some for more than 12 years. Many thought they could never be reunited.

Captain W J Long, the council's secretary, interviewed most of them. They either contacted the council on their own initiative or were introduced by probation officers and other voluntary welfare organisations.

"No case is too difficult for us", Captain Long told me. "In most cases of separation one or other of the parties is anxious for re-union, but lacks the initiative. That is where we come in.

"Co-operation is necessary, and if the rift between the parties appears to be too great our trained counsellors get on the job. We have very few failures.

GIVE AND TAKE

"It is surprising how far a little give and take will go to patch up domestic rifts.

"Childless parents are the most difficult to reunite. There is no doubt that children help to keep together parents who would otherwise drift apart."

Captain Long added that business for the council, which has the backing of the churches, is booming.

In the first five months of this year 300 per cent more cases were dealt with than in the same period last year.

The council also deals with problems of engaged couples, who are given free lectures by experienced officers.

Medical specialists give free examinations, treatment, and advice. Last year 53 medical cases were dealt with successfully.[26]

In October 1949, *Reynolds News* reported on the lecture series 'on just those subjects which should have an appeal to young couples' being run by the Council in Belfast:

LESSONS TO HELP ON LIFE'S WAY

Cooking for instance. That is a subject which will be taught by qualified instructors, who will also give lessons on homecraft. Then there will be lectures on the economic problems of family life, such as house purchase, hire purchase, and generally "how to make ends meet."

SEX LECTURES

The course, to last a month, will also include lectures on physiology and sex psychology.

"We are starting the course because of the great need for it," Captain Long, the secretary told me. "Lack of knowledge of the essentials of life accounts for the growing number of people who come to us for assistance."[27]

By June 1950, *Trinity College Mission Magazine* reported, trained counsellors and specialists were providing help and advice without prior appointment on Monday and Tuesday, 10 to 12.30 and 2.30 to 5; Wednesday and Friday, 2.30 to 5; Thursday, 2.30 to 5 and 7 to 10; and on Saturday, 10 to 12.30.[28] The *Sunday Chronicle* informed its readers that Henry Yellowlees, OBE, FRCP, DPM, the Harley Street specialist who had given expert evidence at several famous trials and whose father had been an elder of the old Fisherwick Presbyterian Church in central Belfast, would be addressing the third annual general meeting in Bryson House on 15 February 1951. The report added:

Since the Council was established three years ago it has been expanding steadily. But unless its funds are now supplemented from official sources it is feared it will be impossible to continue the work on the present scale.

If the service is cut there could be a sharp rise in the divorce rate.[29]

Lobbying the politicians: raising the minimum marriage age

The Northern Ireland Labour Party discussed issues raised by the Council at its annual conference in May 1951. The Pottinger branch put forward a resolution calling on the government to 'to make an order that biology and sex education be put on the curriculum of all State schools as soon as the necessary arrangements can be made by the Ministry of Education.' Captain Long was asked for his opinion of the impending debate in *Reynolds News*. He said:

We feel that a proper attitude to sex is essential as part of the preparation for marriage. It is one of the foundation-stones, although perhaps not the most important. I consider that sex adjustment is the first adjustment that a young married couple has to make.

The report continued:

ADD 'S FOR SEX' TO THE THREE RS

While not going as far as to suggest that sex matters should be taught at school, Capt Long believes that information on the subject should be available to older pupils and that it should be imparted only by medical men.

Aid to parents

"That," he said, *"would be a great help to parents. They might then be able to avoid answering many questions by their children."*

Many parents have thanked the Marriage Guidance Council for its courses on physiology, psychology and household management.

At its April meeting, the Committee of the Marriage Guidance Council is to consider joining with other bodies in an approach to the Government for legislation to raise the age for marriage.

As the law stands, a girl can marry at 12 years and a boy at 14, provided, in the case of Protestants, that parental consent is given.

An attempt to raise the marriage age to 16 for both sexes was made in 1946, but the Bill, meeting with opposition from Government supporters, was withdrawn.[30]

The Council had considerable success in stimulating a debate on the marriage age. Bishop John Hind, a member of the executive, effectively launched the campaign when he wrote to the press early in 1951. He asked whether or not the public was aware in Northern Ireland that girls could marry at 12 and boys at 14, after the banns had been issued. The consent of parents was not even required for marriages in the Catholic Church. A clause in the Matrimonial Causes Bill, before parliament at Stormont, had been withdrawn – 'we are told...because a majority of the members was opposed to this much-needed and long overdue reform – a reform which was passed in Britain many years ago'. He continued:

The explanation is not convincing...Is the Northern Ireland Parliament not as free as the British Parliament? I would suggest that all the civilised electors in Northern Ireland write to the members who represent them in the Ulster Parliament and demand that the clause be put into the Bill.

This is not merely an academic question. Several cases of child marriage have come to my notice in recent years. China, India and other non-Christian lands are rapidly reforming their laws to abolish child marriage. Ulster claims to be a Christian land. The withdrawal of this clause from the Bill is tantamount to framing legislation sanctioning child marriage.[31]

The objection to allowing child marriages, even with the consent of parents, was that this led to 'marriages of necessity' which frequently proved to be an unhappy solution. On 16 September 1951 the *Sunday Chronicle* reported that welfare workers in Northern Ireland were to start 'a new drive' in support of a campaign to raise the legal marriage age:

Appeals sent recently to the Ministry of Home Affairs, I learn, have been rejected on the ground that when a similar move was made in 1946 it claimed only limited backing.

The Ministry, though sympathetic, feels that the position has not changed since then. Officials of the Northern Ireland Marriage Guidance Council and the Church of Ireland Moral Welfare Association are not satisfied that this is the case. They believe there is a strong body of opinion in favour of an immediate revision of the Act.

"I have not yet met anyone who approves of the existing legislation," said Bishop John Hind, hon Secretary of the association, yesterday. "It is a deplorable state of affairs. I can't imagine what our MPs are thinking about to allow it to continue."

Bishop Hind, who is to state the case for the raising of the marriage age in the national magazine of the Marriage Guidance Council, will also make a new appeal to members of the Northern Commons when they return after the summer recess.[32]

The Northern Ireland Marriage Guidance Council submitted a memorandum to the Minister of Home Affairs, pointing out that 'medical men' considered 16 years as the most appropriate minimum age for marriage as it 'is certain that neither a girl of 12 nor a boy of 14 could possibly have reached a state of development and stability sufficient for marriage'.

The Minister, Brian Maginess, was won round. Within his own circle, Maginess was noted for his liberal views and soon after he was to infuriate many of his colleagues and backbenchers by banning some Orange parades and by proposing that Catholics should be allowed to join the Unionist Party. In his reply to the Council's memorandum the minister expressed sympathy with the proposed reform but recalled the unfavourable attitude of the Northern Ireland Parliament in 1946: 'Since then he has obtained the support of the Cabinet for a new Bill but this has yet to receive the approval of the Unionist Parliamentary Party'.

Then, the *Belfast Telegraph* reported on 24 October, the Age of Marriage Bill introduced by the Minister of Home Affairs 'is likely to be passed without opposition from Government supporters'. No objections were offered by the Unionist Parliamentary Party. The newspaper's explanation for this change of heart was that most of the MPs refusing to countenance legislative change in 1946 'are no longer in the House'. The Registrar-General issued a Blue Book which was a guide to the requirements of the marriage laws 'in each of the territories of the British Commonwealth and in Eire' (Éire had actually become the Republic of Ireland in April 1949). The *Belfast Telegraph* produced a summary:

Minimum ages for marriage differ widely. In Tasmania it is 18 for the man and 16 for the woman. In Ontario 14 for both sexes; in Saskatchewan 15. New Brunswick has no statutory restrictions as to age.

In England the minimum is 16, but in Northern Ireland and Eire, the ages are 14 for the man and 12 for the woman.[33]

The amending legislation duly made its passage through Stormont in November 1951 but in the following spring the National Marriage Guidance Council was suggesting that the minimum age of 16 was too low and should be raised by the Westminster parliament. A J Brayshaw, the National Council's general secretary, spoke in Belfast in April 1952 at the Northern Ireland Council's fourth annual general meeting. He said that the National Council was advocating the raising of the legal age for marriage above the present minimum of 16 in Britain. He said that the 'equality of the sexes' movement had led to an increase in marriage breakdowns in many parts of the world. He added hastily that he was no Victorian 'with side whiskers and drain pipe trousers', and continued:

I do not mean that the sexes should be regarded as unequal, but that it is an outmoded pattern of marriage which is breaking down. In the old days what Grandpa said was law.

Nowadays husbands and wives had got to discuss things, he said, and it was inevitable that there should be more opportunities for disagreement. He believed that this state of affairs had made marriage richer and more worth while, with fuller opportunities, but also more difficult. The breakdown of the 'old patriarchal form of marriage' meant the difference between a dictatorship and a democracy. 'We have the adventurous task of learning how to make the most of the new pattern of marriage'. The report in the *Belfast News-Letter* continued:

Other reasons for marriage breakdown given by Mr Brayshaw included the decline in religion, war and the fear of war, the housing shortage, and living with in-laws. Incompatibility, often given as a reason, was a lovely word that usually excited great sympathy. He was not quite sure what it meant.

Of all the immediate causes of a breakdown the two outstanding ones from which others sprang were selfishness and emotional immaturity.

Marriage today was something for mature men and women, and the Council hoped that eventually the marriage age would be raised from 16 to 17 or 18.

In England and Wales in recent years for every six new marriages contracted one existing marriage had broken down to the point of going to the courts.

The Marriage Guidance Council was trying to prevent the desire for divorce from arising, by education, preparation and conciliation. In England and Wales the taxpayer was paying 100 times as much to subsidise divorce as to marriage organisations which tried to prevent the desire for it.[34]

An item in the *Belfast Telegraph* on 14 May 1952 demonstrated that the amending legislation raising the minimum marriage age to 16 had created a new problem. Speaking at the Church of Ireland General Synod, Mr J M Lamb, representing Down, seconded a report submitted by the Temperance and Social Welfare Society. He said that the amending legislation had:

created a new Border traffic. When a licence has been refused in Northern Ireland the children concerned have been known to cross into Eire and after the necessary residence period have been married without difficulty.

The Society should press for amendment of the law in Eire to bring it into line with the law in Northern Ireland.[35]

Training volunteers in a fast-expanding organisation

The grant of £150 from the Northern Ireland government – extremely modest though it was – enabled the Council to train up more volunteers. The *Daily Express* reported on 15 September 1952 that fourteen 'men and women volunteers for the work of mending broken marriages will shortly go through a searching test at a Northern Ireland seaside hotel'. The location was to be kept secret and over the weekend the volunteers were to be under the constant supervision of a psychiatrist and four other specialists and headed by Mr A H B Ingleby, Education Secretary to the Northern Ireland Council. The report continued:

The object of the meeting is to find suitable candidates for training as counsellors at the Guidance Council's Northern Ireland headquarters in Belfast.

The system of selection is similar to that employed during the war in the choice of Service volunteers for special duties, and its new use has been approved by the British Home Office.

The council handles about 500 cases a year in Northern Ireland. This number could be doubled by the enlistment of a part-time staff of unpaid experts.[36]

Indeed, the activities of the Council were almost unfailingly reported in the local press and, on occasion but to a surprising degree, in the national press. The fifth annual report, surveying the work of the year 1952 and issued in March 1953, demonstrated how its services had expanded since 1947. Out of 278 new cases of substantial matrimonial difficulties in which counsellors took a hand that year, success 'in restoring happy relations' was achieved in 105 and there were 41 cases in which efforts proved unsuccessful. Most of the successes were in the 'adjustment' group, where there was some difficulty but husband and wife were still living together. The report observed: 'It is very important that we should be able to help people at the earliest possible moment, for as time goes on the chances of success diminish'. In adjustment cases the Council found that many more husbands than wives refused to cooperate, but, when a reconciliation was required, it was more often the wife who refused to cooperate. Wives approached the Council more often over minor difficulties but more husbands sought help when a separation had occurred. The Council also dealt with 223 minor cases during 1952, making a total of 501, 13 more than in 1951. There were 888 separate sessions and 27 people were visited in their homes.

Proposed changes in legislation on marriage seem to have been in contemplation almost every year. In 1952 the Royal Commission on Marriage and Divorce, was sitting in London and, in November the Law Society presented its recommendations. Its memorandum suggested that measures should be taken to prevent the possibility of young persons marrying within a few days of meeting. Another proposal was a change in the definition of the term 'desertion' to ensure that there should be no stumbling block to reconciliation, and that a petitioner should not lose his or her right to a decree merely because, in a genuine attempt at reconciliation, the parties had lived together for a period during the time of desertion. The abolition of collusion as a bar to divorce was also recommended. It suggested that no special machinery should be set up to effect reconciliations. The Society opposed any provision being made for deduction of maintenance from pay:

We consider that the proposal is undesirable as it would put an undue burden on employers. Further we take the view that an employee's personal affairs should not have to be disclosed to his employer.

If the proposal were adopted, in our view it might well result in some cases in the employer terminating the employee's appointment.

In recommending the abolition of proceedings for judicial separation, the memorandum quoted five such petitions by husbands and 78 by wives in 1950 and continued:

The experience of solicitors has been that proceedings for judicial separation, since the decree does not enable either party to remarry, have generally been abused and have been instituted or threatened for vindictive reasons or for purposes of extortion.[37]

The Rev D L Graham, Headmaster of Portora Royal School, was the principal speaker at the Council's annual general meeting in Bryson House on 12 February 1953. He said that he did not believe that sex education should be given in classes but that it was a matter for 'private talks'. In its report, the *Northern Whig* continued:

It should, he holds, be mixed up with the teaching of Scripture throughout the whole school, so that at the end a boy has absorbed the Christian idea of marriage without knowing it. He himself did it most by virtue of being a parson rather than a school master...

At a dance, he told the meeting, he had asked all his partners for their observations on preparations for marriage, and they all said that the only thing that mattered was to have a happy home life, and that if one had that then one was sufficiently well prepared for marriage. It was extraordinary how unanimous they all were.

He went on to say that much could be done in marriage preparation for children in the elementary schools because up to the age of 14 a child was 'not very interested in the subject'. That meant that ninety per cent of the population leaving school were not of an age to think about marriage, and so were left mainly to the Churches. This observation is a striking indication that, even at this late date, the Northern Ireland Education Act of 1947, providing secondary education for all, was very slow in its implementation, most notably in Co Fermanagh, where Portora School was located.

Rev Graham felt that the Marriage Guidance Council had a role to play in assisting the clergy:

Sometimes he asked the clergy how often they preached on marriage. It was extremely seldom, and yet marriage was a subject of immediate interest to anyone over 15. In Northern Ireland 92 per cent of the marriages were celebrated in a church and every engaged couple went to see a minister or priest.

The Marriage Guidance Council, Mr Graham said, should make a drive at the clergy. He thought, too, that the Council should press for a primary court to be established in Northern Ireland where before a divorce was granted there should be some attempt at curative treatment and reconciliation.[38]

Not all, however, particularly on the other side of the Irish Sea were content that the clergy should be playing such a central role. On 16 April 1953, Mrs Enid Watson, MP for North Watford and secretary of the Divorce Law Reform Union, told the national conference of Labour women in Edinburgh that Marriage Guidance Councils were 'a very good idea' but that they were in the wrong hands – 'They are ridden by parsons', she said. She continued:

Any sitting of counsellors generally consists of a parson, a lawyer, a middle-class woman who is happily married, and anybody who has wealth and leisure enough to attend these things. A rich person cannot enter into the conditions of the poor, so we cannot expect that a happily married person can understand all the conditions that make a marriage intolerable.

Marriage Guidance Councils did not touch the real problems, she argued. They never advised a woman as to how to get a separation or the proper steps to take for a divorce. 'They concentrated on sending back married couples to try again. This is all to the good, but it doesn't go far enough', she declared. She thought they ought to be reconstituted so that they could do their work fully. Mrs Watson was opposing a motion deploring a 50 per cent cut in grants to organisations providing marriage guidance services. Miss Mary Sutherland, chief woman officer of the Labour Party, did not agree with her: 'I don't think the national joint committee of the Working Women's Organisations would accept these strictures. They will continue to oppose any reduction in the grant.'

Certainly, the Northern Ireland Council was becoming ever more anxious about resources. The treasurer, Mr F McIlreavy, in presenting the accounts in March 1954, referred to the poor financial support given to the council by the public. Subscriptions the previous year had amounted to only £155 18s. 'This would not pay a labourer's wages for six months', he said, 'and I think it is time the public recognised the service this Council is giving to the community'. He continued: 'I wonder if the public fully realise how much we are doing to settle broken homes and save children from growing up in an unhappy family atmosphere'.

More money was required primarily because demand for the council's services was growing. 'We have as many cases on hand as our present staff of counsellors can deal with effectively', Captain Long explained. 'Unless we have more trained people it will be almost impossible to take on any more cases, especially from outlying districts'. He said that of the 244 substantial cases dealt with, the difficulty had been overcome in 44. In 48 cases an improvement had been made, but owing to lack of cooperation from husband and wife, there had been failure in 37 cases. Referring to the fact that in 90 cases the result was uncertain or unknown, Captain Long said, 'Some may have been successful'.

Mrs Irene Evans, a member of the National Marriage Guidance Council, gave the main address, entitled 'Making the Most of Marriage'. She said that Leeds Corporation had provided the council in that city with £500 a year over the past five years. She earnestly hoped that Belfast Corporation would follow the example of Leeds. The *Belfast Telegraph* report continued:

She expressed the hope that Belfast Corporation would recognise the valuable work of the Northern Ireland Marriage Guidance Council in the form of an annual grant. If a grant were made it would be possible not only to promote human happiness but also to save a large amount of money. In the "problem" family, where there was need for the children to have special authorities to look after them and where there were delinquents in the home, assistance would have to come from the local authority.

In many cases, this resulted from a lack of understanding between husband and wife, she said. Mrs Evans contrasted the pattern of Victorian age marriages, when the husband was the "boss", with those of the present day.

Between the wars, the emancipation of women not only through the right to vote but through the way in which so many of them went out to work and pull their weight in society had resulted in an enormous change today.

She found that criticism of divorce was much stronger in Northern Ireland than in the rest of the United Kingdom. 'I think you have, as a country, held on to principles more than we have in England', she said. Young people were reading of film stars being married 'three, four or five times', and it was difficult for them to sort out how grown-ups really behaved when the 'illustrations of married life were so diverse and in some cases even immoral'. On the question of the Press she said: 'We have much to be thankful for, for the services rendered by the Press, but there are some stories in which too much emphasis is put on the physical side of marriage, and there is a tendency to make too much of abnormalities.' She referred to the fact that the marriage rate in Northern Ireland was lower than it was across the Irish Sea – 13.7 per 1,000 of the population, compared with 16.4 in England. That meant that the expectation of marriage for 'Irish girls was not so high as for English girls'. If the present trend of marriage continued in England, 95 per cent of girls under the age of 30 were likely to marry, she believed.[39]

Emigration, particularly of young women, leaves its mark

Actually, the figures quoted by Mrs Evans for 'Irish girls' were for Northern Ireland only. The marriage rate in the Republic of Ireland at that time was extraordinarily low. This was primarily the result of an extraordinarily high rate of emigration – nearly 200,000 left the state, mainly for Britain, between 1951 and 1956, the average annual loss of 39,353 persons being the highest recorded since 1900. Most of the migrants were young and the rise was largely accounted for by the doubling in the numbers of women leaving between 1946 and 1951. For every 1,000 males emigrating there were 1,365 females. The strong demand in Britain for nurses largely explains why 72 per cent of female emigrants were under the age of twenty-four; most of these young women left Ireland in order to take up training in nursing. This great outflow naturally led to major distortions in social patterns. 'In short,' John A O'Brien concluded in *The Vanishing Irish*, a book published in 1954, '64 per cent of Ireland's population is single, 6 per cent widowed and only 30 per cent married – the lowest in the civilised world'.

Emigration figures from Northern Ireland to Britain (by far the favoured destination) were not available. More urbanised and industrialised than the twenty-six counties, the six counties certainly were not losing its young people at the same rate as in the south. However, the habit of emigration was strong in Ulster and had a longer history there than in the rest of the island. Small family farms – smaller on average than in the Irish Republic – predominated in Northern Ireland and it was in the countryside that the marriage rate had been falling and the age of marriage had been climbing ever since the Great Famine in the 1840s. Only one son inherited the farm and he generally delayed marriage not only until his father died but often until his mother (usually considerably younger than his father) had also died. The son inheriting might well be in his forties by the time he was seeking a wife and, if his farm was small with a low income, he might experience great difficulty in persuading a girl to accompany him to the altar. His plight was memorably versified by 'The Bard of Tyrone', the Presbyterian minister and broadcaster, W F Marshall (1888-1959) in his ballad 'Me an' me Da':

I'm livin' in Drumlister,
 An' I'm getting very oul',
I have to wear an Indian Bag
 To save me from the coul'.
The deil a man in this townlan'
 Wos claner raired nor me,
But I'm livin' in Drumlister
 In clabber to the knee...

But cryin' cures no trouble,
 To Bridget I went back,
An' faced her for it that night week
 Beside her own thurf stack.
I axed her there, an' spoke her fair,
 The handy wife she'd make me,

I talked about the lan' that joined
– Begob, she wudn't take me!

So I'm livin' in Drumlister,
 An' I'm gettin' very oul'
I creep to Carmin wanst a month
 To thry an' make me sowl:
The deil a man in this townlan'
 Wos claner raired nor me,
An' I'm dyin' in Drumlister
 In clabber to the knee.[40]

Other siblings who opted to stay on the farm (sharing the house with the proprietor or brother) almost always remained celibate. Others left to work in the towns and cities or to take advantage of the opportunities opened up by the 1947 Education Act to join a profession. In Ireland, uniquely, young women emigrated in greater numbers than young men in the 1940s and 1950s and it is likely that this was also true of rural Northern Ireland. Farming was then Northern Ireland's biggest industry – a situation which would change markedly from the 1960s onwards.

In March 1954 W F McCoy, Unionist MP for South Tyrone, announced his intention of putting forward a Private Member's Bill at Stormont, with the full backing of the Northern Ireland Marriage Guidance Council. This was to enable a minor to apply to a Summary Court for permission to marry where consent was withheld, unreasonably or arbitrarily, by a parent or guardian. Because the proposal 'has aroused the fears of some', Dr W R Sloan, Chairman of the council, wrote to the *Belfast Telegraph* in support:

I am informed a similar provision is made in England. Although its operation to some extent is dependent on the judgment and ability of the individual magistrate it is regarded by the National Marriage Guidance Council (whose counsellors are now in regular attendance at matrimonial courts in Belfast) to assist him to determine whether in fact there is a stable attachment between two young people and whether they are in a position to support themselves in the world.

If such is the case, then unreasoning or unreasonable parents may impose a cruel strain on such young couples with very undesirable results.

Illegitimate conception and forced marriage alike constitute a poor start to marriage. A measure such as this seems likely to diminish the incidence of both.

I would, therefore, take this opportunity to express the hope that this provision of a human and sensible protection against possible parental injustice will find its way on to the Statute Book.

Extending 'activities from the city to the country districts'
Meanwhile, the Northern Ireland government had increased its grant to the Council by £50, raising the annual subvention to £250, with promise of an additional £50

the following year. Belfast Corporation had for the first time made a grant of £200. Nevertheless, Mr F McIlreavy, the hon Treasurer, warned the annual general meeting in March 1955 that the Council required an annual income of £2,500 if it was to maintain its work. The present income was under £1,000 per annum. 'Unless the public comes to our aid, we cannot continue working at our present rate, let alone expanding', he declared. Captain Long, presenting the annual report, said that the number of cases dealt with continued to rise in 1954. There were 572 new cases and of these 259 were of a substantial nature requiring the help of counsellors. The council now had a panel of sixteen counsellors. The first training course for counsellors had been completed in March 1954. The vice-chairman, Wilfred Brennen, told the meeting that the organisation needed to extend its services beyond Belfast:

Many country people travel to Belfast to seek the advice of the Northern Ireland Marriage Guidance Council it was stated at the Council's annual meeting last night, when the need to extend its activities from the city to the country districts was put forward.

The vast majority of all the cases were brought on their own initiative by the people concerned and this, remarked Mr Wilfred Brennen, vice-chairman of the Council, stressed how deep was the need for marriage guidance.

It would appear that many other sources of advice, which were open to people were either not offered or were unknown. The clergy, for example, who had for many years done notable work in this field did not seem to know of the facilities offered by the Council and it was strange that during the past year only six cases were referred by clergymen.

The main address was given by the Rev E C Urwin, formerly secretary of the Department of Christian Citizenship of the Methodist Church in Great Britain. He said that marriages often came to ruin because there had been insufficient recognition of the spiritual basis of the institution. The *Northern Whig's* report continued:

The Church, he remarked, had sometimes been assailed because it had held fast to the principle of a lifelong union with complete fidelity within marriage and chastity outside it. This, he declared, should be regarded as the basis of real love which was something different from romantic love which was, he felt, largely an illusion.

Mr Urwin touched on the problem of mixed marriages and said that although there was no prima facie reason why they should not be a success they did usually come to grief because there was no fundamental unity between husband and wife.[41]

Professor Charles Carter was elected the Council's chairman in 1955. In August he addressed the Belfast Rotary Club. He said that a great deal of juvenile crime and difficulty among adolescents arose from the youths concerned spending their lives in homes subject to marital conflict. While there were 170 divorce cases annually in Northern Ireland, many more cases did not get as far as the divorce court. The Council was dealing with about 600 cases annually, and of this number between 250 and 300 were classed as being 'substantial cases of marriage difficulty'. Those cases were drawn from Belfast and its immediate surrounding areas.

The side of the Council's work which was attracting most notice was the remedial side, which was undertaken by counsellors – part-time voluntary workers – who were willing to go through a rigorous programme of selection and training. Their work did not begin until they were able to have the cooperation of both partners and, of course, the work had to be confidential. 'We have been very fortunate in the type of counsellors we were able to recruit, although there is still need for more workers here', he said. So far as could be judged, he continued, a fair degree of success was being achieved and it was noteworthy that to restore harmony the cost was about £20 per couple, whereas divorce proceedings might cost several hundred pounds. The Council's contention was that the answer to the problem of marital disharmony lay in prevention and early help and not by allowing a case to drag on and reach a hopeless stage. The *Belfast Telegraph* report continued:

There was something wrong with a State which provided on a fairly lavish scale for the dissolution of marriage. In England and Wales provision was made for free legal aid.

Professor Carter said the problem was especially apparent to four groups of people – the clergy, lawyers, doctors and social workers. The causes of the problem, which were complex, included very often the lack of preparation for marriage.

The educational side of the Council's work aimed at reaching people before they got married, and there was a need for reaching young people after leaving school. Young people were often influenced by false ideas they got from films of perpetual bliss and by rather shallow propaganda reaching them from the cheaper forms of the Press.

Professor Carter concluded by reminding the Rotarians that the number of people seeking divorce in the United Kingdom quadrupled during the First World War and rather more than quintupled again during the Second World War. In 1937 about 6,000 were seeking divorce, while in 1939 the number was about 10,000. In 1947 the figure had risen to 47,000, and in 1955 the stabilised figure was around 30,000 per year.[42]

'The council is one of those organisations which remain very much in the background, and one seldom hears much about its work, which, of course, is of a highly confidential nature'. This was included in an article 'by our correspondent' entitled 'Woman's View: Work of the Marriage Council' in the *Belfast News-Letter* on 10 October 1955. Actually, the Northern Ireland Council continued to receive regular and supportive coverage in the press. This feature began:

The "happy-ever-after" ending of many stories and films has led a lot of impressionable young girls into thinking that this rosy future is in store for most of us. Some of them even enter into matrimony with an entirely false conception of what a real and happy partnership should be. It would be quite wrong to say that this is solely responsible for the majority of broken marriages; but the Northern Ireland Marriage Guidance Council does regard it as one of the general causes.

She explained that the sixteen counsellors now were covering the counties of Antrim, Down and Armagh. After stressing how thoroughly they were trained, she continued:

It is not possible to give accurate figures of the successes as counsellors do not follow the cases up. People who go to them in time of trouble, they say, do not want to be reminded of it a year or so later. In a number of cases, however, the people themselves come to tell them what the result has been, so they do know that they have a reasonable standard of success.

The work of the council is divided into two departments – education and conciliation. The former aims at assisting couples to achieve the greatest possible happiness and satisfaction in their married life, and the latter at bringing husband and wife together again when a marriage has broken down, or is in danger of doing so...

The first thing that the counsellors learn is to understand the difficulties of both husband and wife. A great deal of care is taken to persuade both partners to give their full co-operation. The chief advantage to the pair is that they are able to tell their troubles to a sympathetic, understanding impartial person who tries to get them to see each other's point of view, and so find a solution of their problems.

Shortly afterwards, the same correspondent reported that the council would be joining with the Mothers' Union (Church of Ireland dioceses of Connor, and Down and Dromore) and the Church of Ireland Moral Welfare Association (northern dioceses) to host the first 'Home Making' conference to be held in Northern Ireland. She continued:

They are of the opinion that young people today are surrounded by influences which encourage a cheap and superficial view of marriage. Although they admit that it is easier to see the need for action than to know what to do about it, I feel that they are taking a truly progressive step forward with the sponsoring of this conference.[43]

Seeking to advise young people
Interest in the conference was stimulated by the recent publication of a report published by the King George's Jubilee Trust, *Citizens of To-morrow*, in which the Trust 'attempted to sift all the available evidence on what was wrong with the younger generation, and to make suggestions as to what should be done'. The aim was eventually to create a special body uniting the specialised organisations and so offer comprehensive advice to young people. Introductory addresses were to be given by Patricia McLaughlin, MP, and Professor Finnegan, principal of Magee University College, and Professor Carter would preside.

The conference was being held in the belief that 'it can by no means be taken for granted that young people in this province will come to marriage adequately prepared for the practical problems of home making, or with a sufficient understanding of the spiritual nature of the great adventure they are beginning'. More than 150 delegates from 57 churches, youth and welfare organisations, and schools gathered in Bryson House on 5 November 1955. Opening the conference, Professor Carter said of the subject before the conference:

We see it as a problem in education; not in any narrow sense, but as a spiritual problem, to teach people to think of important and eternal values, and make them dissatisfied with the external and purely trivial.

Mrs McLaughlin certainly got attention when she praised Princess Margaret for her decision not to marry Group Captain Peter Townsend. The decision, she said, 'was an example of the wonderful triumph of upbringing and faith. It should inspire them to do their best in their own way to pass on to other people that faith and help to make their own upbringing a triumph over problems'. A great many children, she continued, through the lack of a decent upbringing or not being connected with any church, are growing up completely unfitted for present day citizenship. However, taking into account two world wars, it was 'amazing' that the youth of today were 'as good as they are'. They had had to survive many shocks and upheavals in this life and time. The broken homes of the future were not the direct concern of the conference: the 'second and third class marriages were'. The child who got into trouble with the police and was classed as a juvenile delinquent came from what she would describe as 'the casual home' with no church background.

Professor Finnegan said that 'the surest way of transmitting from one generation to the next the accumulated experiences of the technique of home-making was by tradition in the true sense – the handing down by parents to children of the values by which the parents had lived'. They need not be surprised, however, that two world wars had damaged the continuity of that method of transmission:

If we apply the techniques of successful marriage relationships which worked well in a previous generation we need not be surprised if they fail to work today. The family has been stripped of many of its characteristics, which seemed in the past to be essential; but there remain the fundamental functions of the provision of a home with its combination of material and spiritual demands.

The change in the position of women has as its consequences a change in the position of men, he continued. The result was that the male-dominated patriarchal family had largely disappeared. Indeed, 'the traditional social function of the family has greatly diminished as the State has taken over so many responsibilities which formerly rested on the shoulders of parents'.

Bessie Maconachie, MP, told the conference of the Home Advice Centre, recently opened by the Women's Home Mission of the Presbyterian Church, she hoped that as the centre became known there would be some who would attend it and meet a friendly and sympathetic adviser. She was convinced that many people, without being preached at, could be influenced by knowing that the Church was taking an interest in them and was anxious for their welfare. Mrs W J McCappin, representing the Mothers' Union, said that sometimes parents who tried to hold their children after marriage caused trouble – 'Our young people are not ours to keep; they are ours to give life'.[44]

Professor Carter, presiding, suggested that a committee be formed consisting of members attending the conference and a few co-opted people to see whether suggestions made that day could be put into practical effect. This was accepted.

On 11 November 1955 the work of the Council got indirect support when Professor Max Rheinstein, of the Department of Law at the University of Chicago, gave a public lecture at Queen's University entitled 'Divorce Legislation and Marital Stability'.

Young people, he said, should not be allowed to slip into marriage unprepared. Preparation should aim at making them aware that marriage could not be expected to be a continuous journey of bliss and happiness. Troubles and difficulties can be expected in every marriage, but they do not indicate that the union is a failure. The *Belfast Telegraph* report continued:

Divorce figures meant very little. The actual breaking up of the family could happen without divorce taking place. Something could be done in the way of legislation to attack the broken-home problem – not by tinkering with the divorce laws, but by legislation for marriage guidance.[45]

The year 1956 saw no diminution of the Council's work. Bryson House continued to host lectures and talks. One advertised to begin on 27 January for engaged couples, according to a *Belfast Telegraph* reporter, was designed to 'catch the attention of those who plan marriage before April 5, when income tax concessions are most attractive'. He reminded readers that the Chairman of the Council was 'Professor Charles Carter, who does not allow economic theories to obscure the importance of human relationships'. Another course for newly-married couples was promised 'if sufficient people are interested'. The presentation of the annual report always provided an opportunity to showcase the Council's work. Captain Long reported that the number of new cases continued to increase year by year. In 1955 there were 607, compared with 572 in 1954. Of these, 271 were of a 'substantial nature' requiring the help of counsellors, and 336 were inquiries for advice and information. A great deal of work was still being done with couples who first contacted the Council in 1954 and previous years. Summarising, the secretary said that the efforts of the Council overcame the difficulties of one-third of those who seek their help. In one-third of cases they are not and in the remaining third they are not certain of the result. He added:

We feel that it is best not to pursue those who lose contact with their counsellors, for our policy is never to intrude into the lives of others uninvited. When we consider that many of the problems brought to the Council are of long standing it is encouraging to know that it is possible to help in so many instances.

Professor Carter pointed out that in 1955 legal costs for the dissolution of marriages in Northern Ireland totalled approximately £20,000. At present the work of the Council was confined to Belfast and the surrounding district – 'the remainder of the Province, as far as they were concerned, remained untouched'. He said that the Council did not take any narrow view of the problems that lay before it. Members still found that a great many people had the idea that the Council was primarily concerned with the physical problems of marriage, or even to promote birth control. That was not the case:

Indeed, we have given much more attention in the past year to the spiritual problems of marriage. Our work is in the support of the Churches in the maintenance of the Christian ideals of marriage.

The guest speaker for the 1956 annual general meeting was Canon Bryan S W Green, Rector of Birmingham and a well-known evangelist. He said that the divorce rate of one in fifty marriages in Northern Ireland contrasted favourably with the rate of one in eleven in Britain, and it was a great improvement on the rate of one in six which existed in Britain just after the war. He continued:

For the one in 11 that reaches the divorce court I would have to add regretfully another three that are not really happy. I do not see why you should expect these to be happy marriages in a disillusioned age. Some people seem to think that you can have a world all going wrong and happy marriages standing apart.

Housing difficulties, which forced so many young couples to share a house at the start of their married lives, were one of the main material difficulties today. Christian training on sound spiritual values from a very early age was one of the best preparations for marriage – 'spiritual tit-bits dished out by a parson to an engaged couple is no adequate preparation for marriage'.[46]

Sex education 'without any kind of subterfuge with silly fables like fairies and gooseberry bushes'
On 12 March the actor Richard Attenborough delivered the 1956 Mothering Sunday BBC Appeal in aid of the national council.[47] Four days later a second 'Home-Making Conference' took place in Bryson House and here it was decided to form a Standing Joint Conference associating all organisations whose work was concerned with the promotion of better conditions of home and family life in the community. Hugh Lyon, chairman of the Executive Committee of the National Marriage Guidance Council and a former headmaster of Rugby School, gave a talk entitled 'Education for Family Life'. Christian marriage had to be put back on its proper pedestal, he said:

We have got to convince young people that marriage is the most noble and a life-long contract, not just an experiment which, if it doesn't work, you can break off and repeat with somebody else.

At the same time, he went on, something must be done to de-glamourise marriage. Young people must be told that marriage was going to mean harder work than they had ever done before, and a calling which would summon up all their reserves of energy, tact, humour and patience. In a reference to sex education he said:

I think it is an accepted fact that in the best homes questions are answered as soon as they are asked and, that the right parents see to it that their children grow up knowing at each stage what they need to know and what they wish to know, without any kind of subterfuge with silly fables like fairies and gooseberry bushes.

To be worth anything at all sex education obviously must advance along all fronts at once – physical, emotional, intellectual and spiritual. If we were going to have good homes we had to have good husbands and wives, and everything else was subordinate to that. Almost the principal need of a child was security. Children also needed a good example of the right values. Asking how boys and girls could be educated to be good husbands and wives, he said he would put very much in the forefront religious and spiritual education, which children could not learn too early. With that would go a training of the character to withstand difficult influences later on. Tolerance, too, was important, and the only thing children should be taught not to tolerate was intolerance. He thought that too little was done to train the emotions of the young. What was needed in marriage was agreement on the fundamental things that mattered. A husband and wife should have the same sense of humour and the same values in life. The loveless or forced marriage was one of the tragedies of today, just as a breach of promise case was a ludicrous way of getting some kind of justice. Engagements should give young people a chance to get to know each other in their own homes when they were not on their best behaviour. Too short or too long engagements were both dangerous. He quoted two phrases which, he advised, should be omitted from arguments between husbands and wives. They were: 'I told you so' and 'And another thing'.[48]

'fortunate in having such selfless voluntary workers'

The Council succeeded in persuading the Education Committee of Belfast Corporation to introduce some of its work into its programme. The committee had responsibility not only for all 'controlled' schools (in effect state schools with Protestant clergy on their governing bodies) but also for the further education sector (which, apart from Queen's University, was the only area of education then in Northern Ireland to which the label 'integrated' could be properly applied). The newspaper advertisement read:

County Borough of Belfast
Education Committee

The Education Committee intend to provide, if there is adequate enrolment, a ten week "Home Making" Class in the Further Education Centre, Stanhope Street, commencing MONDAY, February 4th, 1957.

The Course will consist of talks, demonstrations and discussions on the practical aspects of running a home, including cooking, furnishing and budgeting, and five one hour talks with discussion on "The Secure Home".

Copies of the Syllabus may be obtained from the Further Education Department, Education Offices, Academy Street, where intending students may enrol.

The Fee for the Course is 10s 6d.

The *Belfast Telegraph* provided further details in an article entitled, NEW 'COURSE' CATERS FOR THE YOUNG BRIDE:

How many young housewives know how to read their gas and electricity meters? How to mend a fuse; put a washer on a tap? These are only a few of the practical household jobs that will be taught in a course on home-making organised by the Further Education Sub-Committee of the Belfast Education Authority...

In addition to the practical aspect of home-making, which will be under the direction of Mrs G B O'Hara, domestic science teacher in Edenderry Secondary School, Mrs J H McLachlan will give five talks on the importance of "The Secure Home".

The course is intended primarily for young brides and brides-to-be, but any men who are interested will be welcome.

The opening lecture was to be on the selection of a house, with advice on such matters as ventilation, drainage and building fabric. 'The financial problems regarding house purchase by instalments and the renting of houses will be explained'. Mrs O'Hara in her lectures was to deal with budgeting of income, cookery, choice of furniture and utensils, schedules of work for daily, weekly and monthly cleaning, laundry, safety measures in the home, and the treatment of minor injuries and illnesses.[49]

This course was the outcome of the work put in by the Standing Conference of Home and Family which sent out circulars to bodies affiliated with it and to youth organisations.

The 1957 annual general meeting was preceded by one of many fund-raising events for the Council. A 'Coffee Party' in Bryson House was opened by Mrs W W B Topping, wife of the Minister of Home Affairs, and succeeded in raising £130. Lady Wakehurst, wife of the Governor of Northern Ireland, chaired the AGM and the principal speaker was Mrs Eric King, chairman of the house committee of Glendhu Children's Hostel. Mrs King began by saying that she was impressed with what the Council was doing to prepare young people, particularly engaged couples, for the future. Stressing the importance of a happy home, she said that at Glendhu they were sometimes asked to look after children from broken homes. In nearly every case such children were insecure and unhappy, and many of them might, unfortunately, end in juvenile courts. The unhappiness of children from broken homes in the hostel manifested itself frequently in bad temper or more often in general cantankerousness. The *Northern Whig* report continued:

At that hostel they had what appeared to be a very large staff. That was necessary because of the nature of the work and also by the fact that the girls had to have time off during the day, leave during the week and holidays. These things were taken for granted among working girls, but no mother could look forward to any leave as a "right". It should, however, be granted to her if she were to retain her sense of proportion, her humour and her good temper.

Mrs King gave this advice:

Where 'sitters-in' are not possible father should be good enough to stay in the house one night in the week and let mother get out and follow some outside interest. It may be politics or parents' associations; it may be doing welfare work or going to the pictures; it may be having tea with a neighbour – it doesn't matter what, so long as it is an outside interest. The homes where mother can get out regularly one evening every week are never the unhappy homes.

The outgoing chairman, Professor Carter, said that the case work in 1956 had continued to expand. There was a prospect of extending the work to centres outside Belfast. 'In the past year', he said, 'interest in marriage guidance has been developing in Larne, Ballymena, Portadown and Londonderry'. During 1956 there were 644 new cases, compared with 605 in 1955. Of these, 294 were cases of substantial marriage difficulty and 350 were minor cases, mainly requests for advice and information. The Council was successful in solving the difficulties of one-third of those who sought their help. He continued:

We must again record our thanks to our counsellors and consultants. Most counsellors have given between 100 and 150 hours to interviewing in the past year – the equivalent of two to three weeks' full-time work. We are very fortunate in having such selfless voluntary workers, in spite of the rigorous system of selection and training.

Professor Carter informed the meeting that Belfast Corporation and the government, which gave grants the previous year of £200 and £250 respectively, had each promised to give an additional £100 in 1957. He explained that the Council's work had two sides – educational and remedial – rather like that of the medical profession. The educational side was concerned with preparation for marriage and the spreading of the right ideas about home life. There was no lack of opportunity for such work, only a lack of the right kind of people to undertake it. It was 'a matter for considerable satisfaction' that the Standing Conference on Home and Family Life had, with the backing of the Belfast Education Authority, largely taken over this task and had sponsored a course in home-making which had been extremely successful.

The council branches out

On the remedial side the Council was 'rather limited' by geography. 'At the moment all the work had to be done from Belfast, but there were plans to extend it to other centres'. Professor Carter announced that a meeting was to be held in Larne that night with the object of forming a centre there and that there were plans afoot to branch out elsewhere. The nature of their work was such, however, that it could be done only in centres of fairly large population if the necessary secrecy were to be maintained.

Lady Wakehurst, the patron of the Council, said that in England and Scotland there was an average of 25,000 broken homes every year and 'to this concrete evidence of unhappiness' had to be added all the misery that had preceded the break and the distress of the children:

All of us who believe that we are living in a Christian country, must have a feeling of responsibility in this matter and be anxious to do anything we can to help. Fortunately, in Northern Ireland there is very much more religious allegiance to the Churches than in England and there is more social pressure against divorce, which is not recognised here in quite the same way as in England.

It was wonderful that so many counsellors had been willing to train for a year to fit themselves for this very fine work and she hoped that many more would come forward.[50]

The *Ulster Protestant* published a full feature on the Council in February 1957. It began by outlining the origins of the regional organisation:

During and after the war many people became gravely concerned over the breakdown in family life which was revealed by the great number of divorces. They realised that very little was being done to prepare young people for marriage and family life and that the lack of practical help for marriages in difficulties encouraged separation and divorce. One of the steps taken to deal with the problem was the foundation of the marriage guidance movement.

It explained that the Council had taken an active part in the setting up of the Standing Conference on Home and Family Life which aimed to 'improve the standards of education for marriage by helping those who provide it' – 'parents, teachers, social workers, etc. and by arousing interest among adults through discussions in organisations like the Workers' Educational Association and in evening classes. It has justly been said that we would never think of allowing anyone to embark on a skilled job without technical and practical training and yet we permit people to enter marriage with wrong ideas and no training at all. No wonder it is not always successful!'

It noted that there were now twenty counsellors and, while it acknowledged the grants made by Belfast Corporation and the government, it observed:

Unfortunately, the Council's work has not commended itself to the public as a charity. This is largely a result of the fact that all counselling is done in confidence and case records cannot be used to lend human interest to any appeal for financial support.[51]

The press noticed that the Council was finding it difficult enough to entice engaged couples to attend its courses. The *People* ran this article in October 1957:

Lovers shun marriage talks

Meetings where engaged couples could discuss marriage problems were arranged in Belfast. But at the first meeting not a solitary girl or young man turned up.

"Very disappointing," said a Northern Ireland Marriage Guidance member last night. "Why, we even had a cup of tea ready for them to put them at their ease."

Why don't the would-be brides and bridegrooms attend? Do they think they already know all the answers or are they just shy?

"Couples have no need to be shy about the physical side of marriage," said the chairman, Mrs C E Thompson, of Newtownards, yesterday. "We don't lay undue emphasis on that.

Only one of the three evenings we are planning will be about anatomy. The other two will concern social life, home-making and money matters.[52]

'An Ulster Log' in the *Belfast Telegraph* provided a similar report and outlined what was being offered. It observed that in 'comparable cities in England the talks are welcomed by grooms and brides-to-be...The Council provides a valuable service, and it would be a pity if this side of its work should have to cease.'[53]

Comments in previous annual general meetings to the small number of cases referred to the Council by clergy were being heard. In January 1958 the *Irish Times* reported on the calling of a preliminary meeting in the Clarence Place Hall in Belfast on 'a series of lectures for the clergy designed to give them the necessary background for their ministry in preparing couples for marriage'. The lectures would be sponsored by the Church of Ireland Moral Welfare Association in collaboration with the Council. The Rt Rev F J Mitchell, Bishop of Down and Dromore would open the series with 'Christian Ideal of Marriage as set forth in the Prayer Book' and then two clergy would report on a conference they attended recently in England on the same subject.[54]

Thereafter, at monthly intervals, lectures would be given on 'Understanding the Law', by J R Lindsay, Chief Registrar of the Probate Court of Northern Ireland and the Lord Primate's Chancellor, dealing with the laws on marriage, divorce, nullity and judicial separation. Rev T McCracken MD, a psychiatrist, would speak on sex instruction, problems of adolescence, pre-marital chastity, and other moral principles in his lecture entitled 'Understanding Youth'. With the title 'Understanding Ourselves', Dr W R Sloan would talk on fertility and allied problems and Rev. Charles Davey would speak on adjustment in marriage. The series would conclude with a lecture by Rev A T Bartlett, of the Church of England Moral Welfare Council.

The Presbyterians followed suit in May. The Presbyterian General Assembly adopted a resolution (discussed in private) at their meeting in Dublin that it should arrange instruction for engaged couples or others desiring it. The motion also recommended that instruction in sex and marriage should form part of the curriculum of the Theological College and 'that full use should be made of the Marriage Guidance Council'. The clergymen and ruling elders accepted another resolution stressing the importance:

in those undertaking Christian marriage, of the intention of permanence and of the acceptance of responsibility for the procreation of children, except where, in the latter case, there is medical evidence against it.

A third resolution condemned 'those who use sex appeal commercially without responsibility or moral standards'. The motions were adopted after consideration of the observations of the presbyteries – twenty of the thirty sent in their observations – on a report on marriage and sex problems.

Some clergy decided to give those they had married an opportunity to renew their vows. In 1957 the hundred couples wed by Rev E A Jones since he became Church of Ireland rector of Larne in 1951 attended a special service in Larne Parish Church at which married vows were renewed, wedding hymns sung and the Wedding March played. After the service a reception was held in the church hall, where there was a wedding cake and toasts were made to all the brides. On St Mark's Day, 25 April 1958, the rector of St Mark's Parish Church, Newtownards, Rev R J Chisholm, and his wife acted as host and hostess to all those whom the rector had married since he took up duty in Newtownards eight years before. The occasion also included a service embracing the Wedding March and renewal of vows, followed by a reception in the parochial hall, highlights being the cutting of cake and toasts.[55]

Dr Wilfred Brennen wrote to the press in June 1958 to appeal for more counsellors:

Sir, – The response to our last request for marriage guidance counsellors was so gratifying that I desire to make a further and most earnest appeal.

Where marriage difficulties arise, people are turning to us in increasing numbers, both in Belfast and throughout Northern Ireland.

To provide skilled and sympathetic help we need, especially, more men, but also women, who will accept this challenge and opportunity to undertake difficult but thoroughly rewarding voluntary service.

These men and women must be mature, well-balanced and fully confident, through experience, of the spiritual values upon which true marriage is founded.

They must be ready to offer regular times of attendance during the day or in the evening.

Volunteers, if deemed suitably qualified, will be invited to attend a weekend residential conference at which a final selection will be made.

There follows a period of part-time training, both theoretical and practical, before a volunteer becomes a counsellor.

I hope that people of good heart and broad vision, and especially men, will earnestly consider this appeal and will write, offering their services, to the secretary at the address below.

The Northern Ireland Ministry of Education asked the Council to give lectures to domestic science teachers. In July 1958 a report in *The People*, entitled 'Recipe for happiness', began: 'Bad cooking may not break up marriages, but good cooking allied with marriage guidance should ensure lasting happiness'. Referring to Dr Brennen's appeal, it added:

Dr Wilfred M Brennen, chairman of the council, recently appealed for people of "good heart and broad vision, and especially men" to train as counsellors. He was overwhelmed with replies.

But his phrase "especially men" raised some quizzical eyebrows until Dr Brennen explained that it was no reflection on women's abilities as counsellors. It's just that people generally prefer advice from men.[56]

Notes

1   Mary Pat Kelly, *Home Away From Home: The Yanks in Ireland*, Belfast, 1994, p. 138
2   *Belfast Telegraph*, 24 January 1946; Brian Barton, *Northern Ireland in the Second World War*, Belfast, 1995, pp. 106-7; Jonathan Bardon, 'Northern Ireland, Americans and the Second World War', *The Journal of East Tennessee History*, (No. 77), 2006, pp. 48-9
3   *Belfast Telegraph*, 6 March 1946
4   *Belfast Telegraph*, 3 March 1946
5   *Belfast News-Letter*, 5 September 1947
6   *Northern Whig*, 5 September 1947
7   *Belfast News-Letter*, 5 September 1947
8   Ibid.
9   *Northern Whig*, 3 October 1947
10   *Belfast News-Letter, Northern Whig* and *Belfast Telegraph*, 21 October 1947
11   *Belfast News-Letter*, 25 October 1947
12   *Northern Whig*, 27 October 1947
13   *Belfast Telegraph*, 24 October 1947
14   *Northern Whig*, 27 October 1947
15   *Belfast Telegraph*, 24 October 1947
16   *Northern Whig*, 4 November 1947
17   *Belfast News-Letter*, 24 October 1947
18   *Belfast News-Letter*, 26 October 1947
19   *Belfast News-Letter*, 29 October 1947
20   *Belfast News-Letter*, 26 November 1947
21   *Belfast News-Letter* and *Northern Whig*, 21 May 1949
22   *Belfast News-Letter*, 6 October 1949
23   *Belfast Telegraph*, 16 April 1949
24   26 November, 1949
25   *Charities Yearbook 1949, Relate archive*
26   *Sunday Dispatch*, 12 June 1949
27   *Reynolds News*, 9 October 1949
28   *Trinity College Mission Magazine*, June 1950
29   *Sunday Chronicle*, 28 January 1950
30   *Reynolds News*, 18 March 1951
31   1951, Relate archive
32   *Sunday Chronicle*, 16 September 1951
33   *Belfast Telegraph*, 19 October 1951
34   *Belfast News-Letter*, 25 April 1952
35   *Belfast Telegraph*, 14 May 1952
36   *Daily Express*, 15 September 1952
37   *Belfast Telegraph*, 17 November 1952
38   *Northern Whig*, 13 February 1953.
39   *Belfast Telegraph*, 13 March 1954; *Northern Whig*, 13 March 1954; *Belfast News-Letter*, 13 March 1954
40   J A Todd (ed.), *Livin' in Drumlister: The Collected Ballads and Verses of W F Marshall 'The Bard of Tyrone'*, Blackstaff Press, Belfast, 1983, pp. 32-33.
41   *Belfast Telegraph*, 11 March 1955; *Northern Whig*, 12 March 1955; *Belfast News-Letter*, 12 March 1955
42   *Belfast Telegraph*, 1 August 1955
43   *Belfast Telegraph*, 10 October 1955 and 31 October 1955; *Belfast News-Letter*, 31 October 1955
44   *Belfast Telegraph*, 5 November 1955; *Belfast News-Letter*, 7 November 1955; *Northern Whig*, 7 November 1955
45   *Belfast Telegraph*, 12 November 1955
46   *Belfast Telegraph*, 27 February 1956; *Belfast News-Letter*, 28 February 1956; *Northern Whig*, 28 February 1956
47   *Belfast News-Letter*, 12 March 1956
48   *Belfast News-Letter*, 17 March 1956
49   *Belfast Telegraph*, 15 February 1957
50   *Belfast Telegraph*, 21 February 1957; *Belfast News-Letter*, 22 February 1957; *Northern Whig*, 22 February 1957
51   *Ulster Protestant*, February 1957
52   *The People*, 6 October 1957
53   *Belfast Telegraph*, 5 October 1957
54   *Irish Times*, January 1958
55   Relate cuttings file
56   *The People*, July 1958

CHAPTER TWO

Growing in the years of hope

The problem of matrimonial trouble now 'a frightening one'

On 27 March 1960 the Northern Ireland Marriage Guidance Council held its first formal dinner since it had been set up in 1947. Wilfred Brennen, FRCS, Chairman of the Council, presided at the function in the Midland Hotel, Belfast. He described the dinner as 'a signal moment to mark the acceptance by the public of our work and its importance throughout the Province'. This, clearly, was an occasion which provided a significant opportunity to raise public awareness. Dr Mary Macauley, member of the National Council's Medical Advisory Board on the National Council, travelled over to be the keynote speaker. Vice-President of the Merseyside branch, a family planning specialist and a justice of the peace, Dr Macauley had written *The Art of Marriage*, a book now attracting considerable media attention. Before joining the diners, she was interviewed on 'Roundabout', UTV's teatime news magazine programme. After the guest of honour, the Countess of Roden, had commended the work of the Council to the public, Dr Macauley proposed a toast to the government of Northern Ireland, saying that the amount of public support accorded the work in the region indicated that its value to the community was appreciated. The *Belfast News-Letter* continued:

Marriage is not just a question of here and now, or this country or this age. Ever since people began to live in tribes they found they did not want to care for other people's children – the Welfare State is the only tribe that does it…

One of the most important things to the making of a happy marriage was that the partners could on occasion agree to differ and that each partner was prepared to admit at times that he or she might actually be in the way.

In trying to help the present generation the movement was really helping generations as yet unborn. One of the main causes of family trouble was that there was too little said about "thou shalt and thou shalt not". It was important that there should be a basic framework in every family to determine what children should do and should not do and the willingness on the part of each parent to respect the other's point of view.

She stressed that, in a time of rapid social change, it was important to reinforce preventative work through the forces of education.[1] When a marriage broke down it was often too late to do anything about it. Preparation for marriage by courses for engaged couples and adolescents in the schools could help young people to understand their responsibilities. When a marriage was in danger of breaking there was a strong possibility of its being mended if both partners wanted it to be mended. Even if only one partner wanted to save the marriage there was hope. She gave her recipe for a happy marriage as an agreement to disagree and a willingness on both sides to admit they might be wrong. 'But', she added, 'it must not always be the same one who admits to having been in the wrong'.

Brian Faulkner, Minister of Home Affairs, then rose to his feet. Nothing was more calculated to promote social insecurity in the community and to produce juvenile delinquency than broken homes, he declared. For that reason, he said, his Ministry had always been interested in the work of the Council and had given it financial support. After noting the rapid rise in the number of cases dealt with since 1947, Faulkner said that his department's probation officers had dealt with more than 1,700 matrimonial cases in the past year. Though matrimonial trouble was not as widespread as it was in the big cities of Great Britain, the problem was 'a frightening one' and was not fully realised by the mass of the people.

Dr Stuart Hawnt, Director of Education in Belfast, supported Dr Macauley's emphasis on the role of education. He foresaw closer cooperation between education authorities and the Marriage Guidance Council. 'Education today is lagging behind the needs of society', he said. 'There is too much education for examinations and literacy instead of as a preparation for life. Life for most people involves living in partnership in marriage, and we must envisage education for marriage through the school or the youth club'. Councillor J Dixon, chairman of the Belfast Corporation Welfare Committee, said that while voluntary and statutory bodies could work closely together, people were more likely to bring their marriage problems to a voluntary body. He added that the cost of keeping a child of a broken marriage in a home was £400 a year – 'and I am not assessing the cost of human suffering'.

The Council's report for 1960 did indeed lay emphasis on the value of education:

The Council is concerned that education for marriage should be provided for all young people, so that they can establish right attitudes and a sound set of values before they get married. This to be fully effective requires a national effort, but the Council has its own contribution to make, and it attempted to interest others in the solution of the problem.

The report explained that 'Marriage is now regarded as a partnership of equals, and people have come to expect a great deal from it. People now got married much earlier than in previous generations. Successful marriage has thus become much more difficult at a time when very little preparation is being given for it, and the way out of difficulties, through divorce, is very much easier'. The Council was concerned that, while in the past education for marriage and family life was given mainly at home and by the church, 'nowadays many parents do not even attempt to prepare their children for marriage and many of them are out of contact with the church'. It intended to secure the interest and advice of educationalists and was arranging a training course for speakers. It was planned to appoint a part-time education organiser in the near future.

In Belfast the suitability of Bryson House as a venue for those seeking guidance was emphasised. After all, it was also the headquarters of a number of other voluntary organisations: 'This means that enquirers seeking the help of the Council need not fear that their calling at a certain building would tell the world what their problems were'. For the same reason it was difficult to provide a counselling service outside of Belfast. There were 'considerable difficulties in small and intimate communities such as existed in most Ulster provincial towns':

It was difficult to secure premises where it was not obvious that those who called there were seeking marriage guidance. Local people would often be unwilling to discuss their problems with other local residents with whom they might be acquainted.[2]

Sex Education – rather strong meat?

Education in preparation for marriage was kept to the fore when, in May 1960, Mr A H B Ingleby, education secretary of the National Marriage Guidance Council, accepted an invitation to address headmasters and headmistresses of grammar and intermediate schools in Belfast 'on the problem of education for marriage as it concerned schools'. 'The best family life educators in the world are parents themselves', he opened. Many parents, however, were not doing their job in that field for various reasons, and he believed that there came a time in the lives of most children – even in well-adjusted homes – when the parents were not the people to whom young people turned with their really personal problems. That applied particularly during the adolescent phase.

Since the root of 'most social evils' sprang from relations in the family, 'the self-evident solution' was to strengthen the family as the basis of family living. In England there was a steadily increasing trend towards earlier marriage – although at the other end of the scale 'young people's dependency' was being increased by the raising of the school-leaving age. The earlier the marriage, the greater the danger of breakdown. Mr Ingleby pointed out that in England, of the marriages of people between 16 and 18 years, there was a risk of a breakdown in one in every four in twenty years' time. Young people were freer than before 'to escape from a mediocre home where they were not getting the understanding they should'. They then took the results of 'tension, distress and mal-adjustment' into their own marriages. At the top of his list of reasons for the breakdown of these early marriages were 'a sheer inability to run a home, to make ends meet, to cook a decent meal and to budget'. Mr Ingleby stressed the importance of sex education. Sex education, he believed, was going on all the time – 'in the school yard, on the playing fields, as boys and girls thumbed through Sunday newspapers and periodicals, and as they looked at the television screen – but those things gave them a one-sided view of sex, which was concerned with the purely physical side'. He continued:

Stressing the need to integrate sex education in the whole school curriculum, Mr Ingleby said that over the last 50 years it had tended to become separated from the rest of life. The heart of the problem, he believed, was to create an atmosphere in which young people could ask questions freely and be helped in finding an answer for themselves.[3]

This insistence on the incorporation of sex education into the school curriculum, even at this date, was undoubtedly rather strong meat for many of the school principals listening to him to swallow. Ingleby, a wartime Lieutenant-Colonel before becoming education secretary in the National Council, ruffled some feathers within the organisation by arguing forcefully that women should not be tied to the kitchen sink. At the National Conference at Buxton in May 1961 he said to the 250 delegates:

It is often much better for a family for the mother to go out to work if that is what she wants. Then when she comes back she's refreshed in body and mind and much more able to show the way she loves her children. This surely is far better than having a mother who resents being tied to the kitchen sink and the home when the rest of the family is out and who becomes cross and irritable in her frustration. Having her own outside interests can mean a better mother.

However, he did not want to see a mother forced to go out to keep up hire purchase payments on the TV set or the car 'to keep up in the rat race'. If possible 'mother should have a part-time job which does not tire her too much'. Mrs B Hume, chairman of the National Council's Education Committee, took issue with Ingleby:

I cannot agree with all these views. I'm sure the vast majority of the members of this movement would never agree to a mother being out when the children got home. I certainly feel very strongly about it. I have had four children, and although I have often gone out doing voluntary work, I have never been away from home when the children arrived back.

I would not object to a mother having a part-time job when the children got older, provided she was always home by the time they got back.

Mrs Hume, however, had a comfortable life as the wife of a distinguished surgeon. Lady Bragg, Chairman of the National Council (and wife of Sir Lawrence Bragg, winner of the Nobel Prize for Physics) was more emollient. 'I have two married daughters with small children', she said, 'and I know how bored and frustrated they get tied to the house all day. Both are university graduates, and I really wish they could get part-time jobs which I know would make a tremendous difference to them'.[4]

Ingleby's new book, *Learning to Love*, was stacked on the hotel tables at Buxton. A reporter found that he was worried in case his wife Betty, Liberal candidate in the Barnes Borough Council election, might be elected:

"Who," he said in rather cool tone, "is going to cook my meals?"

The problems arising from early marriages was a theme which cropped up again during the thirteenth Annual General Meeting of the Council in March 1961. The Lord Mayor of Belfast, Alderman R G C Kinahan, presided. He did feel that 'in Northern Ireland we hold our marriage vows better than in most parts of the British Isles'. 'Marriage has a very special place in Northern Ireland', he said, adding that while he was in the Army he was always impressed by the way Ulstermen and their wives 'stuck together'. Alderman Kinahan's association with the Council was to prove close and enduring.[5]

A conference sponsored by the Council on the same day arrived at this conclusion:

Young people engaged to be married are so much in love that it does not occur to them that marriage is one of the most difficult of human relationships, about which it is as necessary to be informed and educated as any of the major aspects of life.

A recurring theme in these years was a general feeling that the influence of the media was having a baleful effect:

The conference discussed the influence of Press, radio and TV in disseminating widely ideas and values about marriage and family life which to some degree corrupted and distorted proper values.

In creating the impression that the teenager was a separate and problem member of the community, mass media might in fact be doing much to confuse young people and lead them towards forms of behaviour and conduct, which at their extreme, became anti-social, it was said.[6]

The Northern Ireland Council kept in constant touch with its parent body, the National Marriage Guidance Council. Wilfred Brennen, surgeon at the Mid-Ulster Hospital at Magherafelt and chairman of the Northern Ireland Council, flew to London in September 1960. He had been invited to the formal opening of the National Council's new headquarters in Queen Anne Street, Marylebone by the Home Secretary, R A Butler. The minister acknowledged that the £75,000 required to move to the new premises had come from voluntary contributions. Hinting that the Home Office might increase its annual grant of £15,000, Butler seemed to go further than giving recognition to the work of the Council. 'When it is considered that it costs about £400 a year to keep a child in a local authority home, I think we can stir local authorities up – and stir me up – to give a little more'. Much of the Council's success, he continued, was due to the fact that it was scientific and idealistic at the same time. It could succeed only if it combined the heart with the brain. Another reason was the careful training given to persons used as group counsellors – it was not haphazard but based on knowledge and character. In trying to prevent unhappy marriages the Council was engaged in territory which was the most precious to mankind.

The impact on marriages of six years of war had led to a soaring in the divorce rate in 1946, reaching a peak of 60,254 in 1947 in the United Kingdom as a whole. Thereafter the rate had declined steadily to 22,654 in 1958. However the divorce rate began to rise again in 1959, a trend which continued through the next decade and beyond.

On 12 May 1961 the *Daily Herald* published a major feature on the work of the National Council. Journalists Joyce Chesterton and Tom Baistow contrasted the cost of broken homes across the country each year – a total of £22¾ million, £16¾ million of that sum spent on children in public care – with the annual total expended by the government and local authorities on all marriage guidance work, a sum of £40,000.

The £15,000 provided by government covered only half the National Council's expenses of administration and training. The feature reported that around 1,200 counsellors had been trained, after a rigorous vetting:

First they must be approved by the local M G C. Then they must pass a residential week-end selection conference. This has been developed from methods used by wartime officer selection boards. A psychiatrist takes part in the selections.

Nobody divorced or separated is accepted.

Single people are rarely taken. Anybody with strong personal prejudices or a powerful urge to run other people's lives is weeded out.

Forty-five per cent fail at this stage.

Of course the divorce rate in Northern Ireland remained consistently lower than in the UK as a whole. This fact was expressed with some satisfaction by the Lord Mayor, Alderman Robin Kinahan, when he presided at the 13th annual meeting of the Council in Bryson House in 1961. The vice-chairman, Mrs P M Thompson, was able to report that the government had increased its grant from £400 to £600 and Belfast Corporation from £300 to £500. This was a reminder that the Marriage Guidance Council, both nationally and locally, benefited from the consistent support of the great and the good. Robin Kinahan had thrown himself into the work of the Council and would give his services to it for years to come. The fact that he was one of Northern Ireland's most successful businessmen and a Lord Mayor did the Council no harm at all. Kinahan was not unusual. Lady Bragg, wife of the famous scientist, Sir Lawrence Bragg, a member of the 1951 Royal Commission on Marriage and Divorce, had been Mayor of Cambridge in 1945-46. In 1961 she was chairman of the National Marriage Guidance Council and was due to come to Belfast to address the annual meeting, but for the fact that her plane was grounded by fog.

The *Belfast News-Letter* carried a column, 'by AIM', in January 1961 which reported in detail on the Council's new educational policy. This columnist began by admitting initial reservations:

We all have a deep-rooted objection to being preached at. The corollary to this proposition is that we all have a deep-rooted prejudice against those who (we think) might possibly preach to us, whether in fact they really wish to do so or not. We seldom wait to see: it is quicker to unload the clever sneer and move on.

The work of Marriage Guidance Counsellors has been consistently praised on public platforms and denigrated in private conversations. Whereas the glow from the dais is occasionally more roseate than most counsellors would wish in the interests of strict accuracy, it is certainly true that any critics I have listened to have in the main been grossly misinformed as to the qualifications of the counsellors or to the modesty of their claims.

The columnist went on to report that the educational policy embarked on by the Council was a direct result of the work and experience of the counsellors – 'Prevention is not only better than cure but, they feel, the only real bulwark against the wreckage of hopelessly unsuitable marriages'. Specially trained group leaders had been asked to undertake work in three spheres: with engaged couples, with young people in clubs, and with teenagers in schools. Since it took time to train leaders and since the scheme had been under way for scarcely two years, it was too early to judge how successful it was being – indeed, 'AIM.' thought 'the possible results for good will not be assessable, if indeed they ever admit of assessment, for another 10 to 20 years'. The columnist continued:

It is felt that by encouraging girls and boys to talk about themselves – leisure interests, work, friendships and relationships with other people – it is possible to arrive at some idea of the problems as they see them and to encourage them to sort out their own ideas. The experience of one lady, a doctor, by profession as well as a housewife and mother, in a girls' school was that teenagers want, first of all, factual information. The way in which this is given may set the whole tone for further discussion and development.

The emphasis here is on the young people (they are being got at rather, but maybe it will really help them) and on group discussion. One notices that this group business is increasingly used in all forms of social therapeutic and preventative work and apparently it is very satisfactory. It seems that it is very helpful to humans to discover that other humans are in the same distressful boat as themselves. It would worry me to death.[7]

The Council's 1962 annual report indicated a fresh intention to expand counselling and educational work outside of Belfast. 'Counselling work has reached the stage when we are ready to move onwards from our well established centre in Belfast to others in the Province'. Larne and Portadown were being earmarked as the first outcentres. Some 1,210 interviews had been conducted by counsellors in 1961, an expansion on the previous year; courses for engaged couples were continued 'but we still find difficulty in contacting people at the right time and the numbers are smaller than we would like'. The Council had more success with courses for young people in grammar schools, church groups and youth clubs and, it continued, 'an interesting development was the arranging of a series of discussions for apprentices in a Belfast engineering works – as part of their course in liberal studies'.

There was 'a welcome increase in subscriptions and grants from public funds' and accounts for the year showed 'an excess of income over expenditure, but this happy state of affairs was not likely to continue'. In addition to the increased grants from Belfast Corporation and the Ministry of Home Affairs, the Council for the first time received grants from Down Welfare Department (£75) and County Tyrone (£15).[8]

One reason why the Northern Ireland Marriage Guidance Council was in a modest state of financial surplus in 1962 was that it had robust sales of books and pamphlets produced by the National Council. The latest publications often attracted considerable attention from the local press. One of these was a new booklet, *A Home of Your Own*. Of course in 1962 many of those just married still had no choice but to share the parental home. In that case the newlyweds were urged that privacy is just as important for the older couple as for the younger couple – 'intrusion is horrible whether by people, animals, noise or overflowing bath water'. 'It is impossible to overstress the need for the expenses and responsibilities of both families to be as separate and defined as possible', the advice continued.

Do sort out all arrangements for paying for conversion, rent, rates, decorations and repairs at the very beginning of the idea. The use and payment for gas and electricity, the use or share of the garden (including that clothes-line), the disposal of rubbish, keeping of animals, cleaning of any shared passages or stairs, and, most important, the sharing of the bathroom, where unavoidable, should be discussed while the actual conversion is being planned.

Those about to set up a home of their own were strongly advised: 'For heaven's sake, right from the start, forget about the Jones'. In view of the fact that 'Government freezes, squeezes, and pauses' were making it particularly difficult to find even the minimum outlay for a house or flat, the real emphasis must be on cultivating a good relationship:

…a home is what you make it by the sort of life you lead in it, and this has nothing to do with the colour of the walls, the number of labour-saving gadgets, and all the latest furniture on the HP. Real married happiness can make a home out of one room, a mattress and some orange boxes…Building up your home from practically nothing is immensely satisfying. Wealthy folk who can just buy everything all at once have no idea of the fun of saving for one thing at a time, and the thrill of coming upon a bargain in a junk shop.

This was one of a series of booklets produced by the national council, prepared with the advice of a husband and wife team, Mr and Mrs J Howden Cook (she was a marriage counsellor and group leader and he was an architect) and two BBC gardening and do-it-yourself experts, Joe Brashaw (who was also general secretary of the council) and Barry Bucknell.[9]

The National Association of Retail Furnishers decided that it must reply to the advice in *A Home of Your Own* to avoid hire purchase. Its main point was that 'the stresses and strains of early married life are quite bad enough without the frustration, for the wife, of trying to make a home without the barest necessities, and the physical discomfort, of the husband, to return after a day's work and to be faced with an orange box'. Juliet Leigh interviewed Mrs C E Thompson, vice-chairman of the Council, to seek her comments for the *Belfast Telegraph*. The outcome was a detailed article – entitled 'From orange blossom to orange boxes or HP.' – in March 1962 which gave extensive coverage to the work and philosophy of the Northern Ireland Council.

Mrs Thompson, while not opposed to hire purchase for 'established' couples, 'did not believe in building a life on it'. She thought a marriage should be 'big' enough to 'stand up to a lack of comfort at the beginning. If it could not do so then, what hope was there for the future?' Based on her experience as a counsellor, her view was that it 'was not so much a lack of material possessions as a lack of respect for one another's ideas or way of life: wanting one's partner to be what one would like him to be, instead of accepting him as he is'. She continued:

There must be give and take and understanding of one another's rights. Too often it is not recognised that marriage is a partnership. There is a lack of common kindness and courtesy. Too many young people get married with the idea that it is for their own happiness and when they come to the Council for help it is all too frequently the other person's fault. Happily married people have problems also, but they have learnt to face them together.

Juliet Leigh then went on to interview the Northern Ireland Council's educational secretary, Mrs Thelma Greeves. She confessed that she was not an 'orange box' enthusiast herself but added that group leaders in the Council were divided on the issue:

Mrs Greeves thinks that when two young people, both earning, get married, they should contrive to live on the husband's salary, keeping the wife's income for furniture or savings, so that when the wife gives up her job there is no appreciable difference in their way of life… "I am all for couples being realistic about the difficulties," she said. "They should try to furnish decently at least a bedroom and a living room for a start. Yes, I do believe in a bit of comfort when it is at all possible!"

She told the *Belfast Telegraph* columnist that at least half the engaged couples who had come to the Council over the past three years intended to go in for hire purchase. It was the unfortunate people who had no idea what they were in for who suffered, 'and this could lead to a great deal of unhappiness in marriage'. 'All this made me eager to hear more about the work of the Council', Juliet Leigh continued. The work of counsellors was outlined and if the problems encountered required more specialised treatment the client could be referred to 'a panel of consultants – medical, psychological, spiritual, social or legal'.

There was 'plenty of room' for more counsellors, the ideal candidates being happily married people aged between 30 and 50. 'No academic qualifications are required', Thelma Greeves continued, 'but the right qualities of personality and temperament are important, such as a sympathetic understanding of people in difficulties, a liberal and tolerant outlook, a genuine liking for and interest in people and the ability to be a good listener'.

Voluntary part-time group leaders for educational work were also carefully selected. Talks and discussions were arranged for small, friendly and informal groups of engaged and newly-married couples on such themes as 'Getting to know the in-laws', 'Sharing the chores', 'Money', 'Spiritual background', 'Planning a family', 'Sex in marriage', 'Lasting romance', 'Furnishing and decorating', 'Housekeeping and budgeting', and 'When children come'. Sometimes these groups were held in the home of a married couple where husband and wife are both group leaders. Mr and Mrs J W Russell of Newtownards worked together in this way. This educational work was based on the Council's belief that if young people are helped to understand more about themselves and their relationships, to approach moral problems in an informed and responsible way, sound foundations will be laid for the full and enriching experience that marriage should be.

The group leader 'gives a short talk on some aspect of the "facts of life", and then the meeting is thrown open for questions and discussion', Thelma Greeves said. She did not 'agree with the idea that the majority of young people nowadays, in Northern Ireland at any rate, have pre-marital intercourse. Going by their questions she finds them amazingly innocent'. Juliet Leigh concluded:

With the present day trend towards earlier maturity and earlier marriage, this educational work is of growing importance, and the Council believes that many marriage difficulties would never arise if issues had been faced beforehand and the need for mutual adjustment clearly understood.

So whether it is to be orange boxes or hire purchase to furnish the new home, maybe it does not matter so long as both parties are agreed and have it all worked out in advance.

Just a thought – what about covering that orange box with a foam cushion, or something?[10]

During his long service with the Council, Wilfred Brennen wrote frequent appeals for volunteers, often at considerable length, in the form of letters to the editors of local newspapers. These were urgently needed to act as group leaders for educational work 'to help young people and engaged couples understand more about themselves and their relationships, and to approach moral problems in an informed and responsible way'. Since this was 'responsible work calling for certain personal qualities…we make no apology for the fact that group leaders, although voluntary part-time workers, are asked to undergo a most careful selection and training before being accepted for this work'. The Council was looking for men and women of wide sympathies, between 25 and 45 years, happily married, and preferably parents. 'As a matter of expediency and not censure', he added, 'we cannot consider divorced or separated persons for this work'.[11]

Moira Douglas, writing for the *Belfast Telegraph*, reported that the Council was somewhat disappointed at the numbers of couples applying to attend its educational groups. 'The winter round of evening classes has returned, with thousands of students eager to improve their store of knowledge', she began. 'Yet curiously enough there does not appear to be a waiting list for one particular study course which should be of vital interest to hundreds of young people in Northern Ireland'. Around seventy couples had participated in these courses over the past three years. She talked to some of those who had completed these courses. Denis Ringland, a bank official now married and living in Bangor, told her:

The classes certainly brought my wife and me much closer together…I would definitely recommend them to all engaged couples. I think what holds most of them back from attending is shyness.

He felt it was particularly important to have the opportunity to talk over the problems of setting up a home with other young couples facing similar difficulties, and 'getting things off your chest' with a neutral arbitrator. He thought the classes were 'very good crack' as did Desmond Porter from Newtownabbey who liked the relaxed atmosphere when discussing serious matters. 'Things were discussed informally, yet without anyone being at all embarrassed – this was very good', he said. He and his wife Pat were particularly appreciative of the legal advice and information regarding housing matters.

Moira Douglas also talked to Mr and Mrs J W Russell, trained group leaders who had run several courses at their own home in Newtownards. Mrs Russell thought that a 'private home does allow for a more informal atmosphere'; on the other hand, 'some people feel it is too personal, and would prefer to attend courses in Belfast'. Shyness, she believed, was what held most couples back from attending courses. 'Girls, in fact, seem to be more interested to come than boys', she commented. Male reluctance was what prevented most couples from joining the courses offered, the Russells had discovered.

In addition to the regular courses at Bryson House, the Council was also cooperating with churches in the running of small 'closed group' for engaged couples:

"In the closed group we have the advantage of being able to go a little further in pointing out the significance of the marriage ceremony, and its follow-up in the Christian community," one minister, who wishes to remain anonymous, explained to me. The courses are very similar to those run at Bryson House – the clergyman introducing his group to the leaders, and then retiring into the background, with the exception of the final evening session, when he joins in to discuss the moral and spiritual side of Christian marriage.[12]

On 27 March 1963 the Northern Ireland Council held its fifteenth annual general meeting. The keynote speaker was Joseph Brayshaw JP, General Secretary of the National Marriage Guidance Council in London. 'People still think that we are nosey parkers prying into their private affairs' he declared. In spite of its educational programme, many still thought that the work of the National Council was concentrated on marriages that had gone wrong. He continued: 'From the very beginning we have always attached as much importance to the avoidance of marriage difficulties as to the solving of them.' The increasing number of teenage marriages made the educational aspect even more important:

Attitudes to marriage are formed long before a couple has even met and become engaged...it is a mistake to think that you should never quarrel in front of your children. It is much more important to let them see that you are ready to make it up – this is tremendously important in later life.

Nowadays, he continued, both partners could continue to work, the great majority deferred having families at the start of marriage. Hire purchase made it easy to set up a home. Despite this, statistics for England and Wales in 1961 showed that two-thirds of brides under twenty had conceived before marriage. The teenager was bombarded with sex in advertisements, films, plays and novels. The answer to this, he believed, was not to refuse to discuss matters of sex with teenagers, but for people with ideals and principles to be prepared to defend these. 'If we refuse to discuss such matters', Brayshaw maintained, 'it makes young people think that we are incapable of defending them. We must be open minded about this'.

At the sixteenth annual general meeting, in 1964, Sir Robin Kinahan, who presided, went out of his way to welcome the recently-inaugurated Roman Catholic Marriage Advisory Service. The vice-chairman of the National Council, Mrs P R Allen, was the main speaker. In her address, entitled 'Marriage in Modern Society', she said that young marrieds today had optimism, but that their problems were due to them not being ready for the responsibility involved.

The press showed more interest in the speech given by Denis P Barritt, secretary-designate to the Belfast Council of Social Welfare. Two years earlier Barritt had created quite a stir when his book, *The Northern Ireland Problem: A Study in Group Relations*, written jointly with Professor Charles F Carter, had been published – this at a time when very few of their Protestant contemporaries thought that the region had a group relations problem at all. Barritt opened with this arresting observation: 'A car licence puts one in control of a lethal weapon; with a marriage certificate you have a weapon which can be lethal to human happiness and family life'. He went on to say that it had struck him as an extraordinary fact that while the most intensive training and qualification was required for almost every situation in life, apart from the work done by the churches and the council, there were no formal or statutory requirements for marriage. With the changing tempo of modern life, he continued, the Marriage Guidance Council should be looking into the factors which will govern family life in the future.

Wilfred Brennen, in presenting the annual report as chairman of the Council, emphasised the value of the educational side of the organisation's work. Group leaders were in agreement that the teenagers were 'a splendid lot' and, given the right guidance at the crucial stage in their lives, should prove worthwhile citizens:

These leaders were finding that with the lowering of the age of marriage the work of group leading for the young unmarried people was overlapping with the work of counselling for young couples, many of whom were still teenagers themselves. Mr Brennen drew attention to the fact that at the request of two prisoners serving sentences, counsellors had been allowed to visit them in prison and that every facility had been accorded to them with the warm approbation of the Governors concerned.[13]

In September 1964 the Council had a stand for the first time at the Ideal Home Exhibition at the King's Hall in south Belfast. The *Belfast Telegraph*, sponsoring the exhibition, took the opportunity to interview the vice-chairman, Mrs C E Thompson, about the work of the Council. She said that, even though the organisation now had fourteen counsellors, demand was fast increasing:

More and more people are seeking our help. We are steadily expanding our educational programme in schools, colleges, youth clubs, churches and in industry, and we hope that through this families will be better prepared to meet a crisis.

There is still a great amount of work to be done. Voluntary workers are needed to give a better service in the outlying areas of the province.

But not anybody can take up the work of marriage guidance. The people who come forward must have a mature and balanced personality; be able to cope with their own family problems, and have a friendly approach to others.

A home cannot be in any sense ideal if the people in it are not happy, she continued. Alcoholism, gambling and unemployment are still big factors in the break-up of many homes, but another problem is causing concern to Ulster marriage guidance counsellors, as she explained:

Ulster is a closely knit community and people have close family ties – young married couples are inclined to turn to their parents for emotional support, even in times of minor difficulties, when it would be much better if they tried to solve the problems themselves. But we are now in the midst of a transition period. We are getting away from the "extended family" idea, where grandparents, parents, aunts and uncles all play a part in the running of the family home. Newlyweds are setting up homes of their own in new housing estates away from close family ties. And while it is better that they should live away from home, many young people are not yet prepared emotionally to meet the change.

While Northern Ireland had a comparatively low divorce rate compared with many other areas of the United Kingdom, this did not mean that 'everything in the garden is rosy', Mrs Thompson believed. 'Figures can be very misleading', she added. 'In a religious, closely-knit community like Ulster people generally are not willing to face the stigma of divorce. And those who are not prepared to stand up to the social consequences just go on putting up with each other, although the marriage is past breaking point'. She continued:

You cannot solve a marriage problem by giving someone a new house – it might ease matters temporarily, but it is not a solution. Where you get dissension and lack of understanding between husband and wife a marriage will break up irrespective of the material benefits. Anything can act as the spark that causes the break – like a kitchen not being kept tidy or a row over overspending at the week-end.

If there was more love and understanding in homes there would be fewer heart-breaks.[14]

To highlight the work of the Council the *East Antrim Times* and the *Ballymena Weekly Telegraph* set up a competition for engaged couples, with a free honeymoon in Jersey as a prize. Mrs Thompson joined a Ballymena travel agent, Margaret Cameron, and Doris Craig, the wife of the Home Affairs minister, William Craig, to choose the winner. In a letter of thanks to the *Belfast Telegraph*, Mrs Thompson wrote that 'a great number of books were sold, appointments made for consultations, and a real contact made between the Council and the public'.[15]

Notes

1   *Belfast News-Letter*, 23 March 1960
2   Ibid.; *Belfast Telegraph*, 23 March 1960
3   NIMGC cuttings file, May 1960
4   *Daily Express*, 13 May 1961
5   NIMGC cuttings file, March 1961
6   Ibid.
7   *Belfast News-Letter*, January 1961, NIMGC cuttings file
8   *Northern Whig*, 13 April 1962; *Belfast News-Letter*, 13 April 1962
9   NIMGC cuttings file, 1962
10 *Belfast Telegraph*, 16 March 1962
11 *Belfast News-Letter*, 25 October 1962
12 *Belfast Telegraph*, September 1962, NIMGC cuttings file
13 *Belfast News-Letter*, 12 March 1964
14 *Belfast Telegraph*, 31 August 1964
15 Ibid., 23 September 1964

CHAPTER THREE

Coping during the Troubles (1968-79)

The year 1968: resources 'strained to the utmost'

Prime Minister of Northern Ireland from 1963, when Lord Brookeborough resigned, Captain Terence O'Neill had set out in an optimistic spirit to regenerate the economy of Northern Ireland and to ease intercommunal tensions. Despite his mould-breaking gestures of conciliation, however, O'Neill eventually created intense frustration within the nationalist minority by his inability to deliver thoroughgoing reform, while more and more loyalists were convinced that he was conceding too much, and turned against him. At the beginning of 1968, however, even the most experienced political observers were not predicting that before the year was out the region would be plunged into a state of near-revolutionary crisis.

In 1968 the Council had its offices half a mile south of Belfast city centre at 76 Dublin Road. The Patron was the Prime Minister's wife, Jean, listed as 'The Honourable Mrs Terence O'Neill'. She had formally opened the Council's new premises in November 1967. In her message for the year 1968 she pointed out that 'the general growing awareness of the vital importance of this welfare is making great demands on its service. Every effort to meet all these demands is being made and as a result the reserves of the Council in personnel and finance are strained to the utmost'.

Though the Council's resources were, indeed, being 'strained to the utmost', at least it continued to have the support of the establishment. It was entirely appropriate that Wilfred Brennen, founder member and stalwart activist, should be President; and that Captain W J Long, former Secretary and now a junior government minister who would become Minister of Home Affairs in December 1968, should be a Vice-President. Other Vice-Presidents included the Church of Ireland Bishop of Clogher, the Moderator of the Presbyterian Church in Ireland, and the President of the Methodist Church in Ireland. Since the Catholic Church had its own marriage advisory organisation, it was inevitable that the establishment represented continued to be a Protestant one. However, women increasingly were playing a pivotal role in the Council. Mrs Phyllis Thompson was Chairman; Gladys Jeffery was a Vice-Chairman; Mrs Peggy Musson was Education Secretary; two of the three Representing Counsellors were women, Mrs M C Perceval-Price and Mrs J Unwin; and half of the Executive Committee was female, those members being Mrs K Kinahan, Mrs T Greeves, Dr Joyce Neill, Mrs N Stevenson and Mrs Margaret Keith.

The Press continued to report annual general meetings and to publish regular appeals for volunteers to come forward – still almost always written by Wilfred Brennen – and in January 1968 the *Belfast News-Letter* referred to the National Council in an editorial entitled 'Noli me tangere'. Gerald Sanctuary, the National Secretary, had made a speech saying that he thought there was not enough physical contact between parents and their children when they are in need of comfort. The *News-Letter* editor did not agree with him:

There is a natural and justifiable prejudice in this country against molly-coddling. In his memoirs published in the "Sunday News" this week Lord Brookeborough recalls an occasion when as a small boy he tripped over a chair and fell heavily. His grandfather, Sir Victor Brooke, rebuked his tears with "Remember, boy, no Brooke ever cries".

It is not bad advice, even if it cannot always be acted upon. A relationship between married couples in which tenderness is shown must be a good foundation for life, but sentiment is a personal thing and should not be paraded outside.[1]

The Council continued to depend heavily on unpaid volunteers, including professional consultants who advised and assisted counsellors by attending regular case discussions and the like. There was regular contact with Medical Officers of Health and Health Visitors. Schools continued to make extensive use of the Council's services including, for the first time that year, Bloomfield Collegiate School, Dundonald Girls' High School, Fivemiletown Secondary School and Annadale Grammar School. Counsellors visited groups of boys and girls in Rathgael and Whiteabbey Training Schools to 'pay special attention to helping delinquent children with their adolescent problems'. The Ministry of Education arranged a residential training course for teachers in July 1968 at Greenmount Agricultural College. A group of Venture Scouts asked a Counsellor to accompany them to see *Helga*, a sex educational film being screened in Belfast and then to discuss it with them back at their Scout headquarters. Following a request from some younger clergy 'concerned about the increase in family problems they are confronted with', the Council held a three-day residential course at Rathmore House in Larne in September. The number of cases handled in 1968 was 293 (an increase of just one case on 1967) and the number of children involved under the age of sixteen was 385.[2]

'I am sticking to my proposal. I say no grant'

The great bulk of the Council's activities was centred in Belfast but the organisation was anxious to widen its reach. The Derry/Londonderry branch moved into better accommodation in Clarendon Street and contacts were being established in the counties of Fermanagh and Tyrone. Then, in November 1968, the Co. Londonderry Welfare Committee decided not to make a grant to this branch. The Derry/Londonderry branch had written to the committee pointing out the additional costs of its recent move and demonstrating that the demand for its services had increased very considerably: 'A large proportion of the people making use of the service came from the county, even from as far away as Portstewart'.

Two years earlier the county had given the branch £50, J L Wilde, the county welfare officer had reported, but this grant had not been renewed in 1967. Now the Welfare Committee members, James Barr and R A Brown, proposed, as a response to the Derry/Londonderry NIMGC branch's appeal for a restoration of financial help, to deny this request. Another committee member, Mrs J T Milligan, asked the committee to think again:

She made the point that if the Marriage Guidance Council could save a home from being broken up it would very probably save the committee the expense of having to take the children into one of their homes.

Mr Barr – I am sticking to my proposal. I say no grant.

Mr Brown – The amount of money is not the important thing here. If people set up on a voluntary basis then good luck to them. But if it is voluntary then it should not be grant-aided in any way.

Mrs Milligan then put forward an amendment, seconded by Mrs J L Stanleigh, that a smaller grant of £25 be made, but on a vote the amendment was defeated by eight votes to four.[3]

That the *Belfast Telegraph* felt able to devote some column inches to the proceedings of the Co. Londonderry Welfare Committee on 6 November 1968 was in itself remarkable. A month earlier, on 5 October, the RUC had used strong-arm methods to prevent a banned civil rights march from going from the Waterside across the River Foyle to the Guildhall.

A few hundred feet of film, captured by RTÉ's cameraman Gay O'Brien, changed the course of Northern Ireland's history. Images of unrestrained police batoning unarmed demonstrators, including MPs, 'without justification or excuse' as the Cameron Commission judged later, flashed across the world. At a stroke the television coverage of the events of that day in Derry/Londonderry destabilised all the six counties of Northern Ireland. The Derry Citizens' Action Committee, formed on 9 October, seized the initiative by launching a major programme of civil disobedience. The climax came on 16 November when almost 20,000 citizens, shepherded by dozens of stewards, defied the law and set out to establish their claim to carry the protest into the heart of Derry/Londonderry. Six days later O'Neill – under pressure from Prime Minister Harold Wilson in London – felt he had no choice but to outline a five-point programme of reforms, but the juggernaut of the mass civil rights movement was not to be halted at once by this announcement.

'We can only attribute this to the troubled state of the Province'
In 1969, a vibrant civil rights movement, inspired by direct action on the streets overseas, dissolved into intercommunal conflict, plunging Northern Ireland into near-chaos. In less than two years Northern Ireland moved from a promising period of cooperation to violence so intense that in news coverage across the world it vied with reports of the Vietnam War. The unchained sectarian dragon leaped from its cage as fear, suspicion, atavistic hatred and memory of ancient wrongs gushed to the surface, inaugurating thirty years of destruction, conflict, forced population movement, mutilation and slaughter.

In the spring of 1969 O'Neill was forced to resign and, as the summer marching season approached, vicious rioting erupted in Belfast, particularly in the vicinity of Hooker Street north of the city centre. On 12 August 15,000 joined the Apprentice Boys march in Derry/Londonderry and, as it concluded, the 'Battle of the Bogside' began. During the afternoon of 14 August troops took the place of exhausted RUC officers – the British Army was now on active service in the United Kingdom. That night intense intercommunal fighting erupted in Belfast: by dawn next day six people had been killed or mortally wounded; at least twelve factories had been destroyed; and over 100 houses had been wrecked and another 300 damaged by petrol bombs. Troops arrived in Belfast later that day but they were unable to prevent further violence after darkness had closed in.

The violence of July and August had resulted in ten deaths in the region; 154 people suffered gunshot wounds; 745 injured in other ways; around 300 treated at first-aid posts for the effects of CS gas; 16 factories gutted by fire; 170 homes destroyed and another 417 damaged; 60 Catholic-owned public houses attacked and 24 of them left in ruins; and in Derry/Londonderry one dairy alone lost 43,000 glass milk bottles during the three-day battle in the Bogside. Catholic-owned or occupied premises accounted for 83.5 per cent of the damage, estimated at £8 million. These figures take no account of the rapid spread of fear and intimidation. The Scarman Tribunal, set up to investigate the disturbances of 1969, reported that in Belfast alone 1,820 families fled their homes during and immediately after these riots; 1,505 of these families were Catholic, making up more than 3 per cent of all households in the city.[4] The Provisional IRA emerged at the close of 1969 and what was universally described as 'The Troubles' now entered its bloodiest phase.

The Council's 1969 Annual Report stated that for 'the first time we are unable to report an increase in our educational work and we can only attribute this to the troubled state of the Province, particularly in the Autumn which is normally the busiest time of the year'. It also reported 'a sharp drop in Donations', though this was more than offset by the receipt of the second of three annual payments from the Carnegie United Kingdom Trust Grant. This grant – together with continued grants from the Ministry of Home Affairs, Belfast Corporation and County Welfare Committees – 'enabled us to continue the task of converting our total internal organisation to cope with the transition to the larger scale of operations necessary since coming to our new premises at 76 Dublin Road'.

Despite the widespread dislocation brought about by violence and intimidation, the Council was able to spread its reach further, particularly in Coleraine and Craigavon. The number of interviews for the year leaped to 782 and the number of children involved under the age of sixteen to 432 – an increase over 1968 of 12 per cent. Eighty-two talks were given, including addresses to apprentices at Michelin Tyre Co., Ballymena, and Bridgeport Brass in Lisburn. The disturbed condition of the city of Derry/Londonderry was illustrated by the fact that only seven outpost counselling interviews were conducted there, but a surprising 32 were conducted in the Co. Tyrone village of Clogher. 'While the disturbances in the Province resulted in a substantial reduction in visitors to our stand at the Ideal Home Exhibition and a consequent reduction in sales', the 1969 report continued, 'the sale of books through the activities of our speakers to outside bodies showed a very big increase'.[5]

'Two main causes of unhappiness for young wives'

In retrospect, a remarkable feature of the early years of the Troubles was the way in which the great majority of people continued with the normal routine of their lives. Only rarely, for example, were children prevented from going to school. This author, who during that time had responsibility for GCE night classes in the College of Business Studies building in the heart of Belfast, recalls that, during four evenings a week in term-time, hundreds of adults regularly came in for this tuition from every corner of the city, even in the depths of winter. News bulletins, of course, were watched and listened to with intense concern, but people had no desire for an unrelieved diet of local gloom. Newspapers continued to report on matters which had nothing to do with the political state of affairs, and that included the activities of the Northern Ireland Marriage Guidance Council.

In October 1969 'Chichester' in the *Belfast News-Letter*, with the headline 'The housewife from Holywood who has all the answers', profiled Mrs Mary Grummitt at some length. The English wife of John Grummitt, who had retired as headmaster of The Royal Belfast Academical Institution ten years before, Mary had reached the final of the BBC's Brain of Ulster competition. Mention was made of her NIMGC activities:

October had produced an unexpectedly sunny day and Mrs Mary Grummitt was "gardening like mad" at her Seapark, Holywood Home…Acting and producing for Holywood Players, giving talks to women's organisations, marriage guidance counselling, and she still found time to dig the corner of an adjacent field into an attractive garden.[6]

Life for the Grummitts was in sharp contrast to that of people in working-class estates who often had good reason to dread the onset of darkness every evening. Some did not go into the city centre for years on end. Men employed in the building trade were particularly at risk, since they had no choice but to travel and work, very often, in districts where the inhabitants did not share their religious affiliation. Incidence of stress, depression and loneliness became more common, particularly for women, too often treated then with the liberal dispensing of valium.

Kay Kennedy addressed the issue of isolation in her regular column in the *Sunday News*. She began by asking whether the following comments had a familiar ring: 'You never take me anywhere. It's all right for you. You get out every day and meet all sorts of people. I'm stuck here in the house with the kids all day'. She spoke to a group of welfare workers and was told that 'loneliness and the lack of adult conversation during the time the husband is out of the home are the two main causes of unhappiness for young wives'. She continued:

"If only more young wives would make an effort and get to know their neighbours," one of the group said. Another remarked: "Through attending their local clinic with their children, young mothers can get to know others and make friends." Is this the answer to the loneliness of the housebound young mother? Not for one, who said: "The last thing I want to do is sit nattering in another house just the same as my own and listening to another woman with the same gripes as I have. I want to get OUT".

This cry of frustration expresses the fear that seems to be the root of much of what husbands unkindly call "nagging". It is the fear of a normal, healthy, mentally alert young woman that life is passing her by.

Kay Kennedy talked to a psychologist who commented that if a young woman was not an 'organiser joiner' by nature, 'it's no use telling her to take up a hobby, become a member of the WEA, WI or turn to good works'. The answer was to accept her position as wife and mother 'and enjoy it. It's a strictly temporary situation'.[7]

Kay Kennedy was describing a situation which prevailed in every other part of the United Kingdom. She did not refer at all to the disturbed condition of many parts of Northern Ireland, where so many had been the victims of intimidation and enforced movement and where opening the front door – let alone to go out – could involve risks unimaginable in other regions. And as children grew up and moved from primary to secondary school, the gnawing anxiety of many couples was that their offspring could well be in the company of 'dangerous others', putting both the community and themselves in peril.

Sex education in troubled times

In the autumn of 1969 the BBC announced that there would be broadcasts across the United Kingdom for primary school children aged eight and nine on sex education. The *Belfast News-Letter* explained:

There will be radio broadcasts with film strips and later television broadcasts. The under tens will see naked male and female bodies, the filmed birth of a baby – but not the actual sex act.

The series, with two programmes "Where Do Babies Come From?" and "Growing Up," were unveiled by the BBC yesterday. Clinical terms like "penis" and "vagina" are used. The sex act is explained simply and precisely.

Pilot versions of the two radio-vision programmes (radio broadcasts followed by brightly-coloured film strips) had been tried out in around twenty schools. Neither the word 'love' nor 'marriage' had been used because 'an attempt had been made to make the programme warm and loving' and 'marriage' was ruled out 'because there were areas of Britain where there was a high rate of illegitimacy'. 'In general the children viewed the pilot programmes with absorbed interest and without embarrassment', the BBC stated. 'Teachers commented on the lively and frank discussion which followed the programmes and welcomed the opportunity this gave for answering questions and removing misunderstandings about sex'.

However, this full *News-Letter* report had the headline, 'TV sex lessons for under-10s in Ulster attacked'. Rev Eric Gallagher, former President of the Methodist Church in Ireland, 'was critical of the plan to start sex education programmes for children'. He said: 'This is not a job for the amateur or the enthusiastic do-gooder any more than it is one for the reluctant or the slick professional'. The plan would help, he continued, if the schools could find sympathetic teachers who were willing to prepare their lessons thoroughly – 'Otherwise the last stage could be worse than the first'. No doubt there were many in Northern Ireland who would have agreed with Mrs Mary Whitehouse, Secretary of the National Viewers' Association, when she declared that she 'had great reservations about this. Already there is evidence children may well experiment because their curiosity is aroused by these lessons'.

The *Belfast Telegraph* acknowledged that in Northern Ireland 'there will be reservations whether this method of instruction should be preferred to the more personal approach in the home. Some parents will be concerned about the most basic of all human experiences being treated with the stark semi-clinical approach of an anatomy lesson'. However, it gave its broad support to this BBC initiative and reproduced one of the illustrations from the radiovision programmes, showing a baby almost at full term in the mother's womb. This newspaper devoted an editorial to the subject. In an ideal world this information should be provided by parents:

Sex education on radio and television is the outcome of a society which still feels embarrassed about discussing the most intimate details of its origin. Sex is too often regarded as pornographic. Sex is still the subject of buxom ladies on seaside postcards. Would this all be so if childhood scepticism about sex was taken away?

Measuring the effect of these programmes would not be possible until these children had grown up. 'It may make them even more permissive than today's society but then again it can serve to remove much of the misery of couples who go into matrimony with an inadequate knowledge of how to behave towards one another':

This scepticism about sex is the fault of many parents. Because they have shown an unwillingness to broach the subject with their children somebody else is having to do the delicate work for them. But radio and television programmes are not enough in themselves. They can be helpful – but they are not a substitute for parental advice.[8]

That autumn sex education on screen was also being provided for adults. This was a German production, entitled 'Wonder of Love', being shown at the ABC cinema in central Belfast. At a special screening on 15 October, the *Belfast News-Letter* reported, 'the invited audience sat through most of the very explicit bedroom scenes in stunned silence'. Mrs Phyllis Thompson, chairman of the Northern Ireland Marriage Guidance Council was there. She was not impressed. Mrs Thompson, interviewed afterwards, emphasised that she was speaking personally, found the film 'boring' and continued: 'I thought it was vulgar and pornographic, also technically it was badly done. The dubbing was so terrible it was a constant distraction'. Talk about love had taken up around a quarter of 76 minutes running time 'and the remainder is an illustrated lesson on how to treat your marriage partner but, as Mrs Thompson pointed out, only in respect of one thing – sex'.

In contrast Rev John McCandless of St Patrick's Jordanstown, said he completely approved of the film's content which he considered 'educational'. He said he would take his teenage son and daughter to see it, and commented:

Before I entered the ministry I was in social work for 13 years and I know that many married couples would benefit from the message in this film. It could be very helpful to many people.

Members of Belfast Corporation's Police Committee had been invited to the preview but none had attended.[9]

Divorce: 'the old rules do not apply any more…the boot is on the other, slender, female foot'

On 23 July 1969 a journalist from the *Belfast News-Letter* interviewed Mrs Peggy Musson, the Northern Ireland Marriage Guidance Council's information officer. This was during what shipyard workers had always referred to as the 'Twelfth Fortnight', when the great majority in Northern Ireland took their annual holidays. The 'Twelfth' itself that year was marked by a ferocious intercommunal conflict by Unity Flats in Belfast, an attack on the Orange march in Derry/Londonderry by youths from the Bogside, and by sectarian clashes in Lurgan. However, an almost eerie calm prevailed during the three weeks thereafter. Mrs Musson took advantage of this to lay out the Council's wares. During the previous year, she said, a total of 736 interviews were given but she emphasises that the Council's work was by no means confined to counselling on marriage problems:

"In the field of education we gave 317 sessions last year to a total of 1,671 people, and there is an increasing number of clergy and youth leaders coming to us for guidance". One of the problems the council has to face continually is finance. It has an annual bill of about £4,500 and in grants from the Ministry of Home Affairs, Belfast Corporation and Down County Council they can only raise £2,300.

"Last year we made an appeal to industry, but we had a very poor response," said Mrs Musson. "We do have a bookshop which brings in some money, and we get donations and hold jumble sales to raise the extra money, but it's always a difficult job, and it's getting more difficult all the time".

The Council had only twenty-six counsellors and Mrs Musson warned that when new centres were set up in Craigavon and Coleraine, 'the already limited numbers will be unable to cope'.[10]

Just over a fortnight later, on 10 August 1969, while the situation in Northern Ireland continued to present the appearance of being under control, the *Sunday News* devoted a centre-page spread to the NIMGC. Written by Bob Cameron, this was based principally on an interview with the chairman, Phyllis Thompson. Cameron began with statistics: during the last quarter of 1968 alone 'over 2,270 couples had walked down the aisle – the highest number for 22 years'. But if it was 'a boom year for confetti' it was also a record one for divorce figures. In 1966 '150 wives pointed out that a £10 wedding ring isn't the current price of a doormat', 211 couples divorced in 1967 and the figures reached a new peak in 1968 of 229. There had only been 118 broken marriages in 1959 – 'so what has caused the divorce rate to practically double in ten years?' Mrs Thompson was asked. Her reply was succinct: 'it's because the old rules do not apply any more. In other words the boot is on the other, slender, female foot'.

The provision of legal aid, introduced in Northern Ireland in November 1965 (fifteen years after the rest of the United Kingdom), had made a great difference. 'In the past, the wife who has been kept "barefoot and pregnant" in the kitchen, has just about managed to scrape enough money together for food, never mind save up for a divorce'. At roughly £150 per divorce, around £9,000 had been paid out under this scheme in 1968, £6,000 more than in 1967. Recipients were expected to pay back at least some of this money over time, leading Cameron to describe this state of affairs as 'divorce on HP'. Legal aid made it possible for wives to take their husbands to court for maintenance orders. The statistics 'show that the Ulster housewife is not prepared to face a life of drudgery and despair – and will take this first legal step towards divorce'. Cameron continued:

So despite Ulster's hot religious climate, the kissing has begun to stop, and the long, cool honeymoon is drawing to its inevitable close.

But not all foundering marriages come to an end in the divorce courts. Many are saved thanks to the vigilant, and tireless efforts of the Marriage Guidance Council.

The MGC's chairman, Mrs Phyllis Thompson, has beautifully young eyes (thanks to 44 years of happily married life), that can turn a serious shade of blue, twinkle mischievously, or look at you without a flicker of emotion. She is an infinitely patient, kind and above all understanding veteran of 14 years as a guidance counsellor. A typically discreet chairman of the Ulster branch which started here 21 years ago.

Twenty-five volunteer trained counsellors, he reported, had to deal with 293 'heartbreak cases' in 1968, involving 736 interviews. The number of children involved in these cases was 385. 'Counsellors also managed to visit borstal children and give a total of 317 discussion-type lectures to 1,600 teenagers all over the Province'. These sessions 'provided a vital personal link between the counsellors and the teenagers in case they should have matrimonial difficulties later on'. Mrs Thompson gave as an example, an invitation to a counsellor to watch the sex educational film 'Helga' with a Venture Scout Group. 'This is just the kind of relationship we are looking for', she said. 'In the past many couples have left their troubles nearly too late before coming to see us. Now there is a growing trend for young couples to arrive here and talk freely about their problems before the rot sets in'.

She explained why she could not discuss case histories:

An ailing marriage is a very delicate affair. We offer complete anonymity for a couple to come and see us and pour out their troubles. In no circumstances could we discuss individual cases, it would simply be betraying a secret and it could do our work untold harm.

Asked for her views on divorce, Mrs Thompson thought that 'divorce is a good thing sometimes'. One of the main reasons for a rising divorce rate 'is the modern trend for independence among married women'. They no longer had to sit around waiting to get money from their husbands – they can go out and earn it. 'And if anything should seriously go wrong with the marriage the wife can always afford to get out of it.' In response to the question, 'what makes a good counsellor, and how would you go about saving a marriage?' she said:

To be a good counsellor I think you have got to be completely unemotional about the person sitting in front of you. Be like a sponge and soak up their problems. Or be a wall for them to bounce their problems off.

Impartiality is also essential. I remember when I first started, wives and husbands used to sit in front of me and tell me the most horrible things their partners had done. And when they had finished I would feel like letting rip. But that is something you must never do. Be clinical and understanding of all the issues, you're like a father-figure really, an emotional outlet for pent-up feelings.

And how would Mrs Thompson go about saving a marriage?

It's not the counsellor who can save a marriage, but it's the couple involved who have their fate in their own hands. It's strange the number of times men or women will come along distraught and on the verge of divorce, but after they have sat and poured out everything to you they often stop and listen to what they are saying themselves. And perhaps they may think well, I shouldn't have lost my head over that, or that I have been a bit of a nagger.

The reporter concluded that the Council's conception of the ideal couple 'appears to be: Companionship. And don't try to mould your partner into the kind of person you want him to be'.[11]

Just two days after this article appeared, the storm in Derry/Londonderry broke and Northern Ireland entered into the most violent period in its history.

'Marriages…serviced, repaired and renovated in the Dublin Road'

Of the nineteen who met with untimely deaths as a direct result of the violence in 1969, fifteen were civilians. Constable Victor Arbuckle, killed by the UVF on the Shankill Road on 12 October, was the RUC's first victim. During the year 1970 the Falls Road military curfew in July brought the Army's 'honeymoon period' with the nationalist population to an end, as the GOC, Sir Ian Freeland, had predicted. The Provisional IRA gained many fresh recruits and launched its bombing campaign. By the end of 1970 twenty-nine people, nineteen of them civilians, had lost their lives in the conflict.[12]

Captain O'Neill had accepted a peerage, becoming Lord O'Neill of the Maine. His wife, now Lady O'Neill, continued as the Council's Patron. Shock waves from Northern Ireland's conflict were frequently felt, quite literally, coming through the walls of the NIMGC offices in Belfast. Here, as Ann Karel reported in the *Belfast News-Letter* in December 1969, the demand for the Council's services was nevertheless growing strongly. Interviewing the vice-chairman, Gladys Jeffery, Ms Karel provided a lucid and detailed account of what was required of a marriage guidance counsellor:

Marriages may be made in heaven, but more than a few of them are serviced, repaired and renovated in the Dublin Road. It is here that the Belfast offices of the Northern Ireland Marriage Guidance Council organise the activities of 28 counsellors. More are always needed but two-thirds of those who apply to become counsellors never make the grade.

As Mrs Jeffery explained:

"There is a very careful selection process followed by a fairly intensive training programme. Counsellors are highly trained people, and they must go through six intensive courses during their first two years, plus a regular visit from London-based tutors, plus a great deal of private reading and study."
    Counsellors delight in exploding popular myths about their work. They are not paid. Every counsellor must undertake to conduct three interviews each week, write up the necessary notes, conduct the necessary study and attend the required group discussions as a minimum. Most of them do much more.

Counsellors did not sit behind desks and deal with couples. The small counselling rooms contained a few easy chairs and an occasional table. There was no firm ruling whether interviews were conducted with either the husband or the wife or with both. 'We don't, of course, give advice to anybody,' explained Mrs Jeffery. 'People sometimes imagine us sitting behind a desk, telling people what they should do and providing a sort of instant magic cure. Nothing could be further from the truth.' The counsellor's job was to sit and listen with understanding, and by assisting to crystalline the client's problem in the client's own mind, to show that the solution lies also with the client. A counsellor could help with direct information on, for example, legal or medical problems but the basic emotional problem, once isolated, must be solved by the person facing it.
    'This strange blend of objectivity, understanding and human sympathy needed in a good counsellor explains to a degree the need for a careful selection procedure', the reporter continued. When couples were facing problems in their marriage they needed the help of someone 'who, at worst, will not make things any more difficult'. 'Sometimes people are disappointed', Mrs Jeffery recalled. 'A wife can be upset because I refuse to tell her husband he must do as she says. And a mother will insist that I tell her daughter to leave her husband before I have even had a chance to talk to the girl'. She was quick to point out that mothers, and all other relatives, were normally excluded form counselling interviews.
    The demands upon counsellors, 'intellectual, emotional and from the point of view of devoting sufficient time to the job', meant that there was among them a greater-than-average preponderance of middle-class women. 'But the hard work, hard training and continued high standards ensure that the soft and elegant do-gooders are eliminated at some stage or other'.

Mrs Jeffery observed that if there was any common root cause of marital trouble it was failure to communicate:

"So often we find that, for one reason or another, a husband and wife are moving away from each other. They need to re-establish a way to communicate with each other. But not all our work is remedial", she went on, explaining that it was better to build a fence at the top of a cliff than to repair broken bones.

Ms Karel concluded the interview by making an inquiry as to the state of the counsellor's own marriage. 'A very happy one', Mrs Jeffery replied, 'and I think it fair to say that the understanding I have learned through counselling has made it even happier'. 'Mind you', she added, 'you need to have an understanding partner'.[13]

'Meeting the challenge stemming from acute social disturbance'

In the 1970 Annual Report the Chairman, Charles H G Kinahan, began his message with these words:

The wind of change has been with us for some time now – political upheaval – industrial unrest – unemployment – inflation – communal strife – has there ever been a year more likely to produce more frightening tensions into ordinary people's lives and, as so often happens, leads ultimately to the breakdown of their marriages? There has never been a time when the work of the Marriage Guidance Council has been more needed in promoting a positive and creative attitude towards making sound family life an integral part of our society.

Despite these challenges, the work of the Council continued to expand. The number of interviews rose to 1,093 and the number of children involved to 550. A total of 1,163 young people attended 162 sessions in youth clubs, schools and other centres. Some casework agencies were able to quote examples of problems presented and the way in which the agency had helped. Because of the particular nature of its work, the Council could not do this. What it could do was to demonstrate the care with which the organisation prepared its counsellors – 'volunteers giving their services without remuneration'. The object of counselling, the 1970 report explained:

is to provide help for people who have difficulties or anxieties in their marriages or in other personal relationships. It is a time-consuming process often involving hours of interviews extending over many weeks during which the client is helped to come to a better understanding of the problem through the relationship of trust built up with the counsellor. It is not a matter of an all-wise, all-knowing expert advising others how to live.

Counsellors had first to be accepted at a nationally-convened Selection Conference. Then they were committed to a course of basic training, involving six residential sessions, followed by continual in-service training, through fortnightly discussion groups and regular individual tutorials. In short, those who volunteered to train and serve as counsellors had to be prepared to devote a prodigious amount of their time, unpaid, to enable the Council to function:

NIMGC, in common with all other MGCs throughout the UK is entirely dependent on the faithful, constant, regular weekly commitment of the counsellors to maintain the service it offers to the public.[14]

Derick Woods joined the Council in 1970. It was Gladys Jeffery who got him involved – they knew each other because her son Keith (now the distinguished historian, Professor Keith Jeffery) was a pupil at Methodist College where Derick was a member of staff. 'Would you like to come on to the executive?' she asked. 'I'm not even a member', Derick responded. 'Just pay your five shillings and become a member', she advised. 'It shows the amateur nature of the organisation at that stage', he recalled.

Derick Woods, one of the longest-serving and most committed members of the NIMGC, explained why he (and, indeed, many like him) was attracted to and drawn in to marriage guidance:

I could see in the school the problems that divorce and family troubles caused children. Of course, at that stage that problem was quite small; but it grew and grew and by the time I retired it was, I suppose, a third of the kids were from broken homes.

But I never saw the Marriage Guidance Council or Relate as a marriage-mending machine – it was a way of counselling people. By the time I was involved it was an enabling organisation to help people get through the trauma of trouble in their marriage. Sometimes it worked – they decided to stay together, and that was great from the family point of view – but they made the decisions.

If the couple decided not to stay together then the organisation would help to ensure that 'a good divorce (if there is such a thing)' was the outcome. Was Derick motivated by his religious convictions? 'My religious convictions play a part in my whole life – so, yes, definitely'. Gladys Jeffery had coaxed Derick Woods into the organisation because she was sure he would make a good counsellor. But the responsibilities of his own full-time position in education meant that there was no point in him undertaking the necessary training – he simply would not be able to devote sufficient time to counselling. He did, however, have the time and experience needed to help run the organisation – something he was to do for nearly three decades. 'When I first went on the executive', he remembered, 'at the first few meetings I was at there was a man called Maurice Smith. He was counselling *me*. Maurice kept asking questions all the time. And it was said to me: "You realise Maurice was counselling you!"'[15]

Organisational cooperation not yet a marriage ... 'but we are doing a very strong line'

When the group owning the *Belfast News-Letter* decided to launch the *Sunday News* in the mid-1960s many wondered whether it could survive. By 1970 wiseacre journalists, trading witticisms with the *News-Letter's* celebrated columnist Ralph Bossence and nursing foaming pints in the Duke of York's public bar off Donegall Street, were observing that Saturday's news made the *Sunday News*. Indeed this was true: Saturdays were so often marked by political rioting, by vicious sectarian murders and by other violent incidents that this newspaper had a ready, if anxious, market the following morning. Nevertheless, throughout its years of publication, the *Sunday News* consistently gave space to the work of the Northern Ireland Marriage Guidance Council.

Peggy Musson, the Council's administrative officer, availed of every opportunity to raise public awareness by writing to the press. In June 1970 she responded to an article in the *Sunday News* suggesting that 'one day marriage bureaux may be as much part of the welfare state as is Marriage Guidance and Family Planning'. She continued:

In fact, the Marriage Guidance Council fills a gap (as does Family Planning) in the social services by providing specialised counselling for people with marital problems and by undertaking preventative educational work…If some of the marriages made in the bureaux prove not to have been made in heaven may I point out that the Marriage Guidance Council at 76, Dublin Road, Belfast, is here to help and also that working from the premise that prevention is better than cure, it offers courses for engaged couples, where those getting married can discuss the various problems and adjustments that face them. Our telephone number is: Belfast 23454. – Yours, &c, Peggy Musson (Mrs) Administrative Officer.[16]

Mrs Musson wrote to the press to remind readers that on 4 October the BBC's Week's Good Cause Appeal would be on behalf of the Northern Ireland Marriage Guidance Council. In October 1970, *City Week* interviewed her. She said that 'we use the word discussion, not lecture or talk' because the Council was adamant that adolescents were more mature than their elders liked to believe. 'We don't like to advise people, we ask questions and help them help themselves as we can never get into anyone's mind to the problem', she said. 'So we give aid to point the way – not lecture.' The feature gave particular prominence to the publications available: the reporter found 'row upon row of inexpensive booklets and paper backs dealing with questions posed by people with every sort of problem. Contraception, of course, is one of the main aspects dealt with…birth control obviously warrants special attention'.[17]

Peggy Musson also addressed a unique meeting of marriage guidance organisations in Dublin on 28 November 1970. This was the first occasion that members of the Catholic Marriage Advisory Council, the Northern Ireland Marriage Guidance Council and the Marriage Counselling Service (a Church of Ireland organisation based at 47 Leeson Street in Dublin, which hosted the conference) had met formally together. As Nicholas Tyndall, Chief Executive Officer of the National Marriage Guidance Council, said to the delegates, 'as yet the non-catholic and Catholic organisations had not sat down together nationally'.

The purpose of the meeting in Dublin was twofold. Firstly, to enable the three voluntary organisations in Ireland concerned with family relationships and marriage reconciliation to come together and inform each other of their respective organisations and discuss mutual areas of interest and concern. The second was to hear Mr Tyndall speak of the experience of the National Council. Mrs Bonita Scott, a marriage counsellor, explained that the Marriage Counselling Service had been founded in 1961 by Canon M Handy. Associated with the Dublin Council of Churches, it drew most of its financial support from church sources and parishes. She outlined the 'extensive training' undertaken by the organisation's nine counsellors and fifteen youth counsellors.

Mrs Celine Regan, a counsellor of the Catholic Marriage Advisory Council, described the structure of her organisation which began in Belfast and was now operating with thirty counsellors in Kilkenny, Limerick, Cork and Dublin. She explained the method of selection of counsellors 'and the training they received over 18 months on marriage, development and behaviour and counselling, with a written examination at the end'. Their counsellors – all married, aged between 35 and 45, and with third level education – worked on either remedial or educational activity with parents, engaged couples, school leavers and teachers. The organisation had over four hundred cases referred to it throughout the country. Mrs Regan emphasised the importance of premarital education.

Mrs Peggy Musson then got her opportunity to summarise the work of NIMGC. She concluded by observing that she felt that there was no difference between the types of marital cases which her Council dealt with and those which had been mentioned by earlier speakers. In his keynote address Mr Tyndall said that, while in the past counsellors recruited were over the age of 30, recent experience indicated that those under that age had been very successful – he therefore suggested that the recruiting of younger counsellors should be considered:

He commented on the need for married counsellors to be trained in working with young people as more and more of their clients are coming from lower age groups in early years of marriage. Similarly, Youth Counsellors previously accustomed to meeting youth in groups are now finding that they need to acquire the experience for working in person to person counselling interviews which was normally part of marriage counsellors' training.

In the closing words of the conference, Father M Browne, Director of the Catholic Marriage Advisory Council, commented on the declared willingness of the three organisations to work more closely together: 'It might not yet be a marriage between us, but we are doing a very strong line'.[18]

'New city neurosis'
As the year 1970 drew to a close, the *Portadown Times* had as its front-page headline; '200 BROKEN MARRIAGES':

More than 200 marriages broke up in the Portadown area last year. And the figures are so startling that the Northern Ireland Marriage Guidance Council are considering opening a full-time office in town.

At the moment the Council are served by fortnightly sessions at the Citizens' Advice

Bureau office, but this is completely booked out and will be increased to three in the near future.

Gladys Jeffery, described as a 'top official from the Council's headquarters in Belfast', had come to Portadown to look into the possibility of setting up an office there. Certainly the demand was there, she said. 'We would hope to eventually start a comprehensive marriage education programme in Portadown', which would include talks in schools and youth clubs about all aspects of marriage including personal relationships and budgeting. 'Many young people rush into marriage without much prior thought', she added. 'These marriages are shaky from the start'. Other reasons she gave for breakups were lack of communication between the partners and the immaturity of one partner. The following week the *Portadown Times* reported that 'last week's front page story' had been 'received with dismay in the area'.[19]

In the wake of the news from Portadown, Patrick Boyce of the *Sunday News* wrote a feature with the headline, 'Rising Living Costs Blamed for Jump in Broken Marriages'. He reported that 'Northern Ireland is in the middle of an epidemic of broken marriages'. In the new housing estates throughout the region 'the incidence of couples breaking up has risen dramatically during the past year'. Referring to the statistics for Portadown, Boyce wrote that the NIMGC administrative officer, Peggy Musson, 'hit out' at what she described as 'new city neurosis'. A call had gone out for more people with marriage problems to seek advice before couples reached breaking point. 'It is vitally important that couples should come to see us as soon as things start to go wrong', she said. 'We are hoping to have counsellors in most of the big estates soon in a bid to curb this rise in broken marriages'. She thought that the move to new housing areas puts different strains and pressures on a marriage:

"The new house is usually more expensive for a start," she said. If it has electric underfloor or central heating, the family faces big fuel bills where before they used to buy bags of coal as they were needed. "Then when this big bill comes in they can't pay it and this financial worry leads to increased friction between husband and wife".

She also hit out at the lack of community and entertainment facilities in the new estates, which tends to encourage a drift back to old haunts for men in search of a social life. "When you take people from a small tightly knit integrated community you have to rehouse them in a similar community if the move is to be a complete success. Too often these new estates have no pubs or cinemas close at hand, so husbands drift back to their old areas to have a drink with the boys. And in new areas where they might not know many people, a couple will find it difficult to get a baby sitter if they want to go out. This, plus the added expense of having to travel into town, means that some couples seldom go out together. This leads to resentment on the woman's part because she doesn't like being stuck out of town".

She said that a high proportion of the '800 couples we interviewed this year came from housing estates, and that is only scraping the surface. A lot of people seem to think there is something shameful in coming to seek help about their marriage, but surely it is worse to break up and mess up their own lives as well as the lives of their children'.

Adam Turner, the NSPCC inspector for Co. Armagh, reinforced Gladys Jeffery's observations. 'There has been a big increase in the number of broken marriages in the New City area,' he said. 'And we are very worried about these families because often if the father runs off, the wife and the children are left on the poverty line'. He agreed that the move to new housing estates was partly responsible 'for the large number of separations in the area'. County Welfare departments had begun to take some action. Family casework visitors had been sent in to offer help and advice to families in difficulties. Edward Malone, recently appointed Community Development Officer for Co. Down, said:

My job is to try and involve people in the day-to-day running and living on the estates… We are trying to educate them to take an interest in local tenants committees and community organisations. By doing this it is hoped to generate a better, integrated, independent community with local recreational facilities and thus get rid of the attitudes that you must go into Belfast for a night out.[20]

In retrospect, the startling feature of all these newspaper reports on the rise in the incidence of separation and divorce, and on social problems arising in new housing estates poorly supplied with ancillary facilities (in common with many other parts of the United Kingdom), is the complete lack of reference to what then made Northern Ireland a place apart – the political violence and internecine struggle then convulsing a deeply divided community.

'The third successive twelve months of strife and bitterness in our community'
The year 1971 witnessed a further intensification of the Troubles. Brian Faulkner, who became Northern Ireland's last Prime Minister in the spring, obtained the approval of the Westminster government to introduce internment on 9 August and this was followed by a steep rise in the death rate. The year ended with the Ulster Volunteer Force's bombing of McGurk's bar, killing fifteen people, and a bomb on the Shankill Road which caused four deaths, including a baby aged seven months. That year a total of 180 people died directly as a result of the violence.[21]

Naturally, this impacted on the work of the Council as the 1971 report acknowledged:

This year saw the third successive twelve months of strife and bitterness in our community. The resulting tension had a marked effect not only on our service but also on that of all welfare organisations. During the year the Catholic Advisory Service's premises were destroyed and they expressed their thanks to us for the help which we immediately offered.

Domestic problems multiplied and our counsellors were called upon to deal with a large number of cases resulting from the upset state of the Province.

Our evening sessions were hit by the reluctance of clients to come out after dark and the dislocation, and sometimes the absence, of public transport had its effect on clients' ability to come to 76 Dublin Road.

There was a sharp decrease in the number of young people attending Youth Clubs and as a result our education work was adversely affected, likewise there was a reduced demand for our speakers to address outside organisations which meant that we lost valuable publicity and a reduction in the sales of booklets which normally results from this activity.

The 1971 report's message was written that year by Mrs Gladys Jeffery, Vice-Chairman and also the Council's representative for both Northern Ireland and North-West England on the National Executive. She wrote:

Living in Northern Ireland today we can all too vividly see and read and hear the problems of our Province with all its resultant trail of tragedy and bitterness. It is not a time to stand idly by and just look or criticise – it is time for action, especially for all those people who continually devote unsparingly of their time and energies in the many voluntary social welfare organisations working within our community.

'The need to establish and promote a positive and creative attitude towards making sound family life an integral part of our society', she continued, 'has greater pertinence today than ever before'.

In March 1971 the BBC broadcast a thirty-minute radio programme, presented by Pat Lindsay, on marriage guidance entitled 'The Counsellors'. It was reviewed in the *Belfast News-Letter* by Ian J Hill. At first it did not seem to him to be the 'style of programme likely to brighten up my Sunday afternoon's listening…it looked as if it was going to be one of those worthily intended neo-public-service-devices of which provincial radio is so fond'.

Gradually his opinion changed 'as the information bank released its information and built up a picture of the service' and became particularly interesting when it dealt with the educational work of the Council – 'and actually mentioned sexual problems, a facet of the overall scene which had been, up to then, conspicuous by its absence'. It was the last section of the programme which most engaged Hill's attention, which attempted to answer: 'How were counsellors really chosen, did they really push a certain moral line, why do people want to become counsellors?'[22]

'Craigavon…turning into the headstone on a multiple grave of broken homes'

Population concentration ensured that the cities of Belfast and Derry/Londonderry recorded the highest number of violent incidents during the Troubles. However, mid-Ulster was disproportionately affected and journalists and Army officers alike often referred to the 'murder triangle' in this area. In the 1960s Captain O'Neill's government had set out to implement a grandiose scheme to create a new city, Craigavon, in the Lurgan-Portadown area. Multinational firms were persuaded to set up branch factories here but some stayed only for a short time and those remaining did not provide as many employment opportunities as had been hoped. Mistakes made on the outskirts of Liverpool, Glasgow and other large cities across the Irish Sea were repeated here. Above all, these housing developments were bleak, too often devoid of character and severely lacking in facilities which would turn these estates into communities.

The exceptionally high rate of marriage breakup in the Craigavon-Portadown area had attracted considerable media attention in 1970. In September the Council set up a committee of ten women in Portadown with the aim of opening a branch of NIMGC in the area. This committee was formally set up and launched at a wine and cheese party in Craigavon House on 10 September. The function of this committee was to be mainly administrative, keeping headquarters in Belfast informed and helping to find suitable people for training as marriage guidance counsellors.

Julie Roy, writing for the *Portadown News*, 'noticed representatives of various women's organisations in the town, together with counsellors from Belfast, who were immediately recognisable by virtue of their lapel badges'. She reported that there was no difficulty in recruiting ten women to sit on the committee. Her article, along with a similar report in the *Portadown Times*, provided readers with ample details on the philosophy and work of the Council, much of it provided by an interview with the chairman, Charles Kinahan, who stressed that 'we are anxious to train local people as counsellors, where they can be more at hand'. The counselling was currently being provided by Gladys Jeffery and Mr M R Smith, both travelling from Belfast.

Ms Roy concluded:

Personally, I believe the Council is providing a most helpful and worthwhile service. But I would like to be able to prove this. Could, therefore, anyone who has been helped by the counsellors, get in touch with me? I would relate your story without betraying your identity. Your story would do more than any advertising campaign.

She did get the response requested and published it in the last week of November.[23]

On 26 September 1971 the *Sunday News* reporters returned to Craigavon's acute problems with a feature headlined, '*New City Neurosis* blamed for divorce rise'. It began by describing a typical case:

Alan and Mary have been married for eight years. They won't be for very much longer. For this young couple are victims of what has been termed "New City Neurosis".

The move from the comforting cosiness of a street in one of Belfast's redevelopment areas to the mushrooming housing estates of Craigavon put stresses on the marriage which are irreparable. Increased rent, hire purchase commitments and attempting to keep up with their new neighbours led them into debt. But instead of making a serious attempt to budget properly Alan tried to run away from his troubles by drinking heavily.

This led to more debt. Mary found herself left at home alone at nights and when she complained Alan struck her. In response Mary started going out to dances at night with girl friends. Unable to get baby sitters, their three children were left alone. Hearing the children crying, a neighbour complained to the welfare authorities. The

NSPCC inspector called, sized up the situation and put the couple in touch with the local Marriage Guidance counsellor. 'But it was too late; all affection had gone out of the marriage. Love had turned to bitterness'. Thus what had begun with a good job and a modern house was now about to end up in the divorce court.

This case was 'just another number in the dismal statistics that show an alarming increase in Ulster's divorce rate'. Over the previous six years the divorce rate had risen by more than 100 per cent. The rise was attributable in part to the provision of legal aid from 1966 onwards. The feature continued:

But there are also other reasons for this epidemic of broken marriages. The unaccustomed pressures of life in new housing estates throughout the Province has led to a dramatic rise in the number of marriage break ups in certain areas.

And nowhere is this more noticeable than in Craigavon, where Ulster's signpost to a new and prosperous future is turning into the headstone on a multiple grave of broken homes.

The reporter was told that there were nine matrimonial cases waiting to be dealt with in Lurgan court in the previous week. Adam Turner, the NSPCC inspector, said that this was an average weekly number. He remarked that more than 70 per cent of his work was dealing with matrimonial cases, 'trying to salvage some future from the wreck of a broken home'.

Peggy Musson said that, to try to have counsellors available as quickly as possible in this 'potential black spot', a special ten-woman committee had been set up by the NIMGC with the aim of opening a branch in the area. For the present the Council was holding two sessions a week, on a Monday morning in a welfare clinic and on Wednesday evenings in the Citizens Advice Bureau. Here two highly-trained counsellors were attempting to cope with the rising number of couples in difficulty. Peggy Musson continued:

But if we are to have any success we will have to have at least two counsellors in the area who will be on call any time they are needed…it is essential that couples come to see us at the first sign of trouble. They have no reason to be shy about approaching us. All the counsellors are specially selected and have undergone a two-year training period. And, of course everything is strictly confidential.

She attempted to explain why the move to Craigavon put different strains and pressures on a marriage. Families were up against all sorts of tension when they move into a new area, making new friends, furnishing a new house and readjusting to a life away from family and friends. Once again she referred to higher bills – including the unexpectedly high cost of electric underfloor or central heating – causing friction, and to the lack of community feeling and entertainment facilities. Not only were baby sitters difficult to get but they had the added cost of travelling to their entertainment. The result was that couples seldom went out together, 'which can lead to resentment on the woman's part because she doesn't like being stuck at home. Or else they leave the children alone, which can be dangerous and illegal.' Adam Turner said that when he came 'across a case of troubled marriage I usually try to get them to go to see the Marriage Guidance people. But sometimes they don't want to or it is too late to help. If only people would ask for help as soon as things go wrong, a lot more marriages could be saved'.[24]

A branch of NIMGC was set up that autumn in Craigavon. The honorary secretary was Mrs Betty Richards who spoke to a reporter for the *Portadown News* and made available the text of a talk given by someone who had been helped by the Council:

After reaching the searching decision myself that my problem was already too big for me to carry alone, I rather reluctantly contacted the Marriage Guidance Council. I was impressed at my very first interview by the complete privacy and quietness in which one was given the opportunity to talk and discuss with such sympathetic yet practical men and women as marriage guidance counsellors.

Their task is to help people, through a series of interviews, to come to terms with their innermost feelings of confusion, shock and emotional turmoil. The counsellor, who became my friend, accepted me without question, without prejudice and without judgement. Slowly a relationship was built up which gave me a sense of my personal worth which my marriage had long since stripped from me. There were moments of despondency for us both but I shall be eternally grateful to the particular counsellor who came to my aid so selflessly.[25]

In February 1972 Portadown Council decided to defer the question of a donation to the Portadown Marriage Guidance Council 'until they had more details about the organisation'. The *Portadown News* writer of the 'Jeanne's Week' was appalled. Under the headline, GIVE 'EM THE MONEY, she had found it particularly alarming that Alderman Harry McCourt had remarked that there was no need for a branch in the area. In his view, 'couples who are having problems with their marriage should go to their minister, and if they cannot find guidance there they should turn to the Welfare authorities'. Her response was that those like Mr McCourt who were not properly trained in marriage guidance work 'should not give advice – more harm than good can be done, however well meaning they are'. In any case most people 'might feel some reserve in discussing intimate problems' with a clergyman. She concluded:

It is far easier to talk to a stranger as three hundred odd callers a year at Portadown Citizens Advice Bureau will find out. As for the Welfare Authorities, they are so overworked that I do not think it is fair to ask them to take on this extra task.

Come on councillors, there should be no doubt in your minds. Give the experts their due and, more important, give them the money![26]

Before the year was out Portadown Council, along with all other local authorities in Northern Ireland, would be voted out of existence. It was only one of many transformations which would occur in 1972, a year which would prove to be the worst year of violence in the Troubles.

'Meeting the challenge stemming from acute social disturbance in the community'
On 26 January 1972, in the words of the Northern Ireland Marriage Guidance annual report, 'we had a visit from the "bomb"...and had all the windows in the front of the building blown in. Luckily, although the staff and some others were in the building at the time, no injuries resulted and the debris was quickly cleaned away and the windows boarded up.' Four days later, on 'Bloody Sunday', thirteen men were shot dead by paratroopers during a civil rights march in Derry/Londonderry. The IRA intensified its bombing campaign, often in crowded places such as the Abercorn restaurant and Donegall Street in Belfast during March. Prime Minister Edward Heath insisted that Westminster take over control of security. Prime Minister Brian Faulkner and his Northern Ireland government resigned. Stormont was 'prorogued' but the reality was that the Northern Ireland Parliament never sat again after 28 March 1972. 'Direct rule' had been imposed.

For the Provisional IRA the war went on. On 21 July that organisation detonated twenty-six bombs in a few hours in Belfast, killing eleven people and injuring 130, in what became known as 'Bloody Friday'. Altogether the Troubles claimed 497 victims in 1972, 259 of them civilians.[27] In spite of plans to restore devolution, Northern Ireland was no longer a devolved region of the United Kingdom; direct rule from Westminster was to be the norm for all but a few months until the end of the century.

'The present troubles have had an adverse effect on the number of clients seen by the counsellors', the 1972 Annual Report observed. 'This has been a disappointing year in the field of education and this can only be put down to the troubled situation in the Province'. However the report added that 'it is remarkable that the interviews have kept up as they have when Dublin Road has had its share of bombs and gunfire. Counsellors have been undeterred from duty and accepted cheerfully the unkept appointments'. It continued:

For almost four years now the Council has been meeting the challenge stemming from acute social disturbance in the community and it says much for the enduring spirit of service in our movement that the work has progressed so steadily and achieved so much in the past year.

Indeed, throughout the year 'the energetic campaign of extension was continued': a self-governing Craigavon Counselling Centre branch was established; counselling services in Omagh, Coleraine and Bangor were bedding in; and work was well advanced in setting up a branch in Ballymena. The rise in the price of books did not cause 'undue sales resistance'. A new National Marriage Guidance Council publication, *Sexual Difficulties in Marriage* by David Mace, though considered expensive at 50p a copy, was proving a best seller. This augured well for *Goodbye to the Stork* by Jill Kenner, due out in 1973.

Ballymena, Peggy Musson and NIMGC counselling explained
The constant succession of violent incidents and atrocities, together with rapid institutional change and political uncertainty, made it more difficult for the Council

to obtain the same level of media attention it had received up to now. However, the provincial press was taking more notice as NIMGC was extending its services beyond greater Belfast. Many of these newspapers simply repeated verbatim Council press releases, almost always written by the indefatigable Peggy Musson.

Anne Montgomery, editing 'Women's Page' in the *Ballymena Guardian*, interviewed Mrs Musson to provide a very full account of the work of the Council. Indeed, it could be argued, that this article was the most lucid and enlightening one yet published in Northern Ireland's newspapers. Ms Montgomery began:

One of the most popular subjects for newspaper and magazine cartoons is the visit to the Marriage Guidance Counsellor. Numerous situations and catchlines with this in mind have been penned over the years but behind all the jokes and laughter lies a very important and essential service to the community.

Though the Belfast headquarters at 76 Dublin Road had branches in Derry/Londonderry, Coleraine, Bangor, Omagh and Craigavon, 'up until now, however, Ballymena, despite all its other amenities and services, could not boast a branch but it is hoped that in the very near future this state of affairs will be put right'. This was due to be rectified by Ballymena's Mayor, Alderman J B Millar, who would be hosting a wine and cheese reception in the Town Hall.

Peggy Musson made her way to Ballymena to explain to her the work of the Council. Mrs Musson stressed that NIMGC, in existence in Northern Ireland for twenty-five years, was 'a completely non-denominational body set up for the welfare of people from all sections of the community'. Having outlined the aims and concerns of the Council, its counselling and educational work, and its publications, she was asked 'what about the counsellors themselves? Who are they, what sort of people?' She responded that 'the selection and training are extremely stiff and when I say that only about 47 per cent of the applicants successfully get through selection, you will understand just what I mean'. The ideal ages for counsellors were between 26 and 46. Academic qualifications were not essential, 'just people with the right personality who don't look on their job as a means of simply prying into other people's affairs. Counsellors have to be sympathetic and understanding and intelligent enough to offer sound advice.' Like the confidential relationship between a patient and a doctor, the one between a counsellor and client was equally confidential – 'no one need have any worries that their problems will become known to other people'.

Counsellors never tried to handle themselves anything which should be dealt with by a professional. Professional consultants, for example legal or psychiatric, could be approached. The job of the counsellor was to recommend their clients to obtain the correct help. The aim of every counsellor was, through a gradually developing relationship, to help the client understand and improve their relationships with a married partner.

What prompted a man or a woman to visit a marriage guidance counsellor in the first place? There was the attraction of talking over the particular problem with an objective party, someone who could give an unbiased opinion. Mrs Musson went on:

The basic problem with human relationships is lack of communication between the parties concerned and for one or both it is very often a tremendous help to share the trouble with someone on neutral ground so to speak, knowing that any information will never go beyond the particular counsellor involved.

After listening to the problem, the counsellor can offer practical suggestions about the courses of action open and very often support from the counsellor encourages the client to make realistic decisions and act upon them, rather than succumbing to the difficulties. There are instances, however, where cases are unsolvable because of one reason or another, but here the counsellor can also help by explaining the reasons why something is happening and in so doing perhaps make the problem more bearable.

The main problems were concerned with money, sex, children and housing, or a combination of these. Because of the nature of the work, the success rate of the Marriage Guidance Council was extremely difficult to determine – only on very rare occasions did counsellors hear of the outcome of their cases. 'However, when someone does come back to say thanks it is really wonderful', Mrs Musson commented.

Ballymena had been chosen because it was a central and fast-growing growth area. As Mrs Musson explained:

We find nowadays that in growth areas, especially in the housing estates, there is increasing need for a Guidance centre. Husbands working on shifts, leaving their wives, who have probably been uprooted from their homes and know very few people, alone for long hours at a time, bring new problems which we can help with.

A centre was always housed discreetly in a building with other firms so that no one need ever be able to suspect a person calling there and it was only on very rare occasions that a counsellor would visit a client in his or her home.[28]

In January 1973 a wine and cheese party was held In Ballymena, hosted by the Mayor, Alderman James Millar, to form a Mid-Antrim Branch of the Council. In December the *Ballymena Observer* reported that the Council was now offering a service through the Citizens' Advice Bureau in Broughshane Street in the town. 'What happens when someone turns to the Marriage Guidance for help?' the article asked and responded:

It certainly is not being confronted by someone behind a desk as depicted in so many cartoons. Interviews, which last for an hour, take place in comfortable, relaxed surroundings in complete confidence.

Counselling has been defined as the intelligent and sympathetic listening based on the belief that the answer to any problem lies in the person facing it. The client finds in the counsellor someone who is unimplicated but concerned, a stalwart, reliable friend to whom he can unburden himself without censure, hurry or interruption and be met with kindness and respect.[29]

'Is this the kind of work you could do?'

Despite a succession of horrific incidents, there was some reduction in political and sectarian violence in 1973: the death toll was 263. The Council was able to report 'a truly remarkable increase in the number of counselling interviews' to 1,304, with the number of children under sixteen involved at 509. Some 3,000 cards providing all NIMGC contact telephone numbers were distributed to general medical practitioners. Fifty-one talks were given and twice as many young people attended groups with counsellors than in 1972.

The Council had to adapt to a changed political landscape: local authorities had been swept away and were being replaced by Area Boards – would there be new grants to replace those which had been given by the now defunct local authorities? The Northern Ireland Health and Social Services, so closely associated with the Council, was undergoing major reorganisation. Plans were well advanced to restore devolution, particularly after the Sunningdale conference in December where agreement was reached on power-sharing and on the incorporation of what was known as the 'Irish dimension'. Structural changes were also underway in the National Marriage Guidance Council following recommendations in the Spoors Report. A working party recommended that the Northern Ireland Council should consider the appointment of a full-time Director – but would the government, whether direct rule or devolved, increase its annual grant to the organisation to make this possible?

NIMGC from the outset advertised its services. In 1973 steps were taken to make these more eye-catching. They included:

MARRIAGE PROBLEMS
SEX?
MONEY?
RELATIVES or CHILDREN?

If you have a problem which is affecting your
marriage you can get confidential help from a
marriage counsellor.

APPOINTMENTS can be made through
THE CITIZENS' ADVICE BUREAU
COLERAINE 4817
NORTHERN RELAND MARRIAGE GUIDANCE
COUNCIL

And:

HOPE
OFFERED
Perhaps you know someone
whose marriage is in difficulties?
An outwardly successful partnership

being undermined by a
seemingly insurmountable problem
Often a problem of the most personal kind
Many people feel hopeless
in the face of this kind of pressure
The Marriage Guidance Council offers
unique confidential assistance to
people with problems

Telephone: **OMAGH 2752**
Monday 9.30 am – 6 pm
Tuesday to Friday 9.30 am – 12 noon

where hope exists
COMPLETE PRIVACY ASSURED

The expansion of the Council's work, of course, increased the need for counsellors. On occasion NIMGC paid for advertisements in the press. 'Is this the kind of work you could do?' one began in the autumn of 1973, and concluded with the words, 'help us to help'. However, the governing body and staff at 76 Dublin Road had been able networkers from the outset and they continued to lobby journalists and broadcasters to publicise the appeal for volunteers. For example, in September 1973 the *Down Spectator* reinforced the appeal in a feature. 'With an increasing demand on its services, particularly in Bangor and North Down', the Council needed more volunteers. The current counsellors were men and women aged 30-50 and all were married. The feature continued:

Most of the women are housewives seeking to enrich their domestic lives with an occupation in which they can apply their previous training in such various spheres as social work, teaching, medicine and nursing. The men are in full time employment. They undertake counselling either to complement their professional work as teachers, ministers, personnel officers or to seek the satisfaction in personal service that may be absent in their work in industry, administration or business. All of them share a deep concern for human happiness.

At selection conferences the selectors were primarily looking for personal qualities rather than academic attainment, qualities such as 'a high degree of personal insight, sensitivity and being able to tolerate stress and anxiety'. Their task was not to diagnose or prescribe remedies but rather to share with clients the troubles, doubts and tensions of their marriages.[30]

Anyone interested in 'this rewarding work' was urged to get in touch with the Administrative Officer, Peggy Musson. When Mrs Musson resigned from her post in June 1974, the Council was certain to feel her departure as an acute loss to the organisation.

The UWC strike and after

The Annual Report for 1974/5 (the Council moved from the calendar year to the financial year for accounting purposes) had little in the way of good news to report. 'Our high hopes of obtaining a full time Director to implement the Spoors Report recommendation sadly has not yet materialised', the Chairman, Mrs Peggy Chalkey, stated in her message. To make matters worse, she added, 'and with the resignation of the Administrative Officer in June this has placed an enormous burden on the tutors, counsellors and office staff'. The Administrative Officer, Mrs Peggy Musson, had obtained a new post with the Churches Central Committee.

On Tuesday 14 May 1974 the Northern Ireland Assembly passed an amendment expressing faith in power-sharing by 44 votes to 28. The problem was that this no longer reflected the opinion of the majority in the region. The power-sharing Executive had been holed beneath the water in the Westminster general election of February 1974 (eleven out of twelve MPs elected in Northern Ireland were opposed to the Sunningdale Agreement). At 6.08 pm on 14 May spokesmen representing a self-appointed junta, the Ulster Workers Council, informed journalists at Stormont that a strike would begin in protest against ratification of the Sunningdale Agreement.

At first the loyalist strike appeared to fail: most firms reported that 90 per cent of their employees had turned up for work. During the first morning the UWC called on the assistance of the Ulster Defence Association and, as Robert Fisk reported for *The Times*, 'by midday, intimidation was beginning to reach epic proportions'. For much of this period most of the people of Northern Ireland were deprived of electricity, gas, transport, fresh food, piped water, employment and other facilities taken for granted in any western European state. As the strike gained momentum it left security forces, civil servants, public services, trade-union leaders, moderate politicians and the Westminster government ever more impotent. The *Daily Mail* described the state to which Belfast had been reduced during the second week:

You can't have a breakfast egg or bacon – the shelves are bare. You can't make a hot drink because there's no electricity. You can't catch a bus because there aren't any. You can't post a letter because it won't arrive. Petrol is so scarce that some people are trying to run their cars on paint fillers.[31]

On Monday 27 May Brian Faulkner, head of the power-sharing executive, resigned. The first attempt to create devolved community government representing both unionists and nationalists had collapsed. During fifteen days the UWC in league with loyalist paramilitaries had made an entire region of the United Kingdom ungovernable. Little wonder that the Council reported that the 'counselling interviews showed a slight decrease at the end of 1974 compared with 1973, but this was most attributable to the UWC strike in May when little or no counselling was done, during a normally busy month'.[32]

A second attempt to get agreement on power-sharing in a 'Constitutional Convention' soon ran into the sand and the political vacuum was filled by a succession of squalid, violent incidents. By the end of the year, 304 had met with untimely deaths as a direct result – 206 civilians, 52 soldiers, 15 police, and 24 republican and 6 loyalist activists.[33]

The Irish Republic could not but be affected directly by the northern imbroglio. The eventual death toll from loyalist bombs detonated in Monaghan and Dublin on 17 May 1974 was thirty-three, the greatest number of people killed in any one day in the Troubles. Though the great majority of unionists hated the very idea of an 'Irish Dimension', those with responsibility for governing in both Dublin and London saw merit in closer cooperation – however clandestine – between the two jurisdictions.

'An even more developed Irish dimension in counselling for marriage'

Those concerned with marriage guidance, north and south, also saw merit in closer cooperation and collaboration. In October 1974 the All-Ireland Marriage Counselling Conference was held at Greystones, Co. Wicklow. Greystones no doubt had been chosen with some care: this seaside resort some seventeen miles south of Dublin still had its own Orange lodge and, before the Troubles, had long been a favourite summer retreat for Ulster Protestants, evangelicals staying at Carrig Eden guesthouse and the better-off booking in at the La Touche Hotel where the conference was held. The conference involved the Catholic Marriage Advisory Council, the Marriage Counselling Service (a Church of Ireland organisation) and the Northern Ireland Marriage Guidance Council. Its programme covered 'the skills of counselling, the roles of social workers and teachers in ensuring that young and old had good marriages in all senses, and the aims of marriage guidance and counselling'.

This conference was given extensive coverage in the press, the *Irish Times* in particular. Brendan Corish, the leader of the Irish Labour Party, now the Minister for Health and Social Welfare in a coalition government, addressed the delegates. How statutory and voluntary welfare agencies of every type could combine their resources was a fundamental question, the Minister began. The question was to define the right role for voluntary agencies. Following a recent seminar on community care services in Sligo, he would be inviting public discussion on a document being prepared. While his speech was of most relevance to southern delegates, Mr Corish's observations on the relationship between voluntary and statutory agencies could be applied with little difficulty to Northern Ireland.

On the conference's final day, 6 October 1974, Nicholas Tyndall, chief officer of the National Marriage Guidance Council, addressed the delegates. He emphasised the changing expectation of marriage which was linked to how society had changed. He told of the state of the counselling services in the Council of Europe countries, and observed that marriage which had once been regarded as the basic unit in society, 'may now not be so'. There were, for example, a million British children growing up in one-parent families.

Dr Jack Dominian, of the Catholic Marriage Advisory Council in Britain, said that people – particularly the young – were worried about the quality of their marriages, not their traditional roles. The lot of most of mankind had increased materially. Man could, therefore, see past his desire for food. Free from starvation, he could look to the quality of his relationships. Brian Howlett of the Catholic Marriage Advisory Council in Ireland continued on the same theme. Young people, he said, look to marriage for satisfaction and sexual fulfilment far beyond what their parents would have expected. These parents would not have felt the need for a pre-marriage course, but now rising living standards had helped to make life more complicated. But the goals of fulfilment were vulnerable to personal failure. Young people realised this and wanted advice on practical and personal matters. They realised the part sex could play in a happy marriage, and they wanted to see it in more than legalistic terms.

The speakers and delegates devoted a good deal of time to discussing sex. Nicholas Tyndall told of a pilot project in Rugby aimed at curing sexual dysfunction in six couples. It was 'fairly dynamite territory', he said, and also too early to say if it had anything approaching the 80 per cent success rate of Masters and Johnson in America (it differed from the US courses in that it was non-residential and financed by the National Health Service). Dr Dominion followed on by saying that the sexual act had to find a new meaning. The Bible described it as an act of knowing, but instead of adhering closely to this, Christianity took a wrong turn by emphasising the biological, procreative component. But procreation was now being controlled more and more, and Christianity had been left empty of an alternative meaning to sexual intercourse in the absence of procreation. The *Irish Times* report continued:

It had taken refuge in fear and expectation of calamity. The body, however, was the vehicle through which two people communicated. This was the positive aspect. It was negative thinking to regard it as a form of temptation.

During intercourse, partners to a marriage were saying to each other that they were the most important people in the world. The body with its powerful sensuous messages became the source of communication, of acknowledgement, acceptance, and appreciation of each partner. In intercourse, the couple confirmed each other's sexual identity as men and women, and their personal identity.

That intercourse could be discussed so frankly and openly in 1974 demonstrated how fast attitudes had been changing in Ireland over the previous decade. Dr Dominian referred to changes in attitude within his own church (on nullity, for example) and concluded expansively that 'the time had come for denominational differences to disappear…All people wanted to know was, did the Church understand the meaning of love'.

Delegates of several organisations explained what they did, including Nightline for students at Queen's University, the Samaritans (whose speaker said that the main problem today was emotional starvation) and the Mater Dei Institute, whose representative, Rev Richard Copsey, suggested that marriage guidance organisations should prepare literature on marriage suitable for school counsellors.

How marriage guidance services should be funded was considered briefly. Mr Tyndall noted that in Britain the service cost £2.50 per client per hour, even with volunteers. John Phillips of the Northern Ireland Marriage Guidance Council, in outlining work with teacher counsellors, 'indirectly referred to the colossal drain on resources that counselling involved'. The *Irish Times* continued:

His contribution ended with his stated pleasure that there should be an even more developed Irish dimension in counselling for marriage, although in Northern Ireland the marriage guidance council wanted to retain the British link from which it gained much.[34]

The *Irish Times* devoted a leading article to the conference. The editor concluded that 'there was a lot of good sense at the seminar' but that 'any line of disagreement, particularly on matters such as contraception' was 'either avoided or allowed to fit in to tactful expression'. This could not continue forever – 'the counselling bodies, if they are to come even closer (and this should not require any loss of independence) will have to discuss their differences'. Only with such could there be unity of purpose, if not of practice: the purpose being to ensure that as many of Ireland's marriages are happy, 'based on right education, which must go on through life and not be crammed into the last year of school or a crash course before the big day'. Counselling to ensure relationships 'which sustain and grow...on each side of the Border can only be a source for more widespread good, not only to the partners in marriage, but to the whole island'. The editor's overall assessment was a positive one:

A happy event is perhaps the best description of the weekend seminar involving the three Irish marriage counselling and guidance services. For the first time, the Northern Ireland council, and its Catholic and Protestant counterparts in the South, joined together to share their experiences on how marriages on both sides of the Border could be nurtured, not merely saved from breakdown.

Such a positive attitude would indeed be welcome in the wider context of North-South relations, the seminar being perhaps only a small element, but a vital one, dealing as it does with the most important of unifying forces.[35]

Couples

Though there was only a slight reduction in political and intercommunal violence in 1975, there were no dislocating episodes that year on the scale of the 1974 UWC strike. Much of the continuing terror was concentrated in urban working class districts where there were savage struggles for supremacy between competing paramilitary organisations. The Northern Ireland Marriage Guidance Council recovered swiftly from the set-backs of the previous year. Daily advertising in the personal column of the press 'and a closer liaison with Welfare and other statutory bodies along with the good co-operation of the Press in their willingness to write articles on our behalf have all helped to make our service better understood by the public'. At the BBC in Ormeau Avenue two counsellors gave interviews in the 'Good Morning Ulster' programme and the Council was asked to take part in phone-in programmes.

The profile of marriage guidance counselling was raised across the United Kingdom in 1975 by an ITV series made by Thames Television entitled *Couples*. These fictional programmes, shown three afternoons a week, included a long session between a counsellor and a client, whose lecturer husband was having an affair with a female student. The main character was Jane Selby, a widow who having decided she had had enough of her own troubles, applies to become a marriage guidance counsellor. The series featured Jane being interviewed by a committee, the ensuing day-long selection conference, six three-day training courses over two years at the National Council's college at Rugby, and constant supervision thereafter by a team of tutors.

Couples received mixed reviews. The *Daily Telegraph* did not like one extended monologue, an analysis of a failed marriage, nor an unconvincingly theatrical 'row between a younger couple, acted out before the troubled gaze of a woman counsellor'. The critic concluded: 'Unless the writing is of extremely high quality, you are left hungry for information, wishing that an investigative documentary could show the actual organisation in action, rather than a fictional substitute.'[36]

No doubt many marriage guidance activists agreed with that critic's final observation, but were delighted nevertheless that *Couples* was moving marriage guidance nearer to centre stage. One of these was Derick Woods, Acting Chairman of NIMGC: for him this was an opportunity not to be missed to showcase the work of the regional council. Writing to the press, he explained that *Couples* was about a *fictional* marriage guidance council, and continued: 'This programme, which is NOT a documentary, has raised questions in the mind of the general public about becoming counsellors'. He encouraged those who had seen the series to get in touch with NIMGC to seek answers to questions raised by the programmes, and he invited 'your readers to write to us at the address below for information about our work in general and the selection and training of a counsellor in particular'. Indeed, readers were encouraged to call in at 76 Dublin Road where there was an exhibition of books and material about the Council running to the end of the year.[37]

The new Director

At last, in 1975, the Council found itself in the position to appoint a full-time Director. The advertisement, placed in the press in June, stated that NIMGC had twenty counsellors working in six different centres in Northern Ireland and that 'the aim is to double the amount of work undertaken within the next two years'. The Council also planned to 'be able to offer training placement facilities to social work students'. Applications were invited from either: professional social workers with supervisory experience to take on 'a demanding job requiring an unusual combination of qualities to enable the successful candidate to adapt his or her experience of the statutory services to a voluntary agency'; or from those with a successful management record – 'experience of one of the counselling disciplines, or of working with a voluntary social work agency would be an advantage'.

John Phillips, a forty three year old Englishman, who had taught at Campbell College and Royal Belfast Academical Institution, was appointed Director. He was able to hit the ground running because, he wrote himself, 'as I had already been working in the Northern Ireland Marriage Guidance Council for twelve years, the move to full-time work in "76" felt in some respects more like a home-coming than a venturing into new fields'. Shortly before taking up his new post, he was interviewed by Jeanie Johnston for the *Belfast News-Letter*. Her article, entitled 'Keeping your marriage alive', began:

With divorce these days becoming almost as fashionable as owning a deep freeze, it is refreshing to find someone more concerned with why a marriage has gone wrong than how quickly it can be ended.

Too often there seems to be no way out of the dilemma of either seeking to end the partnership or continuing to live with the stresses and strains of a marriage which has broken down. The National Marriage Guidance through its counselling service offers a rational alternative.

John Phillips told her that the number of people seeking help from the Council had risen considerably, 'suggesting that people are more easily able to recognise that they have a problem when a crisis faces them'. About half the NIMGC's clients were referred to the organisation by doctors, clergy, solicitors or groups such as the Samaritans. The majority came alone but increasing numbers of couples were seeking help together. He stressed that initially the counsellor's job was a listening one, leading to a joint exploration of the problem. The aim, he said, was not to prescribe remedies – 'counselling is not giving advice, it's not patching up marriages…Our work has been a success when a client can see a solution to his problem, even if that solution is divorce'. As the relationship grows the counsellor could discover that there was a deeper problem, which the client may not even realise existed behind the initial one:

This relationship is the area in which we work…We use ourselves, our skill and understanding, in relation to the client and so help him to understand the quality of relationships with others. For instance, a woman who nags will come to realise she is nagging the counsellor and therefore probably her husband too.

Group counselling, mostly for the present in schools and with youth groups, was very different from remedial counselling but involved the same criteria. This was one of the areas in which the Council hoped to expand but it was restricted by the pressing need for new counsellors. Mr Phillips explained how counsellors were recruited and trained, and he concluded:

People tend to think of us as do-gooders, and feel that we do it out of a sense of duty. This is wrong. Counselling is an enormously satisfying thing to do – you learn about other people, and you also learn about yourself. I personally think that one often gets more out of counselling than one puts in. I think I have.[38]

In an interview with Betty Lowry for the *Belfast Telegraph*, John Phillips had the opportunity to develop these observations. He told her that people nowadays encountering difficulties 'tend to come earlier instead of waiting until the situation is almost intolerable'. Commenting that more couples were coming together than before, he continued:

When they come they do not always come straight to the point. For example, a woman may come in and ask for advice about contraceptives. You might think the obvious reply to her is to say, "Oh you should go to the Family Planning people. Here is their address". But she may really want to talk to someone about sexual difficulties in her marriage. And the sexual difficulties may be the result of some deeper trouble and if we can find out what that is and fix it the sexual problem may settle itself.

He said that the Council's work showed that there were certain periods 'that could be loosely described as pressure points on a marriage'. The first was very shortly after marriage when it did not seem to be coming up to expectations. Then the traditional seven-year itch, and finally 'there is the time when children are grown up and off the parents' hands. Couples who have stayed together just because of the children may then think about themselves and whether they should separate'. He thought that staying together for the sake of the children did not work from the children's point of view. 'Children recognise when their parents' relationship is not happy. Quite young children can sense it and feel a lack of security.'

A number of 'battered' wives sought help from the Council:

Many of them don't want to end the relationship, even though they have been involved in physical violence. Some of them come from families where a certain amount of physical violence was not unusual. There are other forms of violence which can be much more hurtful, for example a refusal to communicate, withholding of response, withdrawal of money, refusal to provide food – too numerous to mention and too individual to pinpoint.

And what about the impact of political and intercommunal violence on relationships? 'Surprisingly the current troubles are not often mentioned by either husbands or wives as contributing to their marital difficulties though Mr Phillips thinks they must undoubtedly add to the stress and strain in many married lives'. One effect 'of the troubled state of the city' was that people were often reluctant to go to the Council office in the evenings.[39]

'We are now speeding forward'

The appointment of a full-time Director, who began work in his office in January 1976, made a great difference. In his Annual Report message, the Chairman, Derick Woods, observed: 'Already we are feeling the benefits of his appointment in many ways, both internally in the easing of the administrative burden from officers, counsellors, tutors and office staff, and externally in the expansion of our work to the areas and the contacts made. Happily after a period of marking time, we are now speeding forward.'

The demand for the services offered by the Council was growing fast. The number of interviews had risen by almost a third in one year. The problem was that, due to retirements and resignations, the number of counsellors had dropped. Only by counsellors giving more of their time and skill was it possible to cope with the expansion of the caseload. The burden on the tutor, Gladys Jeffery, was now heavier than before: no longer assisted by John Phillips since taking up his new post, she now had to undertake all the tutorial work. In the words of Derick Woods, 'we need more Counsellors to help expand the work and extend it to new parts of the Province.'[40]

John Irvine, Deputy Secretary of the Department of Environment and a former chairman of Action Cancer's management committee, became Chairman for 1976/77. However, since he was appointed Permanent Secretary in the Northern Ireland Office halfway through the year, Derick Woods (now Vice-Chairman) had to preside on most occasions. Though three more counsellors retired, nine new ones were selected during the year and Anna Hyland was appointed as a tutor to fill the vacancy created by the elevation of John Phillips to the post of Director.

Along with Derick Woods, and like Wilfred Brennen and Peggy Musson before him, John Phillips seized every opportunity to keep the media informed about the Council's activities. One letter he wrote to the *Belfast Telegraph* in April 1976 was given the prominent headline, 'Ulster's youngest marriage counsellor at 25'. The NIMGC had made regular calls for more volunteers to come forward from its formation, so it was a challenge to keep these appeals fresh:

Our public image tends to be one of the do-gooder in twin-set and pearls, urging people to stay together with generous helpings of "good advice". Nothing could be further from the truth. Counselling is a highly-skilled process which the counsellor offers to the "client" with marital or other problems…

Because the Council 'is increasingly recognised by those in the caring professions as possessing trained skills in the field of marital counselling, so the demand for our work rapidly grows'. Remedial counselling had increased that year by more than 25 per cent. There was also a rapidly-growing demand for group work with young people, and 'a variety of work at the development stage, awaiting the skill and enthusiasm of more trained counsellors'.[41]

'Steadily increasing demand'
New landlords at 76 Dublin Road, Harris Marrian & Co Ltd, required the Council to move its operations to the ground floor. The Council acknowledged the patience and generosity of the landlords 'who worked with us on seemingly endless drafts of permutations of counselling rooms, kitchen, toilets and so forth':

The construction work itself was dusty, noisy and protracted, but in the end the transition was very smooth, and counsellors and office staff quickly settled in to what has turned out to be a most satisfactory suite of rooms. Three counselling rooms on the ground floor are supplemented by a general purpose room on the first floor return which houses the library, but can be used as a group room or a fourth counselling room if needed. And the old waiting room was converted into a small but convenient kitchen.

Three new centres opened during the year: in Downpatrick, Antrim and (after being closed for four years) in Derry/Londonderry and it was hoped that counselling could also become available in the Waterside area. Until recently, all counselling had been provided without payment. Now, after completing three hours of voluntary and unpaid work per week, counsellors became eligible for a small payment. The 'steadily increasing demand for counselling and the very high selection and training costs convinced the Management Committee and the Executive that a system of "paid counselling" should be introduced at the beginning of the new financial year'. Experience of other Councils in England had shown that 'the introduction of schemes of paid counselling give greater management flexibility and increase the cost effectiveness of the service'.

Ties with other social service agencies both statutory and voluntary were being steadily strengthened. For example, a mature student social worker, Mrs Kay O'Hare, joined the Council in February 1976 to begin a six-month placement and this was regarded as the beginning of an on-going arrangement with the Ulster College and other teaching institutions. A visit by Lord Melchett, Minister of State at the Department of Health and Social Service, gave further official recognition to the work of the Council. Twenty counsellors met him over lunch at the end of March and they 'were impressed by Lord Melchett's obvious knowledge about the Northern Ireland Marriage Guidance Council and his ready grasp of counselling problems'.[42]

In the summer of 1977 Gladys Jeffery retired after a long and fruitful association with the Council. Her role as tutor was taken over by Joan Wilson and Margery Cross. Their involvement in development and training in contract work gave valuable support to their colleague Anna Hyland, enabling the Council to undertake more work in this area. Links with teaching institutions were maintained. The Council was delighted with the placement of Sister Brigid McKenna of the Society of St Vincent de Paul; she 'played a very full part in counselling and case discussion and has observed many activities within the Council and in other organisations'. Around 120 people attended a one-day conference in the New University, Coleraine, in November 1977 on 'Marriage, the Family and then Community', chaired by Derek Murray of UTV.

Marital Sexual Dysfunction training: 'certainly being involved with the Project changes attitudes'

Perhaps the most significant new development in the Council, with important implications for the future, was involvement in the Marital Sexual Dysfunction Project. This had been begun in 1973, starting with eight counsellors in Rugby. Councils across the Irish Sea had been invited to send representatives for training. As this was financed by the DHSS in London, the Northern Ireland Council was not eligible for inclusion; but with the help of Northern Ireland's Department of Health and Personal Social Services, 'we negotiated to buy ourselves in'. The 1977/8 Annual Report continued:

The scheme is an extremely ambitious one: two counsellors are trained in co-therapy in the first year; they in turn train two counsellors each in the second year, and another four trainees in the third year make up a total of ten counsellors engaging in this intensely demanding and interesting co-therapy. The first two counsellors began their training course in Rugby in June 1977 (spouses also attended this conference). We have been more than lucky to obtain the services of Dr Ethna O'Gorman, a clinical psychiatrist with a joint appointment at the City Hospital and Queen's University, as our "external trainer". She is involved in co-therapy with both the first trainees throughout the year. Our own Sexual Function Clinic will open in our Belfast headquarters in the Autumn of 1978.

The main purpose of the Marital Sexual Dysfunction project at Rugby was to establish how readily and effectively Marriage Guidance counsellors were able to learn and apply the understanding and procedures derived from the work of Masters and Johnston in the treatment of sexual dysfunction. Pleasing results from the project encouraged the promotion of local training schemes in about seventeen councils, including the Northern Ireland council.

During the first year two male counsellors, John Phillips and Dick McDonald, began work on co-therapy with Dr O'Gorman at the Department of Mental Health in Fitzwilliam Street opposite the City Hospital. The research had not established clearly whether single therapy or co-therapy was to be preferred. However, Dick McDonald reported, 'the advantages during training of mutual support and variety of insight and the possibility of observing by the other trainee of the way the two therapists interacted with couples, were held to outweigh the greater amount of counsellor time involved'. 'As well as this', he continued, 'co-therapy provides a person of the same sex for each of the marriage partners to identify with and can also help to develop the sense that the "dysfunction" is an aspect of their relationship and not just the "fault" or "responsibility" of one or other'.

In the general training programme of two weekends during the year at Rugby, spouses as well as counsellors attended the first. This was so that they could become familiar with its methods and purposes – 'and may have an opportunity of "growing along with" husband or wife – for certainly being involved in the Project changes attitudes'. Dick McDonald continued:

It is of fundamental importance to note how fortunate we are in having Dr O'Gorman as trainer and consultant. She has established a well-deserved reputation in the field of psycho-sexual medicine and is herself interested in actively promoting the development of co-operation between those trained in counselling skills and those using the "behaviourist" models more common in social and medical therapy. Although the actual programme of work with couples presenting with sexual dysfunction was slower in getting started than we had hoped – a spate of unkept appointments and some unsuitable referrals created a good deal of initial frustration – this has meant that there has been time to assimilate Dr O'Gorman's approach and methods and to gain confidence in using the detailed and carefully structured therapy programmes.

Counsellors were thereby brought much more closely into direct working with other professions concerned with therapy. The Association of Sexual and Marital Therapists had been formed, giving a fillip to counselling to become more and more a profession with recognised standards. The Northern Ireland Council undertook to establish a clinic for the treatment of marital sexual dysfunction sponsored by the Department of Health and Social Services at 76 Dublin Road. Plans were made to begin the training of four female counsellors during the autumn of 1978. This was to be through working in co-therapy with the two male counsellors under the general supervision of Dr O'Gorman. In this way a gradual extension of the case-load could be undertaken.

This development made considerable demands on counselling time, since a therapy programme was of much longer duration than that for a regular counsellor. More was demanded of tutors in the way of supervision, tutorial support and, indeed, the participation of counsellors themselves in the scheme.[43] The Marital Sexual Dysfunction clinic was duly established in November 1978; as the Executive Committee reported the following year: 'Its innovation is two-fold – it isolates, for treatment purposes, the sexual aspect of relationship from other aspects, and it employs techniques of behaviour modification which are quite foreign to the traditional training and experience of our counsellors'.

Dick McDonald was certain that 'the Clinic's successful launching has been due in particular to the imaginative, well-organised and carefully presented preparations which were carried through by John Phillips. The development of the clinic is another example of the way in which the appointment of a Director has enabled this Council to identify and respond effectively to new ways of promoting and sustaining the health of marriages in our community'. The perceived success of this new venture was also due, he thought, 'to the planning, effort and support of a whole range of people from Alison Clegg, the Marriage Guidance Project Officer, whose directness, charm and sharp humour have been a continuing source of encouragement, to the members of committee and counsellors who decorated and organised the premises and so helped to make possible excellent facilities for both clients and therapists'. He continued:

Again the fact that Dr Ethna O'Gorman, our initial trainer and now the Clinic's consultant, has been so whole-hearted in her support has been a crucial factor in securing the acceptance of the Clinic by doctors, health visitors and social workers. The way in which the Clinic has been widely accepted as offering a responsible, competent and effectively organised programme of therapy for the treatment of specific sexual dysfunctions is illustrated by the statistics of referrals to it.

Of the thirty-nine couples so far referred to the clinic, some twenty had been referred by doctors, ten were self-referrals, four were from counsellors, three from social workers and two from health visitors. At the time of the annual report for 1978/9 the clinic had been able to interview seventeen of the thirty-nine referrals. A long waiting list was being created by this strong demand for treatment. Because of this the clinic tried to give couples an initial interview when a preliminary assessment was being made, the treatment programme was explained and an assurance was being given that treatment would be offered within two – or at most three – months.

Fifteen couples had been accepted into treatment; five of these had dropped out; one had completed treatment; and nine others were at various stages of treatment. 'Both teams of therapists consider this to be a substantial volume of work to have undertaken', McDonald observed, 'and have come to recognise that it can be quite demanding for those trained in the counselling role to move into the role of the therapist whose knowledge and experience gives authority and who is responsible for planning a course of treatment related to the needs of each particular couple.[44]

Much in demand

By the end of the 1970s the Troubles in Northern Ireland had become the longest-running conflict in Europe since the end of the Second World War. The years between 1971 and 1976 were the most violent. The year 1976 was the bloodiest since 1972, to be the second heaviest year for violent deaths in a conflict which was to stretch over more than thirty years. Following the failure of the Constitutional Convention, tension was racheted up by the killing of ten Protestants at Kingsmills in January. Despite the Peace People movement, founded by two Belfast women in August 1976, 307 lives had been lost by the end of the year. In the ensuing years, however, the number of casualties fell markedly. Terror continued to stalk the narrow streets and lonely country lanes after nightfall, but there was a perceptible reduction in the tragedy and dislocation brought about by these Troubles.

By the end of the 1970s the Council could congratulate itself on having made great strides over the decade. The number of interviews offered in 1978/9 was 3,793 and the number of new clients was 552. There was a striking expansion in contract work. Many seeking help turned to general practitioners, clergy, social workers, the Samaritans and the like and, as a result, some groups of professional and voluntary workers turned more and more to the Council for assistance. The Council was much in demand to provide national training in counselling and counselling skills. Courses were provided for Education and Library Boards, the Department of Health, the Postgraduate Medical Association and Night-Line (the student telephone service at Queen's University). As the decade was drawing to a close, the principal challenge for NIMGC was that divorce legislation was about to be changed in Northern Ireland. There were, however, other unexpected challenges to be faced.

Notes

1   *Belfast News-Letter*, 16 January 1968
2   NIMGC Annual Report 1968
3   Ibid.; *Belfast Telegraph*, 6 November 1968
4   Jonathan Bardon, *A History of Ulster*, 1992, pp.665-671
5   NIMGC Annual Report 1969
6   NIMGC cuttings file, 1969
7   Ibid.
8   *Belfast News-Letter*, 28 October 1969; *Belfast Telegraph*, 28 October 1969
9   *Belfast Telegraph*, 16 October 1969
10   *Belfast News-Letter*, 24 July 1969
11   *Sunday News*, 10 August 1969
12   David McKittrick, Seamus Kelters, Brian Feeney, Chris Thornton and David McVea, *Lost Lives*, 1999, 2007 edition, p.31 and p.47
13   *Belfast News-Letter*, 4 December 1969
14   NIMGC Annual Report, 1970
15   Interview with Derick Woods
16   *Sunday News*, 21 June 1970
17   *City Week*, October 1970
18   NIMGC cuttings file (*Church of Ireland Gazette*)
19   *Portadown Times*, 4 and 11 December 1970
20   *Sunday News*, 13 December 1970

21   McKittrick, Kelters, Feeney, Thornton and McVea, 2007, p.61
22   *Belfast News-Letter*, 13 March 1971
23   *Portadown News* and *Portadown Times*, 17 September 1971
24   *Sunday News*, 26 September 1971
25   *Portadown Times*, 26 November 1971
26   Ibid., 18 February 1972
27   McKittrick, Kelters, Feeney, Thornton and McVea, *Lost Lives*, 2007, p.138
28   *Ballymena Guardian*, 28 December 1972
29   *Ballymena Observer*, 13 December 1973
30   *Down Spectator*, 21 September 1973; *Belfast Telegraph*, 26 October 1973
31   Robert Fisk, *The Point of No Return: The Strike Which Broke the British in Ulster*, London, 1975, p.221
32   NIMGC Annual Report, 1974/5
33   McKittrick, Kelters, Feeney, Thornton and McVea, *Lost Lives*, p.413
34   *Irish Times*, 5 and 7 October 1974; Irish Independent, 7 October 1974
35   *Irish Times*, 7 October 1974
36   *TV Times*, 11 October 1975; *Daily Telegraph*, 13 October 1975
37   *Belfast News-Letter*, 18 November 1975
38   Ibid., 14 October 1975
39   *Belfast Telegraph*, 12 January 1976
40   NIMGC Annual Report, 1975/6
41   *Belfast Telegraph*, 5 April 1976
42   NIMGC Annual Report, 1976/7
43   NIMGC Annual Report, 1977/8
44   NIMGC Annual Report, 1978/9

Formation of NIMGC, 1947

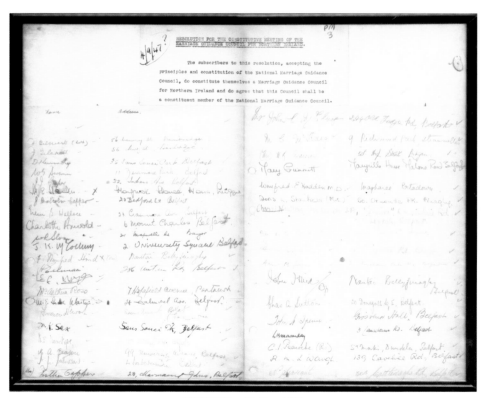

NIMGC Constitution, 1947

Guidance to happiness

1962

THE WINTER ROUND OF EVENING CLASSES has returned, with thousands of students eager to improve their store of knowledge. Yet curiously enough there does not appear to be a waiting list for one particular study course which should be of vital interest to hundreds of young people in Northern Ireland.

Arranged under the auspices of the Northern Ireland Marriage Guidance Council, it has been specially planned for young engaged couples.

By MOIRA DOUGLAS

About 70 couples have participated in these courses over the past three years—not as large a number of "graduates," perhaps, as the Council would have liked, but a very appreciative group, if one can judge from those with whom I talked about these classes the other day.

Shyness

"The classes certainly brought my wife and me much closer together," recalls Belfast bank official Denis Ringland, now married and living in Bangor. They both voted the course as having provided very good information and "very good crack."

"I would definitely recommend them to all engaged couples. I think what holds most of them back from attending is shyness," he tells me.

Mr. Ringland stressed the importance of being able to talk over the problems of setting up a home with other young couples facing similar difficulties, and "getting things off your chest" to a neutral arbitrator.

The informality of the classes, and yet their seriousness, were what Mr. Desmond Porter stressed. "Things were discussed informally, yet without anyone being at all embarrassed—this was very good," he said.

Both Mr. Porter and his wife, Pat, who live at Newtownabbey, were particularly appreciative of the legal advice and information regarding housing matters given at the course they attended. "It has proved very useful to us since then," says Mr. Porter.

A husband and wife team, both of whom are trained group leaders with the Northern Ireland Council, have run several courses at their own home in Newtownards.

"A private home does allow for a more informal atmosphere," says Mrs. J. W. Russell, whose husband is a solicitor. "On the other hand, some people feel it is too personal, and would prefer to attend courses in Belfast.

Reluctant

She and her husband both agreed that shyness was what held most couples back from attending courses. "Girls, in fact, seem to be more interested to come than boys," she commented.

In fact, reluctance on the part of the fiance was what prevented most couples from coming, the Russells discovered.

Several of those who have "graduated" from the Russells' study groups have said later that for them the most important thing had been not so much the actual information provided on the physical and more intimate side of married life, but rather the fact that they had been able to discuss these things frankly and fully with each other afterwards.

Besides the regular courses at Bryson House, the Council has also co-operated with churches in the running of small "closed groups" for engaged couples in their parishes.

"In the closed group we have the advantage of being able to go a little further in pointing out the significance of the marriage ceremony, and its follow-up in the Christian community," one minister, who wishes to remain anonymous, explained to me.

The courses are very similar to those run at Bryson House—the clergyman introducing his group to the leaders, and then retiring into the background, with the exception of the final evening session, when he joins in to discuss the moral and spiritual side of Christian marriage.

"I found the church group most interesting and helpful," says a young married woman who recently attended a "closed" study group. She emphasised the value of holding such groups in connection with the church to which the couple belong, and also the importance of keeping such groups both informal and confidential.

Course

Another series of courses commences at Bryson House next month, Mrs. Thelma Greeves, educational secretary and group leader, tells me.

A firm supporter of the "Prevention is better than cure" theory, she hopes that more young couples will want to learn something of the significance of marriage before rushing headlong into it.

Pre marriage 1961

B. Telegraph 14/9/62

From orange blossom to orange boxes — or H.P.

THE National Marriage Guidance Council certainly started something when they published their new booklet "A Home of Your Own" the other day.

Young couples were advised to "Forget about the Joneses. . . a home is what you make it by the sort of life you lead in it, and this has nothing to do with the colour of the walls, the number of labour-saving gadgets, and all the latest furniture on the H.P. . . . Real married happiness can make a home out of one room, a mattress and some orange boxes. . ."

Not unnaturally the National Association of Retail Furnishers came up with a reply, the main point being that the stresses and strains of early married life are quite bad enough without the frustration, for the wife, of trying to make a home without the barest necessities, and the physical discomfort of the husband, to return after a day's work and be faced with an orange box.

By JULIET LEIGH

In these circumstances, said the Furnishers, young couples would be well advised to take advantage of hire purchase facilities.

STRAIN

I noticed, however, that they said nothing of the intense financial strain and worry which can engulf a marriage when hire purchase is entered into lightly, without any great thought as to the consequences. Curious to know the view of the Northern Ireland branch of the Marriage Guidance Council on all this, I asked Mrs. C. E. Thompson, the vice-chairman, to give me her comments.

Mrs. Thompson had not yet read the booklet, so she very wisely left it to the National Council to deal with any criticism there, but her personal opinion was that, while she was not against hire purchase for established couples, she did not believe in building a life on it. She thought a happy marriage should be "big" enough to stand up to a lack of comfort at the beginning. If it could not do so then, what hope was there for the future?

The chief cause of a marriage going wrong, in her view, and from her experience as a marriage councellor, was not so much a lack of material possessions as a lack of respect for one another's ideas or way of life: wanting one's partner to be what one would like him to be, instead of accepting him as he is.

"There must be give and take with the idea that it is for their own happiness and when they come to the Council for help it is all too frequently the other person's fault. Happily married people have problems also, but they have learnt to face them together."

NOT ENTHUSIASTIC

Mrs. Thelma Greeves, educational secretary for Northern Ireland, confessed that she was not an "orange box" enthusiast herself, although group leaders in the Council are divided on this subject. Mrs. Greeves thinks that when two young people, both earning, get married, they should contrive to live on the husband's salary, keeping the wife's income for furniture or savings, so that when the wife gives up her job there is no appreciable difference in their way of life. She admits, however, that some people find it quite impossible to save and for them hire purchase fulfils a need, provided they do not get in too deep and take on more commitments than they can afford.

"I am all for couples being realistic about the difficulties," she said. "They should try to furnish decently at least a bedroom and a living room for a start. Yes, I do believe in a bit of comfort when it is at all possible!"

At least half of the engaged couples who had come to the Council over the past three years intended to go in for hire purchase, she told me. But they were on the whole serious young people, anxious to discuss it and work it all out beforehand. It was the unfortunate people who had no idea fwhat they were in for who suffered, and this could lead to a great deal of unhappiness in marriage.

All this made me eager to hear more about the work of the Council, which falls under two headings, educational and remedial.

SYMPATHETIC EAR

On the remedial side marriage counsellors are available to give a sympathetic ear and advice to married people who come to them with their difficulties. This is an entirely confidential service, and if the problem requires more specialised treatment the counsellor can refer the client to a panel of consultants — medical, phychological, spiritual, social or legal. Each year more than 12,000 couples seek help—of all types and ages and of every social and religious group.

Marriage counsellors themselves are men and women from all walks of life who have been carefully selected and trained for the work, which is completely voluntary and part time. I am told there is plenty of room for more counsellors, and that happily married people aged between 30 and 50 are ideal candidates. No academic ... and interest in people and the ability to be a good listener.

After attending a special training course and at the end of a probationary year's counselling, there is an assessment of the new counsellor's work for final approval.

The educational side is equally valuable, for the Council believes that if young people are helped to understand more about themselves and their relationships, to approach moral problems in an informed and responsible way, sound foundations will be laid for the full and enriching experience that marriage should be.

Voluntary part-time group leaders are used for this educational work, and like the counsellors, group leaders are carefully selected to undergo a special training.

INFORMAL GROUPS

Small, friendly and informal groups of engaged and newly-married couples are arranged, with talks by the group leader on such themes as "Getting to know the in-laws," "Sharing the chores," "Money," "Spiritual background," "Planning a family," "Sex in marriage," "Lasting romance," "Furnishing and decorating," "Housekeeping and budgeting," "When children come" and so on.

Sometimes these groups are held in the home of a married couple where husband and wife are both group leaders. Mr. and Mrs. J. W. Russell, of Newtownards, work together in this way.

Talks and discussions with young people in clubs and schools are becoming increasingly popular, and Mrs. Greeves told me that there are plans afoot to hold similar groups among apprentices in industry. The purpose of these meetings is not to "lay down the law" but to encourage the young to think for themselves, on subjects such as love, friendship and marriage, or relations with one's family, friends and workmates.

The group leader gives a short talk on some aspect of the "facts of life," and then the meeting is thrown open for questions and discussion.

"INNOCENT"

Mrs. Greeves does not agree with the idea that the majority of young people nowadays, in Northern Ireland at any rate, have pre-martial intercourse. Going by their questions she finds them amazingly innocent.

With the present day trend towards earlier maturity and earlier marriage, this educational work is of growing importance, and the Council believes that many marriage difficulties would never arise if issues had been faced beforehand and the need for mutual adjustment clearly understood.

So, whether it is to be orange boxes or hire purchase to

Orange blossom to orange boxes, 1962

No grant for Derry Marriage Guidance Council

CO. DERRY Welfare Committee by a majority vote has decided not to make a grant to Londonderry branch of the Northern Ireland Marriage Guidance Council.

In a letter asking the committee for a grant the branch pointed out that it had recently moved into new premises at Clarendon Terrace. Marriage guidance work in Londonderry had increased during the past 12 months and it was expected this trend would continue even more rapidly in the future.

A large proporton of the people making use of the service came from the county even from as far away as Portstewart.

The county welfare officer, Mr. J. L. Wilde, said that when the branch was set up two years ago the committee had made a grant of £50 but last year it had been decided not to renew the grant.

Following a proposal by Mr. James Barr, seconded by Mr. R. A. Brown, that no grant be made, Mrs. J. T. Milligan said she would like the committee to think again.

She made the point that if the Marriage Guidance Council could save a home from being broken up it would very probably save the committee the expense of having to take the children into one of their homes.

Mr. Barr—I am sticking to my proposal. I say no grant.

Mr. Brown—The amount of money is not the important thing here. If people set up on a voluntary basis then good luck to them. But if it is voluntary then it should not be grant-aided in any way.

Mrs. Milligan proposed as an amendment, seconded by Mrs. J. L. Stanleigh, that a grant of £25 be made, but on a vote the amendment was defeated by eight votes to four.

The welfare committee has come out in favour of proposals made by the Ministry of Development on the provision of special caravan sites for itinerants.

The assistant county secretary, Mr. R. G. Wilkins said until these people were provided with somewhere to go the problem would never be solved.

B.T. 6-11-68 (Wednesday)

Derry 'No grant'

DIVORCE CHANGE CALL BY Ld GARDINER

'BREAKDOWN' AS GROUNDS

REFORM of the law to make divorce available, subject to safeguards, upon proof that the marriage had irretrievably broken down, and on no other grounds, was suggested by Lord GARDINER, Lord Chancellor, last night.

Opening the annual conference of the National Marriage Guidance Council at Brighton. Lord Gardiner said he believed there was a general wish, at least in England and Wales, that the present divorce law should be radically reformed.

He emphasised that he was expressing a personal view and was not speaking on behalf of the Government.

He said it would do no harm to a happy marriage to allow unhappy marriages to be decently buried. "Their burial may enable those unhappy spouses to enjoy, in their turn, the blessings of a happy married life."

"PLACE IN LAW."
Matrimonial offences

In suggesting reform on the principle of a marriage breakdown, Lord Gardiner said: "I believe that there must remain a place in our law for the matrimonial offence without allowing it to become the basis for relief.

"After all, adultery, desertion, or intolerable conduct towards one's spouse are often very reliable indications that the marriage has, in fact, broken down.

"I would have thought that such offences could properly be used by the law as guide posts—pointing, in the absence of evidence to the contrary, or forgiveness, to breakdown.

"Such a law would enable speedy relief to be available in the undefended case, and would accord with reality."

TRIVIAL ROWS
Discouragement needed

In those cases where there was neither adultery nor anything akin to cruelty, the law must discourage people from coming forward after some trivial row and saying that the marriage had broken down.

That could be done by requiring a period of separation before breakdown could be alleged. The period should be substantial where an innocent and unwilling spouse was involved.

Lord Gardiner said no chance of reconciliation should be discarded.

He welcomed the proposal that solicitors should consider always whether to bring to the attention of their matrimonial client the names and addresses of appropriate persons and organisations qualified to assist in effecting a reconciliation.

"It should be possible for detailed proposals to be worked out, based upon the principle of breakdown, that most of us would find acceptable without causing hardship or injustice."

VIEWS WELCOMED
"Important pronouncement"

Mr. GERALD SANCTARY, National Secretary of the Marriage Guidance Council, said: "This is probably the most important pronouncement on the subject of divorce laws in this country for many years.

"We are delighted that Lord Gardiner has laid so much stress on reconciliation work. The fact that he has made this statement represents the greatest possible encouragement to..."

Grounds for divorce

L'Derry Sentinel — 24th Nov '65.

M.G.C. seeks Counsellors

A North-West branch of the Northern Ireland Marriage Guidance Council has been set up and at a first annual general meeting in Union Hall, Londonderry, the Constitution of the Council was formally adopted.

The Mayor of Londonderry (Councillor A. D. Anderson, VRD, JP), who presided affirmed his interest in the establishment of a Marriage Guidance Council in the North-West, and stressed how the work of the Council would help to promote stable family units in the community.

The Mayor introduced the Chairman of the Northern Ireland Marriage Guidance Council (Mr. W. Brennan, FRCS).

Mr. Brennan formally moved the adoption of the Constitution, and gave a brief account of the preventative and remedial work of the Marriage Guidance movement. He outlined the work of the National M.G.C. which is in contact with the Home Office, and explained that each local council is affiliated to the National Council but is autonomous. The elected Chairman must therefore be a man of some standing in the community and would have the responsibility of incorporating all shades of opinion in one Committee which would work in close contact with the Welfare, Health, Education and Church authorities in the area.

Mr. Brennan also described the work of individual counsellors, their selection, training and responsibilities and sketched future development of the movements.

The proposal that the Constitution should be adopted, was seconded by Mr. H. Bennett, FRCS.

Mrs. Thompson, vice-chairman of the Northern Ireland MGC proposed that the present Committee should be re-elected, with the Rev. Canon H. Fennell, MA, as chairman, Mrs. M. Quinn as treasurer and Dr. Baillie as secretary. Mrs. J. Schofield seconded and adopted.

Mr. John T. McFarland, DL, Londonderry City High Sheriff, proposed a vote of thanks to the speakers, and this was seconded by the Rev. C. H. Young.

Apologies for unavoidable absence were read by Dr. M. Baillie, hon. secretary.

Derry/Londonderry

Derry may get Marriage Council

1/2/65.

A MEETING is to be held in Londonderry to explore the possibilities of establishing a branch of the Marriage Council in the city.

This would be the first branch of the Council outside Belfast.

The chairman of the meeting, to be attended by interested parties in the Guildhall on Wednesday night, will be the Mayor, Councillor A. W. Anderson.

Among the speakers will be the chairman and vice-chairman of the Council, Mr. Wilfred Brennen, and Mrs. C. E. Thompson.

Derry /Londonderry & NIMGC, 1965

Since 1959 the divorce rate has practically doubled in Ulster. Many wives, it seems, are no longer prepared to face a life of drudgery and despair.

In this first of two articles BOB CAMERON talks to the experts who try to patch up an ailing marriage, and shows how a divorce can be financed virtually on the hire purchase.

The Ulster couples who swop their wedding gowns for a law suit

● For most Ulster couples this is where married life begins — in church. It is always a proud and happy day for the blushing bride, but far too often those crucial vows are not taken nearly as seriously as they should be.

'As that sentimental song says: "Love and marriage go together like a horse and carriage" . . . is a catchy call that made last year a record breaking one in the Ulster matrimonial stakes.

For the last quarter ending in December alone over 2,270 couples had walked down the aisle—the highest number for 22 years. But if it was a boom year for confetti, it was also a record one for that horse to bolt in Ulster . . . for the divorce figures have shot up again.

And statistics have made it clear in a wedding bell that thousands of unhappy wives have applied for maintenance orders against their husbands—who are spending their wages on gambling and booze. Leaving the wife and kids to starve.

But many wives are also deciding that they can go it alone and divorce figures reached a new peak of 229 last year. In 1967 there were 211 and in 1966 over 150 wives pointed out that a £10 wedding ring isn't the current price for a doormat.

But in 1959 only 118 broken marriages were recorded, so what has caused the divorce rate to practically double in ten years?

Chairman of the Ulster branch of the Marriage Guidance Council, Mrs. Phyllis Thompson, says it's because the old rules do not apply any more.

In other words the boot is on the other, slender, female foot.

Mrs. Phyllis Thompson and her executive officer, Mr. W. D. R. Vandeleur. Mrs. Thompson says: "The old rules do not apply any more."

Caption: Divorce Court

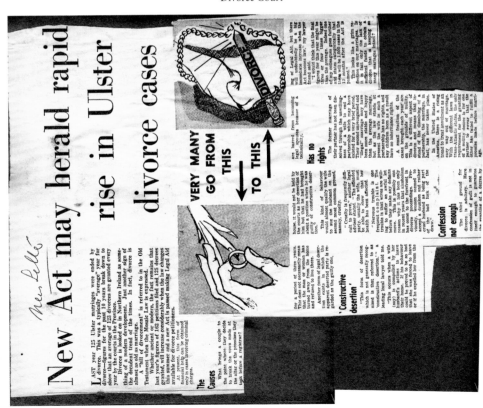

New Act may herald rapid rise in Ulster divorce cases

LAST year 125 Ulster marriages were ended by divorce. This was a typically "average" year for divorce-figures for the past 10 years break down to show that an average of 123 divorces are granted every year by the courts in the Province.

Divorce is looked on in Northern Ireland as something of a modern development. Just another sign of the decadent trend of the times. In fact, divorce is almost as old as marriage.

A 'bill of divorcement' is referred to in the Old Testament when the Mosaic Law is expressed.

Whether ancient or modern, the fact remains that last year's figures of 162 petitions filed and 125 decrees granted, will increase considerably when the law changes this summer and a new Act is passed making Legal Aid available for divorce petitioners.

The Causes

What brings a couple to the point where they decide to break the vows made at the altar or before a registrar?

Caption: Divorce law changes

More marriage-savers needed

Are you happily married and between 25 and 50? Then how about helping other couples whose marriage is in danger of breaking up to achieve the happiness which you enjoy?

The Northern Ireland Marriage Guidance Council would like to recruit more counsellors—people who could help to prevent the Marital state becoming Martial.

But those who wish to become counsellors need to be more than just happily married. They must be mature and tolerant people whose character and integrity are above question.

Those who are finally selected as prospective counsellors attend a training course in England, with all expenses paid.

When finally qualified they have the satisfaction of doing a really worthwhile job on a voluntary basis.

Mr. Gerald P. Sanctuary, who is field secretary of the National Marriage Guidance Council with headquarters in London, has just concluded a brief visit to Northern Ireland during which he met and discussed problems with local officers.

Confidence

Mr. Sanctuary yesterday stressed the fact that people whose marriages were in trouble were assured of having their problems dealt with in complete confidence if they approached the Council. Their partners would not be contacted unless they wished it.

It was felt that the inauguration of free legal aid in Northern Ireland might increase the demands on the reconciliation services of counsellors with more people thinking of divorce when the cost would no longer be a bar to many.

The Council was not solely concerned with the threat to marriages. Valuable courses for engaged couples were held at which advice was given on various aspects of married life.

Marriage Savers

City Week 30.1.69.

LOVE AND SEX IN PLAIN LANGUAGE. CAN THE NORTHERN IRELAND MARRIAGE GUIDANCE COUNCIL HELP YOU? WE HAVE AN EXCELLENT RANGE OF BOOKS FROM 1/- TO 3/6 EACH, WHICH DEAL WITH ALL MARRIAGE, PERSONAL AND FAMILY PROBLEMS. SEND STAMP ADDRESSED ENVELOPE TODAY TO MARRIAGE GUIDANCE COUNCIL, 76 DUBLIN ROAD, BELFAST, FOR FREE BOOK LIST.

1969

6/3/67 News Letter

MARRIAGE GUIDANCE COUNCIL APPEAL

Mr. Wilfred Brennen, chairman, making yesterday's "Week's Good Cause" appeal on behalf of the Northern Ireland Marriage Guidance Council, said that the council had now been fully accepted as a necessary link in our chain of social services.

We no longer asked if its services were needed. Instead, ways were sought to extend them.

He said: "We can no longer find space in our few small rooms in Bryson House, for all those distressed and anxious people who turn to us for help.

"And we have never been able adequately to accommodate there the many groups of young people who want to discuss with us not only how best to prepare for marriage, but the whole business of growing up."

Mr. Brennen said the council now had a home of its own at Dublin Road, Belfast.

But he added: "We must find twice as much for rent as before, and a big capital sum for structural alterations, plumbing, re-wiring, furniture and the rest.

"And we need more counsellors, more especially to meet the increasing pressure on our resources from schools, youth clubs, the churches and the university."

From Bryson House to Dublin Road, 1967

Relate NI's premises at 76 Dublin Road

PM's wife at new offices

Mrs. O'Neill, wife of the Prime Minister, examines some of the publications after opening new offices for the Northern Ireland Marriage Guidance Council in Dublin Road, Belfast. On the right is council chairman, Mr. Wilfred Brennan, the surgeon, and Mrs. Norah Seaby, who is in charge of the bookshop.

Mrs Terrence O'Neill opening 76 Dublin Road, 1967

Industry asked to help mend broken homes

IT COSTS money to mend—and prevent—broken marriages and the Northern Ireland Marriage Guidance Council is looking for £7,000 to increase its work in the province.

At the annual meeting in Bryson House last night Sir Robin Kinahan, the Council's president launched the appeal by presenting a cheque on behalf of Charrington Kinahan Ltd. The appeal is to be made to industrial firms in Ulster.

Mr. Nicholas Tyndall, new chief officer of the National Marriage Guidance Council, guest speaker, discussed the findings of the Seebohm report.

"Marriage Guidance has arrived" he said, "and there is no need to explain it. Proof of this is the Government's 60 pc grant increase to the National Council."

Drawing attention to the Seebohm report he said it was "the social worker's bible".

Another speaker was the Rev. C. A. M. Meldrum, minister of Macrory Memorial Presbyterian Church.

"Young people", he said,

"want sensible and solid guidance on sex matters. They tell us to tell them fair and square what is right and what is wrong. They want to know how far they can go. They want to know the answers to: what is love, what is law and what is lust? I believe that youth to-day are looking for a positive lead".

In his report, chairman Mr. Wilfred Brennan said that the Council's work was much more effective now that it had its own headquarters at Dublin Road. But added that expansion had not been so extensive as

"We have to deal with small populations, so it is unlikely that we can have full-blown Marriage Guidance Councils in Coleraine and Craigavon. But there will be sub-groups", he said.

Sir Robin said it was very sad that only Belfast Corporation and Down County Welfare Committee were

listed in the financial report as supporters of the Marriage Guidance Council. Belfast Corporation's contribution was £900 for last year, and Down County Welfare Committee's £100. The Ministry of Home Affairs' grant was £1,300.

Sir Robin Kinahan and Mr. Wilfred Brennan announced their resignations as president and chairman and their successors will be elected at the executive committee meeting on Thursday.

Mrs. Terence O'Neill is the new patron of the society and recommends the work of the Council in its appeal to industry.

The executive committee elected was — Messrs. W. E. Coe, C. A. Duke, C. H. G. Kinahan, J. M. B. Phillips, Rev. C. G. Kerr, Dr. J. Neill, Mrs. T. Greeves, Mrs. G. Jeffrey, Mrs. M. Keith, Mrs. Price, Mrs.

Sir Robin Kinahan (left), president of the Northern Ireland Marriage Guidance Council, presents a cheque on behalf of Charrington Kinahan Ltd. to Mr. W. Brennen, chairman. Looking on is Mrs. P. M. Thompson, vice-chairman.

1969

Patadown News and Craigavan Times 27th June 1980

Victor Gordon looks at the state of marriages

Why more married couples should seek counsel

MORE AND more people in the Craigavon area are seeking marriage guidance – not because more marriages are floundering, but because married couples are more forthright about their marital problems nowadays.

In the old order, the stigma attached to a marriage breaking up kept an estranged couple together, invariably destroying one another emotionally, and making life turmoil for the children of the home.

But, to the outside world, they presented a picture of a united family, and that's what mattered.

However, the modern husband and wife aren't as prepared as their forbears to endure a life of sheer hell just to maintain appearances, and hence the upsurge in divorces and separations.

COMPLEX

And with the problems surfacing more quickly than in the past, marriage guidance counsellors have never been busier – counsellors like Moyna Tyson who spends every Thursday at Craigavon Area Hospital, helping married men and women sort out the complex problems that can crop up in even the more secure unions.

Moyna insists she isn't in the business of patching up marriages at all costs.

"That isn't my function," she insists. "If a marriage has broken down beyond hope, the most careless avenue open to all can often be divorce.

"In many cases, the problems are so intensive, and there is such a lack of communication between the partners, that opting out is the best solution all round – even if children are involved."

ENRICHED

She explains, "If children are being brought up in an atmosphere of antagonism and hate, it can affect them deeply. Better to live with one parent in a happy atmosphere than with a mother and father constantly at one another's throats."

Having cleared the air on that score, Moyna looks at the many relations that have been saved and enriched with a series of visits to the marriage guidance organisation.

The principle governing all their work is helping the couples work out what they want for themselves. Most are so confused and unhappy that they simply don't know their own minds, and need an expert – and uninvolved – confidant to help steer them to the truth.

The main catalyst on the route to the truth is the fact that the married partner came to see the counsellor in the first place.

SEARCH

Says Moyna, "We are normally approached by one partner initially, although we like to involve both partners in the search for the underlying problems.

"And this is rarely a straight forward affair. Usually, with human relationships in the melting pot, accusations come thick and fast, with neither party admitting 'guilt'."

Indeed, the other partner of the marriage is often told that his or her spouse saw fit to even see a counsellor in the first place.

And this attitude is often at the heart of the matter. The absolute lack of communication is the main reason why many marriages are not working out.

MYTH

"The usual reasons that are invariably paraded – lack of money, sexual problems and blaming in-laws – are often a myth," says Moyna. "It's amazing the number of husbands and wives who simply have nothing to say to each other.

"Often they have nothing more important to say to one another than discussing the weather – and no relationship can be built on that."

Then, things deteriorate into a sullen silence – or even an open and mutual warfare – until one or other partner realises that life wasn't meant to be a constant hell.

Moyna Tyson doesn't mind if she becomes the Aunt Sally when the accusations start to fly – the recrimination stage is the first sign that things could be on the mend. "At least, they're beginning to communicate and that's a start," she says.

But neither can she take sides, and when the recriminations cease, and the couple start to realise that they're making life a misery for one another, then the solution begins to loom.

SOBERING

Whether they realise that the relationship is worth saving – or breaking up – is up to the couple. The moment of truth can be a sobering one – or it can be enriching to realise that, after all, the marriage can be retrieved.

The first step of contacting the marriage counsellor is the most courageous one – and the second is admitting to one's partner that you've taken the step.

After that, things can happen fast, as the search for the truth livens up.

Moyna Tyson reckons there are scores of married couples in the Craigavon area who are yearning for a happy marriage, and yet are living in object misery.

"Perhaps some people go into marriage with their sights set too high," she says. "But a happy marriage is, perhaps, the most enriching of life's experiences."

COUPLES

Anyone with a marital problem is asked to make the first step by phoning Craigavon Area Hospital – where Moyna has her counselling sessions every Thursday from 10 a.m. The number is Portadown 34444, extension 6.

Or if the couples prefer a Portadown venue, there is a counsellor at the Health Centres in Tavanagh Avenue each Wednesday.

That counsellor is Margaret McCarroll, formerly Margaret Cunningham, a well-known face on Ulster Television, and who is involved in Downtown Radio nowadays.

The telephone number at Portadown is 34400, and appointments at both centres can be made from 9 a.m. until 5 p.m., Monday to Friday.

Craigavon, 1980

Lady who works full-time for no wages

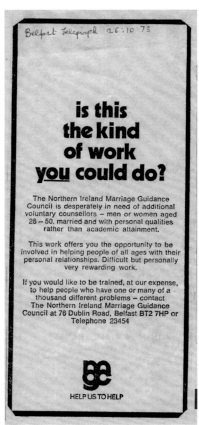

MOYNA TYSON has been a marriage guidance counsellor for five years, and has been in Craigavon since February, where she succeeded Marjorie Cross.

She was originally a secretary, a job which she gave up after she was married. And when her two daughters arrived, she remained a full-time housewife and mother.

However, the girls have now gone their own ways – one to Oxford and the other to France, so mum needed a challenge. She found it in the marriage guidance work, and is now virtually a full-time voluntary worker within the organisation.

CLINIC

Moyna admits, "If I had my life to lead over again, I would definitely have entered social work of some sort – I really enjoy my involvement in marriage guidance."

As well as her Thursday stint in Craigavon, she spends her Mondays in Newry, Tuesdays in Belfast, and she also counsels in a clinic which help work out sexual problems in the Northern Ireland capital.

"The clinic has succeeded beyond our hopes," she says. "It's unbelievable the unfounded hang-ups which still exist."

Her biggest strength is her ability to be a confidant, and it isn't surprising that couples pour out their heart to Moyna Tyson.

NERVOUS

She has a striking humanity, and admits she feels nervous before being introduced to each new client.

"If it's any help, I'm just as apprehensive as the married couples," she admits, adding she was "terrified" about the interview she faced in the News-Times office.

However, nervous or not, the interview soon showed why Moyna Tyson is a successful marriage guidance counsellor. She has all the concern, compassion and astuteness required in the extremely difficult world of trying to help put right human relationships that have gone wrong.

"It can be like walking through a minefield of emotions," says Moyna. "But human relationships are never easy especially when marital problems are concerned."

Craigavon, 1980

Omagh, 1972

Advert for Counsellors, 1973

Marriage guidance comes to Ballymena

THE Northern Ireland Marriage Guidance Council is now offering a counselling service in Ballymena and appointments can be made through the Citizens' Advice Bureau in Broughshane Street.

What happens when someone turns to Marriage Guidance for help? It certainly is not being confronted by someone behind a desk as depicted in so many cartoons. Interviews, which last for an hour, take place in comfortable, relaxed surroundings in complete confidence.

Counselling has been defined as the intelligent and sympathetic listening based on the belief that the answer to any problem lies in the person facing it. The client finds in the counsellor someone who is unimplicated but concerned, a stalwart, reliable friend to whom he can unburden himself without censure, hurry or interruption and be met with kindness and respect.

Contrary to some beliefs it is not necessary to see both partners of a marriage in order that a marriage should be helped, though it is desirable for both to come. The Marriage Guidance Council does not exist to keep marriages intact at all costs and in cases where the marriages have ended in separation or divorce clients have spoken gratefully of the support they have received from a counsellor.

Counsellors, who are voluntary workers, have to go through a rigorous selection procedure and only 30 per cent. get through. There follows intensive training, tutorials and refresher courses.

People with one of the many problems that come up in marriage can now avail themselves of this free service by ringing the C.A.B. office during the following times—Monday and Wednesday evenings—7 p.m. till 9 p.m.; Tuesday and Thursday mornings—10 a.m. till 12 noon. The telephone number Ballymena 42485.

Ballymena, 1972

Gladys Jeffery, 1973

Women's Page

Edited by Anne Montgomery

Marriage Guidance Council looks at Ballymena

ONE of the most popular subjects for newspaper and magazine cartoons is the visit to the Marriage Guidance Counsellor. Numerous situations and catchlines with the in mind have been penned over the years but behind all the jokes and laughter lies a very important and essential service to the community.

The Northern Ireland Marriage Guidance Council is based in Dublin Road, Belfast, and there are branches in Londonderry, Coleraine, Bangor and Lurgan. Ballymena, until now, however, despite all its other amenities and civic pride, could not boast a branch but it is hoped in the very near future this state of affairs will be put right.

In January, at 7.45 p.m. in the Town Hall, Ballymena, the Mayor, Alderman J. B. Millar, will be the host for a Wine and Cheese Reception, out of which it is hoped will spring the enthusiasm to get a branch started here.

It was last week that Mrs. Peggy Musson, the Guidance Council's Administrative Officer, called to see me to explain the work of the organisation and to stress why it was felt a branch should be started here.

The Marriage Guidance Council has been in operation in the Province for 25 years and Mrs. Musson stressed that it was a completely non-denominational set-up for the welfare of people from all sections of the community.

Obviously the aims of fessional counsellors—for example legal or psychiatrists—who can be approached on who never try to handle themselves anything which should they must tackle by a professional. Rather, their client's, to obtain the correct help.

The aim of every counsellor is, through a gradually developing relationship, to help the client understand and improve their relationships with a married partner.

What prompts a man or woman to visit a marriage guidance counsellor in the first place? There is, of course, the attractive problem with an objective party, someone who concerns and expert opinion. Mrs. Musson went on to...

The basic problem with a marriage is usually a lack of communication between the parties concerned and for one or both it is very often a trouble finding someone on neutral ground so to speak, knowing their troubles will never go beyond the particular counsellor involved.

When the counsellor can offer practical suggestions about the courses of action open and available, the counsellor encourages the client to make realistic decisions for himself rather than succumbing to his difficulties.

There are instances, however, where cases are involved where, because of one reason or clients do not get over their troubles, and they simply want to forget the whole thing and so it is all the more vital that counsellors hear of the outcome of their cases. When someone does come back to say thanks it is really wonderful, commented Mrs. Musson.

In many people's minds the Marriage Guidance Council conjures up pictures of interfering busybodies and learned, and that on more than one occasion counsellors have come under fire. From Mrs. Musson's description this picture could not be more ill-

Ballymena, 1972

13

MARRIAGE QUALITY 'WORRIES COUPLES'

Counsellors at conference

By Paul Murray, Social Services Correspondent

MARRIAGE IS NOT just a legal contract, but a relationship with potential for tremendous growth. This was the main theme to emerge from the All-Ireland Marriage Counselling Conference which ended yesterday at Greystones, Co. Wicklow.

It was perhaps best expressed by Dr. Denishan Jack Deminian, of the British Catholic Marriage Advisory Council. Before the young were worried about the quality of their marriages, not their traditional roles, he said.

The conference which involved the Catholic Marriage Advisory Council, the Marriage Counselling Service, and the Northern Ireland Marriage Guidance Council concentrated mainly on the role of social workers and teachers in ensuring that young and old had good marriages in all senses, and the aims of marriage guidance and counselling.

The changing expectation of marriage which was linked to how society had changed was much emphasised. Mr. Nicholas Tyndall, chief officer of the National Marriage Guidance Council, who told of the state of the counselling services in the Council of Europe countries, said that marriage, which had been regarded as the basic unit in society, may now not be so.

There were, for example, 1,000,000 British children growing up in one-parent families, Dr. Deminian brought this a stage further. The lot of most of mankind had increased materially. Man could fulfil his basic desire for food. Free from starvation, he could look to the quality of his relationship.

The sexual act, Dr. Deminian said, had to find a new meaning. The Bible described it as an act of knowing, but instead of adhering closely to this Christianity took a wrong turn by emphasising the biological, procreative component, and the process to grow more controlled of a more and more, and Christianity had been left empty of an alternative meaning to sexual intercourse in the absence of procreation.

It had taken refuge in fear and expectation of calamity. The body, however, was the vehicle through which two people communicated. This was the most eloquent and least negative thinking to regard it as a form of temptation.

During intercourse, partners to a marriage were saying to each other that they were the most important people in the world. The body with its powerful sensuous messages became the source of communication, of acknowledgement, acceptance, which had been reserved only for a partner. In intercourse, the couple confirmed each other's sexual identity as men and women, and their personal identity.

NASTY QUESTIONS

All of which were, perhaps, the more philosophical contribution to the proceedings. Much time was taken up describing organisations like the Queen's University, Belfast, Samaritans (whose speaker said that the main problem today was emotional starvation), the Mater Dei Institute, whose speaker, the Rev. Richard Copsey, stressed that marriage guidance organisations should prepare literature on marriage suitable for use by school counsellors, and Dr. Barnados Homes.

Its senior social worker, Miss Laetitia Lefroy, stressed that social workers, who like marriage counsellors should be engaged in inter-personal relationships, should not be obliged to deal with clients whose needs were rarely practical.

PERSONAL FAILURE

As Mr. Brian Hewlett, of the Catholic Marriage Advisory Council said, young people look to marriage for satisfaction and sexual fulfilment far beyond what their parents would not have felt the need for a pre-marriage course (only part of the work of the three Irish bodies), but we are trying to reach people and help to make life more complicated.

The goals of fulfilment were vulnerable to personal failure, he said. Youth partly responsible, partly advice on practical and personal matters. They realised the part sex could play in a happy marriage, and they wanted to see it in some way.

Marriage, indeed, should be seen 'as affirmation', Dr. Deminian said. It should be regarded as strengthening, as asserting positively, and at the same time as a joint contract, but a relationship. If broke down when the minimum criteria for the last was present.

Much time was spent studying how such problems occurred, and how they should be coped with, rather than resolving how it could be strength-

COLOSSAL DRAIN

Money was rarely discussed. Perhaps the delegates had been educated, by past conferences, not to look for support from the Department of Health and Social Welfare, Mr. Corish, who hinted of being ready to receive applications for State support.

The Rev. Richard Copsey, guest speaker, with Miss Laetitia Lefroy, senior social worker, Dr. Barnados Homes, who attended the all-Ireland Marriage Counselling conference at Greystones, Co. Wicklow, at the weekend.

Mrs. Yvonne Pim (left), and Mrs. Reba Miller, who attended the All-Ireland Marriage Counselling conference.

I don't see anything wrong with living together if you are as much in love as we are

NEXT, a 21-year-old girl looks back at her childhood and explains why she has been living with her boy friend for the last seven months. They share a shabbily furnished flat near Queen's, strewn with coffee mugs.

'When I was a teenager we used to have terrible rows at home. It was always "Who are you going out with?" and "What time will you be home?" and they always sat up and waited until I came in.

'I used to feel furious because I thought they didn't trust me and were treating me as a child instead of a young adult. I couldn't wait to get away from home and get my independence.

'When I went to college I was just 18. I went mad — I think everyone does when they are away from home for the very first time. I had a good time but I wasn't promiscuous or anything like that. I was a virgin when I went to college — I think most of the girls in my year were — only they wouldn't admit it.

'My boyfriend is a student. I've known him for over 18 months. We started sleeping together after we had been going out for seven months and we have been living together since April.

'I don't see anything wrong in living together if you are as much in love as we are. I would never live with, someone I didn't love. My parents don't know and I wouldn't want them to know—not because I'm ashamed of our relationship — but because they would be so hurt if they did find out.

'When I was 17 I might have thought of living with someone just to spite my parents and prove I was an adult. But now I know what love is I would hate to hurt them.

'Since I left home I have grown much closer to them, particularly to my mother. I still get annoyed when I go home and she tells me I shouldn't smoke or go to bed late — the only difference is that I try not to show it.

'It is only now that I realise how much my parents sacrificed for me. They had my best interest at heart when they kept saying "Don't do this," or

'Don't do that.' The trouble is that you never realise it at the time.

'They were strict with me, but I think it was because I was the eldest and they weren't sure of the best thing to do. I've noticed my two younger sisters are having an easier time than I ever had.

'They haven't met my boyfriend yet. I'd like them to because I think they would like him, but I think they would never understand our relationship. If they knew we were living together they would tear their hearts out wondering where they went wrong as parents; and if they didn't know they would make cracks about getting engaged, because I'm devoted either way, the relationship would be devalued.

'You see, we are very happy the way we are now. I don't know if it will last. I hope it does and, if it does, we might get married when he finishes his training.

'We can't afford marriage now and I'm not even too sure that it would be the best thing if we could. I think we are both too independent and too young to settle down and start a family.'

Frank's TV plea is all for funds

Ulster's top comedian Frank Carson will tomorrow night ask Northern Ireland to play Happy Families.

For he is to appeal on Ulster Television for funds on behalf of the Province's Marriage Guidance Council.

Yesterday council director, Mr John Phillips said the council's workload had increased by some 30 per cent since last year and counsellors were working more than the voluntary three hours a week which was expected.

Jobs

He said that counsellors — many have full-time jobs — were giving up as much as 15 hours a week of their spare time to help Ulster marriages.

Mr Phillips stressed that the council is not a marriage mending bureau but a place where couples can be helped in their decisions as to what they want to do with their marriages.

Positive

"If a couple decide their marriage cannot go on and they want a divorce, we will help them break up with as little trauma and pain as possible, especially if there are children involved", he said.

The people who go to the marriage guidance council come from all walks of life. Young married couples seek

Frank Carson in TV cash raising plea.

advice on sexual problems, he said.

"We are trying to draw attention to the positive side of our work. We want to help people to resume happy relationships within marriage.

"I would like to organise group meetings for people who want to improve their marriages rather than just for those who want to save their marriages".

Mr Phillips explained that the council does receive a Government grant to cover part of its expanses but this is not enough.

"All our counsellors have to go to England for training courses which are expensive. They receive travelling allowances but we pay for them.

Tomorrow night's appeal by Frank Carson will be broadcast on UTV at 6-55 p.m.

Frank Carson's Funding Appeal

marriage

FOCUS ON MARRIAGE

The page women turn to first ...

Trend

TO MOST people in this part of the world the phrase "mixed marriage" means one thing — a marriage between a Protestant and a Roman Catholic.

But when Dr. Ethna O'Gorman speaks on mixed marriages at a public meeting organised by the Northern Ireland Marriage Guidance Council tomorrow night she will be talking about the problems faced by couples where one partner is a homosexual.

"The discovery that one of the partners in a marriage is homosexual need not mean divorce," she says, pointing out that sex is only one aspect of marriage. "Married

Betty Lowry talks to a consultant psychiatrist to the Marriage Guidance Council's sexual function clinic who wants more help given to partners with homosexual problems.

couples have so many other bonds — they enjoy the comfort of the same home, the same interests, and frequently children as well.

To an audience that will consist largely of people involved in counselling in various organisations — social workers, doctors and interested laymen and women she will talk about what can happen when a heterosexual and a homosexual are married. Dr. O'Gorman feels very

strongly about the present law in Northern Ireland which still regards homosexuality as a criminal offence.

A consultant psychiatrist at the Belfast City Hospital and lecturer in the Department of Psychology at Queen's University, Galway-born Dr. O'Gorman is also, she reminded me, "a full-time wife and full-time mother." Her husband, a scientist, lectures at Trinity College, Dublin,

and they have a seven-year-old son.

She is honorary consultant to the sexual function clinic of the Marriage Guidance Council and feels that the counsellors who specialise in this particular aspect of the MGC work should be aware of what can happen when a heterosexual and a homosexual are married.

The vast majority of the couples who seek help from the sexual function clinic are, of course, heterosexual. Clinics

operate now, incidentally, not only at the MGC headquarters, 76 Dublin Road, Belfast but also at the health centres in Antrim, Bangor, Ballymena, Coleraine, Limavady, Newry and there will shortly be one in Lisburn.

At tomorrow's meeting, Derick Woods, the chairman of the MGC, will announce the appointment as chief officer of Roy Simpson of Londonderry. Mr. Simpson, a Presbyterian minister, has been a counsellor for some years. The MGC has been without an administrative since John Phillips, who was appointed director in January 1976 left before Christmas last year.

Dr. Ethna O'Gorman interview, 1980

Sex clinic

IN MY piece about the Marriage Guidance Council in Trend on Monday I gave the impression that sexual disfunction clinics were held in a number of health centres. The only clinic of this kind is at 76 Dublin Road, Belfast. People can be referred there from the remedial counselling at health centres.

B.I.

Belfast Telegraph 28/5/80

Relate People Through the Years

l-r: Bruce Stewart, Tutor, Judith Loder, Training Officer, Kate Lewis, Organiser, Family Mediation Service and David Trelford, Executive Member – 1990.

l-r: Granville Lavin, Counsellor, Jackie Graham, Tutor, Barbara Corkey, Counsellor and Philip Hart, Tutor – 1990.

Sir Eric McDowell, Chair, Relate NI – June 1992

Joan Wilson and Gladys Condy – Relate Counsellors – 1992

Jo Noble – Foyle Manager 1992 – 2000

l-r: Des Smith, Chief Executive, UTV, Lady Bloomfield, Peter McLaughlin, Chief Executive, Bryson House – Nov 1993.

Kate Lewis, Head of Professional Services, 1994 -1998

Bob Jordan, Chair, Relate NI 1998-1999

Relate Training, 1994 – Trainer, Barbara Corkey

l-r: Relate Counsellors, Jackie Graham, Barbara Brock and Gillian McClay

l-r: Diane Robinson, Margaret McCutcheon, Frances McGuigan, Carol McConkey, Fran Raine, Jane Sterritt, Reception/Accounts Staff – 1998.

Sex Therapy Team – Yvonne Gilmour, PST Therapist, Relate NI, Marj Thorburn, Head of PST, Relate Federation, Eric Woods, PST Therapist, Relate NI, Avril Brown, PST Therapist Relate NI and Jill Stevens, PST Supervisor, Marriage & Relationship Counselling Service, Dublin.

Lynn Davidson, Margaret McCutcheon, Lorraine McGuigan and Janet McVeigh, Relate Admin Staff – 2012

l-r: Robin McRoberts, Linda Kerr, Rita Glover, Anne Matthews, Jo Noble, Liz Rowan and Gerald Clark – Staff Away Day, Bushmills, 3/4 Dec 1998

Josie Conlon, Receptionist, Newry, Eileen Hamilton, Receptionist, Portadown, Dympna Maguire, Receptionist, Newry and Margot Meehan, Counsellor, Newry – 2012.

Relate Events

Chris Patton MP, Parliamentary Under Secretary of State, Northern
Ireland Office receiving fundraising cheque – from Belfast Marathon
entrant in 1985 with John Chambers, CEO (centre)

Launch of Family Mediation Service on 2 November 1987

l-r: Willie John McBride, Northern Bank, Philip Leonard, Catholic Marriage
Advisory Council and Marie Fitzduff, NIMGC, Counsellor

Joan Wilson, Chair and John Chambers, CEO, at the launch of Relate's new logo outside 76 Dublin Road in 1988

Launch of Relate Fundraising Appeal in 1993 in Belfast City Hall – l-r: Eamon Holmes UTV who launched the Appeal, John Chambers, CEO, Lady Elizabeth Bloomfield, Appeal Chairman and Sir Eric McDowell, Chair, Relate

Launch of RelateTeen Project on 8 December 1993 – l-r Sir Eric McDowell, CBE, Chair, Relate and David French, Director, Relate Federation with the late Diana, Princess of Wales

l-r: John Chambers, CEO, Relate and Bruce Stewart, RelateTeen Supervisor/Trainer with the late Diana, Princess of Wales

l-r: Kate Lewis, Head of Professional Services, John Chambers, CEO and Avril Raitt-Brown, Psychosexual Counsellor with the late Diana, Princess of Wales

The late Diana, Princess of Wales at the Launch of the RelateTeen Service in
Hillsborough Castle on 8 December 1993

The late Diana, Princess of Wales at the Launch of the RelateTeen Service in
Hillsborough Castle on 8 December 1993

Helen McCoy, International Year of the Family 1994
Competition Winner in the 10–16 age category

Relate Counselling Certificate Presentation 1994 – l-r: Linda Wright, Rita Glover, Lorraine Roach, Sir Peter Froggatt, Relate President, Val Kohner & Elizabeth McClelland

Relate AGM June 1994 – front row l-r: Lady Bloomfield, Lady Dunleith, Relate Patron and Anne Hailes

Relate Appeal hosted by UTV in the Kelly Studio in 1995 – l-r: Anne Hailes, UTV, Gerry Kelly, UTV, Des Smith, UTV, Aidan Sherrard, Director of Personnel & Corporate Affairs, NIE plc, Lady Bloomfield, Dermot Davey, NIE plc and Sir Eric McDowell

Relate NI Fundraising Event, 1995 – l-r: John Chambers, CEO, Lady Bloomfield and Bob Jordan, Chair, Relate NI

The Foyle Team at the opening of Relate's Centre in Strand Road, Derry/Londonderry in 1995

Opening of Glengall St premises, 2005 – l–r: Gerald Clark, CEO, Denis Tindley, Chair, Relate Federation, Prof Norman Nevin, Chair, Relate NI and Sir Nigel Hamilton, head of the Northern Ireland Civil Service

Launch of Relate Strategic Plan 2012/15 and Presentation of Couple Counselling Training Certificates to Relate Counsellors on 27 June 2012 – l-r: Jill Downing, Chair, Relate NI, Ruth Hutton, Counsellor, Angie Spence, Counsellor and John Compton, CEO, Health and Social Care Board

Relationships Ireland 50th Anniversary Conference, 30 June 2012 – l-r: Ray Maloney, Counsellor, Brenda McDowell, Supervisor and Marjorie Houston, Senior Supervisor

Jill Downing, Chair and Alasdair MacInnes, Family Policy Unit, DHSSPS

Launch of Annual Review 2011/12 on 22 November 2012 – John O'Doherty, Treasurer and Sue Ramsey, MLA, Chair, Committee for Health, Social Services & Public Safety

Relate Staff at the Launch of Annual Review 2011/12 – l-r: Helen Fry, John O'Doherty (Treasurer), Fran Raine, Margaret McCutcheon, Jacqui Swan, Jean McCauley, Jane Sterritt, Lynn Davidson, Dave Murphy and Marjorie Houston

Relate Anniversaries and Conferences

Marriage Guidance Display Unit, 1952

40th Anniversary– Open Day on 4 September 1987 - l-r: Rev J Toland
(founder member NIMG), Joan Wilson, Chair, Richard Needham MP,
David French, Director National Marriage Guidance Council

Employment Industry Seminar at Malone House, 8 October 1990 – l-r: Sir
Eric McDowell, Nancy Paul, Excel International, John Chambers, CEO and
Derick Woods, Chair

Mental Health and Child Protection Conflicting Agendas Conference
in 1996 – l-r: Judith Loder, Liz Early, Nursing Officer NHSSB, Kate
Lewis, Margaret Black, Assistant Director, Northern Health Board,
Yvonne Gilmour, John Chambers, Marjorie Houston, Peter McBride,
Val Kohner, Eugene Hagan, Sheena Bell, Liz Rowan and Linda Wright

RelateTeen Conference in the Waterfront Hall, 1997

40th anniversary Open Day on 4 September 1987 attended by Richard Needham (far right), Secretary of State for Health & Social Services

Relate Conference, "The effects of Separation and Divorce on Children & Young People", 1996. l-r: Isabel Reilly, Professional Services Consultant, Margaret Fawcett, Family Mediator/RelateTeen Counsellor, Joan Wilson, Chair, Joan Kelly, Executive Director, Northern California Mediation Centre and Gillian McClay, Family Mediator

Robert and Sarah Wylie celebrating 50 years of marriage with Derick Woods (left) and John Chambers (centre), 4 September 1997

Celebration of 50 years of Relate and 50 years of marriage in Government House, Hillsborough on 18 September 1997

65th Anniversary Dinner on 16 November 2012 – Jill Downing, Chair, Relate NI and Edwin Poots, MLA, Minister for Health

65th Anniversary Conference, 16 November 2012 – l-r: John Burnham, Guest Speaker, Mary Jenkins, Guest Speaker and Jill Downing, Chair, Relate NI

65th Anniversary Dinner on 16 November 2012 – l-r: (Relate Trustees) Lindsay Todd, Rosemary Dunlop, Alan Elliott, Jill Downing, Minister Edwin Poots, Paul Rooney, John O'Doherty and Sean Moynihan.

65th Anniversary Dinner on 16 November 2012 – l-r: Dave Murphy, CEO, Relate NI, Jacqui Swan, Professional Services Manager, Relate NI, Fran Raine, Business Services Manager, Relate NI and Edwin Poots, MLA, Minister for Health

65th Anniversary Dinner on 16 November 2012 – Rosemary Frazer, Relate Administrator and Anandi Mahadeo, Relate Counsellor

65th Anniversary Dinner on 16 November 2012 – Barbara McKay, Director, Institute of Family Therapy and Brenda McDowell, Relate Supervisor

65th Anniversary Dinner on 16 November 2012 – Fiona Glass, Relate Supervisor, Andrew Lipczynski Relate Counsellor and John Mellor-Clark, CORE IMS

65th Anniversary Dinner on 16 November 2012 – Owen Donnelly and Kathy Loudoun, Relate Counsellors

Relate CEOs

John Phillips, CEO, 1976 – 1979

Roy Simpson, CEO, 1980 – 1984

John Chamber, CEO, 1985 –1998

Gerald Clark, CEO, 1998 – 2011

Dave Murphy, CEO, 2011 – Current

Into The Future

Launch of Belfast Youth Engagement Project (YEP), May 2013: Back Row – left to right - Mark McCloskey – YEP, Tony O'Neill – Youth Justice Agency, Dave Murphy – Relate NI, Karen Rankin – NIHE, Tina Black – Roden Street Community Development Group, Dermot Magorrian – Youth Justice Agency , Councillor Bob Stoker – South City Resource Centre, Harry Bradley – Youth Justice Agency, Peter Morris – YEHA, Billy Johnson – PSNI. Front Row – left to right - Kathy Watters – YEP, Lisa Barnes – Forthspring, Claire Forsythe – PBNI, Amy Gribbon – Forthspring, Simon Cunningham – BELB, Tommy Boyle – BHSCT, Geraldine Millican – Belfast Regeneration Office, Tommy Latimer – Stadium Youth Project, John McQuillan – Belfast Interface Project, Joe O'Donnell – Belfast Interface Project

Launch of Together For You Project, September 2013: Centre - David Babington, Action Mental Health, Clockwise – Dave Murphy, Relate NI; Anne Townsend, Cruse; Paul Collins, Praxis Care; Siobhan Doherty, Aware Defeat Depression; Fiona Scullion, Mindwise; Julie Harrison, Big Lottery Fund Committee Member, Maire Grattan, Cause, Pam Hunter, Nexus NI.

Presentation of Investors in People Bronze Award in Hillsborough Castle, 2014: John ODoherty, Chair, Relate NI, Maggie Williams, Counsellor/Supervisor, Relate NI, Derek Baker, Permanent Secretary, Department of Employment and Learning and Helen Fry, Accounts Assistant, Relate NI.

Relate NI Investors in People Celebration Event, 2014: l-r; Rosemary Dunlop, Board Member, Relate NI and Elaine McCormick, Counsellor, Relate NI.

CHAPTER FOUR

The Matrimonial Causes (Northern Ireland) Order 1978 – Divorce Reform

An atrocity and a conference

On the evening of Friday 17 February 1978 John Kennedy, Clerk of the Northern Ireland Assembly, reviewed again the arrangements he had made for a major conference next day in Queen's University, hoping it would run smoothly. For many months he had been engaged in consulting elected representatives, legal experts and colleagues and in drafting and redrafting legislation designed to bring about a radical overhaul of divorce legislation in Northern Ireland. This conference was intended to play a crucial role in winning over hearts and minds for a measure which many in the region were certain to find repugnant. Interestingly, Kennedy had invited a distinguished fellow lawyer, William Binchy, to come up from Dublin to attend the conference and to stay as a guest in his east Belfast home – though he was fully aware that Binchy, a special legal advisor on family law reform to the Irish Department of Justice, and subsequently a high-profile opponent of removing the constitutional ban on divorce in the Republic, was implacably opposed to the changes which would be discussed.

That same evening three experienced members of the Provisional IRA hooked two firebombs onto window security grilles of La Mon House. This large hotel, midway between Belfast and Comber, was packed with more than three hundred people attending a variety of functions, including annual prize distributions by the Northern Ireland Collie Club and the Northern Ireland Junior Motor Cycle Club. The devices were of a new type made of recrystallised ammonium nitrate mixed with aluminium filings and attached to gallon tins of petrol.

The warning was telephoned too late and the blasts threw sheets of blazing petrol across a crowded function room and sent a fireball through the hotel engulfing it in minutes. Twelve people died and twenty-three were horribly injured. Some victims had been so badly burned that pathologists had to depend on dental records to identify them.[1]

The next morning John Kennedy and William Binchy were united in mutual horror as they listened to the news of the La Mon atrocity on the radio. A terrible cloud now hung over the conference and perhaps it was understandable that afterwards newspapers carried no reports of it.[2]

'Wives are willing to suffer an awful lot': the delay in divorce law reform

Derick Woods became Chairman of the Executive for the second time in 1978. In the 1978/79 Annual Report he observed that 'two things do not seem to have changed in this period. Firstly, the number of counsellors has not increased in proportion to the demand for their services and thus the work load of tutors and counsellors has increased considerably. Secondly, the expenses of running the Council, in giving this increased service to the public, have risen very rapidly'. He thanked the Department of Health and Social Services and the Area Boards for their increased support, but regretted that 'still we do not seem to attract financial support from the business community and the general public'. These observations would have been appropriate for almost any year in the NIMGC's history. But this Chairman also referred to another development, an indication that the scope of the Council's work would widen considerably in the years ahead. He continued:

It is difficult to look into the future but one thing is clear that due to the new Marital Causes Order, shortly to come into effect, Marriage Guidance counsellors will have an even more important part to play in the life of our community.[3]

Back in 1969 the Westminster parliament had put through epoch-making reforms to the divorce laws. In brief, the Divorce Reform Act allowed couples to divorce after they had been separated for two years, or five years if only one of them wanted a divorce. A marriage could be ended if it had irretrievably broken down and it was no longer necessary for either partner to prove 'fault'. 'New Act may herald rapid rise in Ulster's divorce cases', ran a headline in the *Belfast News-Letter*. Clearly the editor expected that the Northern Ireland parliament would follow Westminster's suit.

Actually the new divorce legislation, applied to England, Scotland and Wales, was not to cross the Irish Sea *for another decade*. One reason for the long delay was that Northern Ireland was, and continues to be, more conservative in social attitudes than the rest of the United Kingdom. Unionists in power at Stormont were cautious about liberalising the law for fear of provoking criticism from their constituents and the Protestant churches. The opposition, overwhelmingly representing Northern Ireland's nationalist minority, preferred to maintain complete silence on the issue, since the Catholic Church was resolutely opposed to divorce. Besides, while the legislation was receiving royal assent, Northern Ireland was being convulsed by the Battle of the Bogside and the violence which led to the deployment of British Army soldiers on active service in the streets. The imposition of direct rule in 1972 brought no immediate change: the Secretary of State and other ministers of state had other issues higher up their agendas: intercommunal conflict; paramilitary violence; housing displaced populations; attempting to shore up a local economy now contracting alarmingly; and, however forlornly, seeking to find a political solution.

And so the old divorce laws remained in force while the rest of the United Kingdom had moved on. Back in the summer of 1969, fully expecting change in the legislation, the *Belfast News-Letter* had devoted almost an entire page to an examination of the current state of play in Northern Ireland. The only significant change in this area had been the introduction of a provision that henceforth Legal Aid would be available to divorce petitioners. The *Belfast News-Letter* expected a dramatic rise in divorce petitions as a result:

Last year [1968] 125 Ulster marriages were ended by divorce. This was a typically "average" year for divorce – figures for the past 10 years break down to show that an average of 123 divorces are granted every year by the courts in the Province…the fact remains that last year's figures of 162 petitions filed and 125 granted, will increase considerably when the law changes this summer…

The high cost of parting from a no longer loved husband or wife has kept many unhappy people bound to a miserable existence. I was told that the average divorce costs about 100 guineas and takes about six months to complete. With the passing of the new Act, we may see the traditional month of weddings becoming renowned this year as the month of marriage dissolutionment…my lawyer friend said,

"I would think that the final figures for this year might be three or four times bigger than the average. Indeed one of my colleagues goes further and states categorically that there will be a 1,000 cases in the 12 months after the Act is passed."

This looks like a grim reflection on our marriages. Is it in fact only the lack of sufficient funds to obtain a divorce that is keeping so many marriages intact?

This article provided a succinct summary of how divorce legislation had operated and would continue to operate in Northern Ireland until the Marital Causes Order of 1978. A lawyer explained. There were the three grounds for divorce: desertion, cruelty and adultery. The commonest ground was desertion, which included 'constructive desertion'. 'This occurs', the lawyer said, 'when a wife (say) is compelled by her husband's actions to leave their home. If his behaviour could be proved to be so bad that she was forced to leave or if he expelled her from the house, it would not be held by the courts as her desertion of him but that he had brought about a position where he was guilty of constructive desertion'.

This kind of behaviour would almost qualify the wife to sue the husband on the second most common ground, cruelty. 'Cruelty is frequently difficult to prove', another legal adviser stated. The offending party, usually the wife, had to be able to show that her health had been affected. He continued:

Nervous trouble is one frequent complaint. The trouble is that wives are willing to suffer an awful lot before they make any definite move. This is possibly one reason why it has been only in recent years that alcoholism has come to the forefront in divorce proceedings. Previously, women seemed to accept a drunken and rather cruel husband as being part of the bad luck of the draw.

This lawyer had expressed succinctly a core reason why a majority of Westminster MPs had decided in 1969 that the divorce laws must be reformed.

The third 'ground' was adultery. 'Here a confession of guilt is not in itself enough to guarantee the granting of a decree by the courts. It is almost always demanded that a confession must be supported by some sort of circumstantial evidence. The one thing which can seriously prejudice the granting of a divorce is the mere suspicion on the judge's part that there has been any collusion between the parties. "The courts do not take a benevolent view of two married people who decide to sever their legal ties," my lawyer friend said sternly'.[4]

Divorce reform

The suspension of Stormont had initially been for one year only. What originally had been intended as a temporary expedient – direct rule – had become a long-lasting feature, particularly after the collapse of the power-sharing executive in May 1974. Republican militants were now referring to the Provisional IRA's campaign of violence as 'The Long War' and, understandably, the attention of the Northern Ireland Office was fixated on how best to bring about the restoration of peace. The number of deaths directly due to the Troubles had risen from 206 in 1975 to 307 (220 of them civilians) in 1976. Thereafter the level of violence fell somewhat: to 113 in 1978 and 88 in 1978.[5] It was now possible for ministers in the Stormont estate to find some space in their busy schedules to address the need to extend to Northern Ireland reforms which had been long in place on the other side of the Irish Sea and the North Channel.

The Office of Law Reform set about applying divorce legislation which had been in force in the rest of the United Kingdom since 1969. This would not be a simple transfer: care had to be taken to set up a consultative process and to recommend articles in the projected Matrimonial Causes Order to take account of regional susceptibilities. John Kennedy had been asked to take over the Office, which had been run by the 'very distinguished' Alfie Donaldson. Kennedy was Clerk to the Northern Ireland Assembly which had not been technically abolished and now, in his new role, he was eager to bring change long overdue to Northern Ireland. The Alliance Party leader, Oliver Napier, had attempted to draw attention to the urgent need for divorce reform in the short-lived Assembly but without stimulating sufficient interest for any practical steps to be taken.

In deciding that the time had come to bring divorce legislation to Northern Ireland which had been in force in the rest of the United Kingdom since 1969, Kennedy was almost alone amongst senior civil servants. The Marriage Guidance Council had long sought legislative change in this area but, perhaps because there were differing opinions within the organisation on this issue, it did not take the lead. Rather, once it was clear that the law would change, NIMGC sought to influence the form that it would take. Kennedy's recollection is that the most resolute support he received was from women's organisations. Mary Clark-Glass, an English woman who then lectured in law in the Belfast College of Business Studies, had been a founder member of the Northern Ireland Women's Rights Movement in 1975. A regular contributor to BBC Radio Ulster on consumer affairs, she acquired a reputation as an authority on legal and human rights issues – she was to be appointed head of the Northern Ireland Equal Opportunities Commission in 1984 and was later a Human Rights Commissioner between 1984 and 1990. Mary Clark-Glass, Eileen Evason, Bronagh Hinds and others in women's organisations gave Kennedy the support he considered vital – 'I couldn't stress too much that those people were my lynch pin and anchor', he remembered.

Kennedy brought those women to Stormont where they impressed his colleagues and Northern Ireland Office staff. In particular they helped Kennedy to win over

James Dunn, the Parliamentary Under-Secretary who would be responsible for steering legislative change on divorce through Parliament. In doing so, Dunn, a deeply devout man, displayed courage: as MP for Kirkdale he was a prominent member of the Merseyside Catholic community. 'He had guts', according to Kennedy, 'I had very great regard for his courage'.

In drafting what became known as the 'Matrimonial Causes (NI) Order 1978' – an Order under direct rule being the equivalent of a Parliamentary Bill – Kennedy consulted widely. The barrister Barry Malcolm and the solicitor Rosemary Chesney were extremely helpful. This was 'very technical legislation' and Kennedy deeply appreciated the drafting skill of his colleague, P J Grant. Finding out the views of the churches was essential. The Catholic Church, opposed to divorce, stood aside; the Church of Ireland was 'very helpful'; the Methodists were 'very helpful'; but the Presbyterians were 'strained' – Kennedy thought that 'the chap they had keeping an eye on it', though much younger than himself, was 'very old fashioned'. There were times when Kennedy yearned for lucid simplicity and he wistfully recalled that eight years earlier Australia had adopted a straightforward law, applying in all its states and territories, providing divorce on one ground alone: a minimum of one year's separation.

It was Kennedy's hope that he could include 'special procedure' – popularly known as 'postal divorce' – as it applied across the Irish Sea in order to keep down the cost of divorce. His problem was that members of the Bar lobbied against its inclusion in the Order – 'they were all barristers wanting the *slightest* bit of work'.

From the autumn of 1977 onwards the Marriage Guidance Council had been attempting to influence this impending divorce legislative reform. The Director, John Phillips, pressed the DHSS, the Office of Law Reform and interested individuals to seek the inclusion of an article in the new Order providing for a conciliation service to be introduced. NIMGC's lobbying attracted press attention. Phillips was reported as commenting on the 'shock revelation that in England and Wales the ratio is now one divorce for every two weddings', a statistic announced by the English High Court judge, Sir George Baker.

In Northern Ireland for every five marriages taking place, one was ending in either divorce or legal separation. On Saturday 8 October 1977 the Director, interviewed by the *Belfast Telegraph*, believed that the figures for Northern Ireland were 'probably lower than elsewhere in the UK because the province's divorce laws were different'. Nevertheless, he added, the rate of breakdown here was increasing: 'Although our figures are not as bad as in England, that is no reason for being smug. Marriage everywhere is under massive pressure and society needs to take the problem seriously'. In the previous year there were 607 divorces granted in the High Court and an additional 1,500 marital orders which granted legal separation. John Phillips continued: 'I think when the law changes here the number of divorces will go up. Marriage break-ups are on the increase, but so is the rate of marriage'. Divorces were easier to obtain in England than in Northern Ireland and 'here an unknown number of people were separating and living apart without going to the courts for legal orders'. Problems leading to marital breakdowns were usually the same universal ones: financial difficulties, sexual problems 'and perhaps cases where relatives "take sides" when a married couple are experiencing personal problems'. The Director did not think that the current Troubles were having any marked effect on the breakdowns, 'although people who were involved in security were often under greater stress and strain'.[6]

The following Monday Phillips made a public appeal, warning that more counsellors, extra back-up services and more money were urgently needed for NIMGC if Northern Ireland was to avoid statistics like those in England and Wales. He said that if children were to be protected from the effects of tens of thousands of broken homes, the public must be prepared to support those who were trying to help in this field:

There is no miracle cure for marital ills. The work is hard and unspectacular. Counsellors are ordinary people, carefully selected and expensively trained and supervised. And they give what time they can voluntarily.

Observing that there were 607 decrees nisi during 1976, out of 10,746 marriages contracted, the Director continued:

If we look a little deeper, however, we find that the courts, through matrimonial orders, recognised that 1,652 marriages broke down during that year. The vast majority of these orders were maintenance orders, whereby husbands were ordered to provide financial support for children and/or wives.

There is no means of recording the number of broken marriages which do not reach the courts – for example, where a childless marriage is broken when a wife leaves a husband who chooses not to seek a divorce.[7]

He pointed out that 'ratios of one in four or one in three are, of course, quite meaningless because it is not those marrying this year who divorce this year but a very large number of divorces there undoubtedly will be'.[8]

In a letter to the *Belfast Telegraph* in February 1978, John Phillips reminded readers that the 'period for consultation on the Draft Matrimonial Causes Order for Northern Ireland is drawing to a close'. On behalf of the Council he expressed his support, 'on the grounds that it will help to reduce the bitterness and distress which have so often attended divorce proceedings'. Again, he pressed the case for inclusion in the Order of a conciliation provision – 'the Council has urged Mr. James Dunn, the Minister of State with responsibility for the Order, to lend his weight to the creation of a service manned by suitably qualified voluntary workers, supervised by experienced professional workers, to help parties to divorce proceedings to discuss their feelings about the break up of their family and to reach agreements'.

The Council's concern was primarily 'with the spirit and emotional climate in which those issues are discussed'. The Director continued:

We are not talking about reconciliation. It seems to us that, if a couple say that they have decided to divorce, no one has the right to tell them that they shouldn't or that they don't know their own mind. What we are talking about is conciliation, offering an opportunity for couples to discuss the break-up of their family in an atmosphere free from bitterness and recrimination.

He added that if the service proposed was to work effectively it would require the understanding and support of the legal profession, the churches and the welfare services, 'and the independent voluntary agencies who will provide the conciliation personnel'. Phillips concluded by stating his belief that the Matrimonial Causes Order – 'coupled with a conciliation service' – would strengthen rather than weaken family life in Northern Ireland 'by enabling marriages in which there is no longer security or emotional growth to be dissolved with dignity and understanding'.[9]

Unionists were amongst those who decided to deliberate the provisions of the draft Order. UPNI – the Unionist Party of Northern Ireland, founded by Brian Faulkner early in 1974 when most of his colleagues rejected the Sunningdale power-sharing agreement – gave its support. In the words of one report: 'UPNI first called for divorce law in Northern Ireland to be brought into line with that in Great Britain at a party conference three years ago. The party believes that the present law is archaic – and it welcomes many aspects of the proposed reform.' Anne Dickson (who had succeeded Faulkner as leader of UPNI after his death in a hunting accident in 1977) led a delegation of her party to meet Parliamentary Under Secretary James Dunn. There were no fewer than twenty-five amendments to the original Order, based on the recommendations of several bodies. The three UPNI delegates 'stressed the urgency of getting the proposed new laws on the statute book'. They could have been delegates appointed by the NIMGC:

They asked Mr Dunn for a commitment to get the legislation through in the next session of Parliament. UPNI asked for a considerable expansion of marriage guidance counselling, urging the Government to back up its commitment to reconciliation by a cash boost to marriage counselling, enabling the introduction of more highly-trained people.

NIMGC would have preferred the word 'conciliation' to 'reconciliation', but this nevertheless was invaluable support. UPNI noted that the special procedure known as postal divorce had not been included – 'In Scotland, however, it was found necessary eventually to introduce the special procedure and this situation will arise in Northern Ireland'. The delegation recommended that there 'should be a marriage guidance office in all the court buildings and this is particularly important at Petty Sessions level where people have their first contact with matrimonial laws'. UPNI also pointed out 'that reducing the cost of divorces was of utmost importance and that in the absence of special procedure the rules governing the new law should be as simple as possible'.[10]

The problem was that UPNI represented a rapidly-diminishing number of voters. In the 1979 general election its three candidates were to obtain only 1.2 per cent of the region's total vote and the party eventually wound itself up in 1981.[11] The view of the Ulster Unionist Party, then representing a majority of unionist voters, was much more significant. Five of the party's Westminster MPs met in a Belfast hotel in March 1978 to consider 'the controversial problem of changing the law governing broken marriages in Northern Ireland'. They were: Enoch Powell (South Down); William Ross (Londonderry); Harold McCusker (Armagh); Rev Robert Bradford (South Belfast); and James Molyneux (South Antrim).

This UUP meeting was described in the press as a 'talk-in' to hear public opinion on divorce law reform. Powell opened by saying that no deadline on the proposals had been reached, 'and the Secretary of State was still willing to listen to any suggestions coming from today's conference, to which everyone with a view to air on divorce was welcome'.

Some wanted the law to be brought into line with England, where divorce by consent of both parties after two years of a breakdown, had come into operation by 1969. Changes had also been made in England in the financial structure for maintenance and division of property between man and wife. In Northern Ireland the husband could still claim all the property after a divorce had gone through. However, as the *Belfast Telegraph* reported, 'some people, including the Presbyterian Church and other religious bodies, are perturbed that changes would make divorce easier'.

The Unionist MPs learned that many organisations had made submissions recommending changes, including the Irish Congress of Trade Unions, various women's bodies, the churches, the Council for Alcohol Related Problems, the RUC, the Salvation Army, the Catholic Marriage Advisory Council and – of course – the Northern Ireland Marriage Guidance Council. The Rev Bradford said he was attending the talk-in 'with an open mind', but he made it clear that his main interest was 'change in the financial set-up in the present divorce law so that both parties concerned could be given a fair deal in any claim involving property'. The Women's Aid Federation wanted divorce proceedings dealt with in the county courts rather than only in the High Court under the present law.

John Phillips was present to press NIMGC's case for the inclusion of a conciliation service in the legislation. 'I want to suggest that we take a much more positive view of conciliation', he declared. 'If we take a lot of the anxiety, hatred and powerful emotions out of the processes of breaking down a marriage we will help especially the children who suffer by hostility between parents than the actual breakdown. We may make it easier for people to look at their relationship and make a fresh start'.[12]

John Kennedy had been an active member of the Northern Ireland Marriage Guidance Council and had served on its committees. He had found that there were 'many fine' people involved in the organisation and he was particularly impressed by Joan Wilson. This, however, was 'in stark contrast to Mr Phillips'. Kennedy was not at all sympathetic to NIMGC's insistence on conciliation but for the present he was more concerned about opposition to the article he had inserted on 'special provision'. Popularly and misleadingly known as 'postal divorce', this provision – which greatly reduced the cost of a divorce – was already in force on the other side of the Irish Sea. 'Unfortunately', Kennedy recalled, 'this provision was spotted by a Presbyterian solicitor and, of course, once he brought it to the attention of James Dunn', the Parliamentary Under-Secretary was 'more than happy to see it go'. This was because postal divorce was regarded by many as making divorce too easy. Dunn, 'being a very devout Roman Catholic', clearly took this view.

Dunn showed great courage in pressing ahead with divorce reform but because of his personal feelings on divorce he left it to John Kennedy to launch the Order to the press at Stormont. Afterwards the *Daily Express* journalist observed: 'Mr Kennedy, you are so enthusiastic – are you planning to divorce yourself?'

The draft legislation continued to receive support from NIMGC, women's organisations, the Standing Advisory Commission on Human Rights and a significant number of representatives of Protestant churches. However, shortly before the Order was to be debated at Westminster, a distinguished Law Lord wrote to the press denouncing its provisions. Baron John MacDermott, eighty-two years old in 1978, had been elected Unionist MP for Queen's University in 1938, had served as Minister of Public Security 1940-41, and had been Lord Chief Justice between 1951 and 1971. According to Kennedy, Lord MacDermott, though revered in the capital for his legal precedents, 'loathed the London scene' as a law lord and was 'happier coming home to take a Boys' Brigade parade'. MacDermott opposed the draft Order in its entirety on the grounds that it undermined family values and would cause increased distress to children involved. This for Kennedy was 'a devastating letter as far I was concerned… the worst salvo of all'.

The debate on the Order took place on 12 June 1978. Kennedy took the opportunity to speak to as many MPs as he could. In London he had private meetings with James Molyneux, the Unionist leader, and Enoch Powell, then the Unionist MP for South Down – Powell, he recalled, was characteristically concerned that the syntax of each article should be perfect. Ian Paisley, the DUP leader, simply observed bluntly that he only believed in divorce on the grounds of adultery.

The vote was taken in the Commons on 20 June. James Molyneux, James Kilfedder, Harold McCusker and William Craig voted in favour, but the majority of Unionists opposed the Order. Nevertheless, the ayes outvoted the noes and the Matrimonial Causes (Northern Ireland) Order came into force early in 1979. The House was not packed on 20 June 1978: four tellers and 126 who voted had been present. A chilling fact noticed later by John Kennedy was that three out of the small number there that day were subsequently assassinated – Rev Robert Bradford, Ian Gow and Airey Neave. Robert Bradford's widow, Nora, later trained as a counsellor with NIMGC and was to give years of valued service to the organisation.[13]

'There is much work to be done to establish an effective service'
In its divorce legislation Northern Ireland was now very nearly on a par with the rest of the United Kingdom…very nearly, but not quite. For Kennedy a particularly disappointing difference was that those who had lobbied for the abolition of special procedure in the draft had succeeded. The absence of 'postal divorce' denied both litigants and taxpayers (since a high proportion appearing in court cases involving marital breakdown received legal aid) the opportunity to reduce the cost of divorce. 'The Bar, of course, love it: with all this legal aid tens of millions must have been spent since April 1979 when the legislation came into force', Kennedy observed. Speaking

as recently as February 2013, Kennedy denounced the 'gutlessness of the current lot' in the Northern Ireland Assembly, and he believes it 'has been so appalling to this day that they have not introduced special procedure…to think that we still have this waste of everybody's time, including that of judges', in addition to the great additional costs involved. He also found the provision to include conciliation and reports on the welfare of children 'very irritating'. This was not the view of the Director of NIMGC.

NIMGC 'are glad to report that the one-man pressure group was successful, as a result of which Article 43 of the Marital Causes (NI) Order 1978, entitled "Reference for Conciliation and the Welfare of Children", makes a provision for a service of voluntary conciliation to be established alongside a statutory referral to a social worker in all cases where there are dependent children'. The Annual Report explained:

Conciliation has nothing to do with reconciliation. It is a counselling service, entered into voluntarily by couples, wishing to make a better divorce and to minimise the effect of feelings of guilt, anger, grief etc on themselves and especially their children. It will operate in premises close to, but separate from, the High Court; and conciliation staff, drawn initially from Northern Ireland Marriage Guidance Council and Catholic Marriage Advisory Council, will work alongside Eastern Board social work staff. It is an exciting venture, breaking new ground in United Kingdom divorce law, which will, we believe, help substantially to reduce the appalling effects of divorce on some children. The new order comes into effect in mid-April and, though it will be some time before applications under it will be heard, there is much work to be done to establish an effective service.[14]

The Director wrote more truly than he then realised. It was one thing to legislate, quite another to make the funds available to get a conciliation service up and running.

Why were the views of the Director of the NIMGC and the Director of the Office of Law Reform so diametrically opposed on this provision in the Order? Kennedy found the inclusion of this article as 'disgusting' because 'there would be no money for conciliation'. In addition, when couples got to the stage of going to court, Kennedy believed they were then beyond the point where conciliation could do any good. If there were problems with children due to marital breakdown, the social workers were 'there already'. Those undoing their marriage vows with children under the age of eighteen were required to be seen by a social worker who then had to compile a report which would become an appendage to a decree nisi. 'Middle class divorcees found this insulting that they should be visited by social workers', Kennedy continued, commenting that the requirement for the report appendage was 'a quite appalling waste of time and money'. However, 'I was very much on my own' in opposing the inclusion of this provision. Provision for this social welfare intervention was revoked some years later because social workers could not cope with the demand. And the provision of a conciliation service proved to be a can continually kicked down the road. [15]

With the exception of a brief interval in the first five months of 1974, Northern Ireland had been governed directly from London since 1972. Indeed, in 1978 the Unionist Party leader, James Molyneux, supported by Enoch Powell, was very much in favour of the full integration of the region into the United Kingdom. The

Matrimonial Causes (NI) Order 1978 came into force in April 1979, on the same day as the implementation of a major overhaul of Northern Ireland's Court Service. Very shortly afterwards, on 3 May 1979, James Callaghan's government was voted out of office and, leading a new Conservative government, Margaret Thatcher entered 10 Downing Street as Prime Minister.

Notes

1   Chris Ryder, *The RUC: A Force Under Fire*, London, 1989, pp.174-5; Patrick Bishop and Eamonn Mallie, *The Provisional IRA*, London, 1989, p.336
2   Interview with John Kennedy, 27 February 2013
3   NIMGC Annual Report, 1978/79
4   NIMGC Annual Report, 1978/79; *Belfast News-Letter*, n.d. NIMGC cuttings file, 1969
5   *Lost Lives*, 2007, p.510, p.608, p.697 and p.742
6   *Belfast Telegraph*, 8 October 1977
7   Ibid., 10 October 1977
8   *Belfast News-Letter*, 11 October 1977
9   *Belfast Telegraph*, 28 February 1978
10 NIMGC cuttings file, February 1978
11 Sydney Elliott and WD Flackes (eds), *Northern Ireland: a Political Directory 1968-1999*, Belfast 1999, p.499
12 *Belfast Telegraph*, 30 March 1978
13 Interview with Julia Greer, 14 August 2013
14 NIMGC Annual Report, 1978/79
15 Interview with John Kennedy, 27 February 2013

CHAPTER FIVE

Widening the scope of the Council 1979-88

'The independent Keynesian Republic of Northern Ireland'

For God's sake bring me a large Scotch. What a bloody awful country'. Reginald Maudling, the Conservative Home Secretary, was infamous for this remark made on his flight back to London after his first visit to Northern Ireland on 1 July 1970. He had also once observed that the government could do little more than make sure that there was no more than 'an acceptable level of violence' – a comment that drew indignant protest at the time, but seemed more realistic to many with the passing of every violent year.

The horrors of August Bank Holiday 1979, when the IRA killed Lord Mountbatten at Mullaghmore and eighteen soldiers and a civilian at Warrenpoint, brought Prime Minister Margaret Thatcher over from London to view the conflict at close quarters. She and her Conservative government, returned to power in May, had been given a grim reminder of the intractability of the Northern Ireland problem. During that year 125 people lost their lives in the violence. Over the next decade, during which a fresh political agreement was hammered out between London and Dublin, another 789 people died directly as a result of the Troubles.

The majority of citizens in Northern Ireland simply got on with their lives as best they could. Security searches, bomb scares, security barriers and cancelled scheduled bus and train journeys were accepted by most with resignation. Detonating bombs, live gunfire, ambushes, booby traps and assassination squads roaming in dark streets created real terror, of course. Untimely deaths and squalid murders affected those of every class and denomination, though those who suffered most in proportion lived in working-class estates or were fatally vulnerable in isolated farmsteads. This was also a decade of acute economic difficulty when the region's traditional export industries either collapsed or were left in intensive care, and when multinational firms, one by one, closed down their operations in Northern Ireland. The De Lorean luxury sports car factory in Dunmurry – seen as a daring act of faith to reduce acute unemployment in west Belfast – collapsed in the autumn of 1982 at a loss of over £80 million to the Treasury.

'Thatcherism' was the term the press gave to the Conservative policies of privatising public utilities and cutting back public expenditure. However, three Conservative ministers in particular swam against the tide and strove to protect Northern Ireland from a strict application of this ideology. Jim Prior, Northern Ireland Secretary of State 1981-84, said himself that he had been exiled to Stormont because of his 'wet' views on economic intervention. Chris Patten, junior minister in the Northern Ireland Office 1981-83, and Richard Needham, who held various posts at Stormont between 1985 and 1992, both actually succeeded in increasing government spending on services and support for industry. In July 1989 the *Guardian* referred to the region as 'the Independent Keynesian Republic of Northern Ireland'.

Both Patten and Needham were to make official visits to the Northern Ireland Marriage Guidance Council's office at 76 Dublin Road in Belfast. Both men played a key part in ensuring that any attempt to cut back annual government grants to the Council were resisted. Indeed the contribution from the taxpayer – via the Department of Health and Social Services and the Area Boards – to NIMGC rose more than was enough to compensate for inflationary pressures. That, of course, did not stop successive chairmen from arguing that the Council needed additional money to meet the rapidly growing demand for its services.[1]

Opportunities for further helpful publicity had been augmented by the launch of BBC Radio Ulster in 1976 which greatly increased local broadcasting coverage. Gloria Hunniford was the first BBC presenter in Northern Ireland to be truly comfortable in front of the microphone without the assistance of typed scripts – it could be argued that Downtown Radio had given the lead in this style of broadcasting. A pioneer of the 'phone-in', she quickly made her regular morning programme, 'A Taste of Hunni', enormously popular. Phillips was a guest on the programme in June 1978 when the *Woman's Own* journalist Angela Willans – then Britain's most famous agony aunt, better known by her nom-de-plume Mary Grant – was being interviewed.

She responded to a question about her qualifications for the job:

The only qualification for being Mary Grant is really just doing it…I'm not really telling people who write to me what to do, I'm comforting, receiving problems, a stranger. Many people ask for advice but are going to go and do just the opposite.

There's a lot of loneliness, fifty per cent are marital problems and I get four to five hundred letters per week. People have a higher expectation of marriage now – they are disappointed and resentful if their marriage does not come up to expectations.

The reason for the columnist's visit was that she was to address an open meeting of the NIMGC that evening. As she said to another columnist, Nikki Hill, she had written two books, *Conflict in Marriage* and *Breakaway: A Family Conflict And The Teenage Girl*.[2]

The *Belfast News-Letter* – now titling itself simply as the '*News Letter*' – continued to run articles on a regular basis featuring the work of the Council. The 'Ulster Woman' column in September 1978 began by dispelling the widespread impression that Marriage Guidance counsellors were 'elderly do-gooders in twin sets and pearls sticking marriages together with cups of tea and emotional elastoplast'. Counsellors were 'not super people nor do they necessarily have super marriages. They are ordinary men and women like you and me'. The feature also stated that NIMGC was 'the only non-sectarian agency which offers a marriage counselling service'. 'Let's have a look at what really happens if you ask them to help you', and continued:

When you phone or call at the office you will speak to one of the two secretary/ receptionists, Mrs Margaret Gordon or Mrs Ethna Robinson. You will be offered an appointment in complete confidence with a counsellor at whatever time suits you – morning, afternoon or at night…Your first appointment will usually be within two or three days of your phoning. You will have up to an hour to talk in a relaxed friendly way with your counsellor about whatever is troubling you.

And what kind of help will be offered by the counsellor? 'It won't be advice of the "if I were you…" kind: you've probably had that before and anyway the counsellor isn't you. Nor will it be a course of pills offered by a doctor'. It went on to inform readers that a new sexual function clinic was being opened in the NIMGC premises in October 1978. The feature explained:

A male and female counsellor work together in what is called co-therapy to help couples (you have to come together to this clinic) with difficulties in their sex lives. The therapy starts with discussion and assessment of the problem, after which all four agree on a treatment programme to be carried out by you and your spouse in the privacy of your home.

If you think you would like to attend this clinic phone the Belfast office. But remember, you will have to wait until October for your first interview at the sex clinic; and you must come together.[3]

The Sexual Function Clinic

As featured in a previous chapter, the Sexual Function Clinic eventually opened in November 1978. The 1978/79 Annual Report made it clear that it was under pressure from the outset. Demand was strong: only three of the four trainees had been able to start, resulting in a growing waiting list. Ten couples were self-referrals. The majority of couples had been referred by doctors, and others by counsellors, social workers and health visitors – 'this has meant that both therapy teams have seen clients from a wide social range and with a wide range of sexual difficulties'. There were two therapy teams and plans were being laid for the third phase of the project for the next year.

'Couples "queue" for sex advice', a newspaper proclaimed. It continued: 'Belfast's new sex advice clinic already has a long waiting list, the Marriage Guidance Council has said'. Joan Wilson, one of NIMGC's most experienced counsellors, had been addressing Belfast Rotary Club. She told club members that advice was not only for married couples but also for those with a 'stable relationship'. The work of the Council was vital 'as it has been shown that when marriages ran into difficulties, there was a sexual problem in six out of ten cases'.

Mrs Wilson felt that the Council would like to be doing more in schools but that it was hampered by a shortage of trained counsellors. She emphasised the need for sex education in schools because, she said, 'young people don't know it all. Many are very ignorant indeed, just as ignorant as the young people used to be in the non-permissive society'. Although sex education should ideally be given at home, Joan Wilson said many parents were glad to have this responsibility taken from them.

An unexpected crisis

John Phillips was the first full-time Director of NIMGC. As he wrote in the 1978-79 Annual Report, he was the only full-time employee which 'has its advantages and drawbacks. For a start you have to be a jack-of-all-trades, you have to mend the fuses and fix the lavatory cistern if it's overflowing, indeed you are finally responsible for just about everything except finding a new Chairman! And you must be available to counsellors and others who want to come to discuss some aspect of their work or just to let off steam…but you couldn't ask for nicer or more willing people to work with…'

Not only did the Director find his work exceptionally rewarding but he was unquestionably an asset to the organisation. He had made sure that the views of the Council were strongly pressed as the Northern Ireland Office, guided by the Office of Law Reform, drafted the Matrimonial Causes (Northern Ireland) Order 1978 – indeed, the inclusion of a clause on the provision of a conciliation service could be said to be a clear indication that Phillips and the Council had left a distinctive, if controversial, mark on the legislation. He had maintained a high profile with the media, and, as he reported, 'a major pre-occupation this year has been the setting up and management of the Sexual Function Clinic'.

Then, as Derick Woods recalled, during his time as Chairman 'we had all sorts of problems': rather suddenly in December 1979, John Phillips resigned as Director and Anna Hyland resigned as Training Officer. The Council was not exactly plunged into disarray by this sudden departure of its chief executive, but it certainly took much time and effort to restore its equilibrium. The outward and visible sign of this was that both the 1979-80 and the 1980-81 annual reports were typed on a typewriter and not, as always until now, typeset. The 1979-80 'Report of the Executive Committee' did its best to be upbeat 'against this background of ups and downs'. 'There can be no doubt that the second half of the year has been overshadowed by the departure, at the end of December, of our Director, John Phillips, and our Training Officer, Anna Hyland', it began, but continued: 'However, your Executive is pleased to report that we have closed the year in very good heart, thankful to those who so quickly took new and extra responsibility and optimistically looking forward to the appointment of our new Chief Officer'. The achievements of both were properly recognised:

John Phillips who for the past four years has been our Director and for many years before that was counsellor, tutor, Executive member and valued colleague, left at the end of 1979. Much of the progress and innovations reported in the Annual Reports of the last few years can be traced to his leadership and influence. Many of the seeds sown by him, such as a conciliation service, have not as yet borne fruit, but most surely they will bear witness in the future to his vision…

Although Anna Hyland had only been in the Training Officer post for six months when she left, her connections with Marriage Guidance go back for a considerable number of years even before she came to live in Northern Ireland in 1972. Her efficiency and high degree of skill marked these years – first as a counsellor, then as a tutor and Executive member.

Nonetheless, the precipitate departure of the Council's key employees naturally created acute problems for the organisation. This is evident reading between the lines in the annual reports. NIMGC was 'indeed fortunate' to have an office 'so efficiently and ably led and manned by three ladies of the experience and calibre of Margaret Gordon, the Council Secretary, Ethna Robinson who mainly looks after accounts and Carol McConkey, with special responsibility for the Sexual Function Clinic…They are in the "front line", settling in their unassuming way, the queries of counsellors, clients, committee members and Chairman, and they have been a tower of strength during the last few months by taking on extra tasks and working many extra hours'.[4]

The Executive Committee, in its report for 1980/81, observed that it has 'been called upon to work extremely hard during this last year'. 'At its own direction the Management Committee was disbanded and the Executive, by meeting monthly, has dealt with all the business previously divided between the two committees'. The result of this was 'a much greater involvement by most of the Executive members in the day-to-day running of the Council, but as they are all busy people, the strain of such frequent meetings was heavy'. Five members of the Executive (Roy Blair, Eileen Warnock, Mary Carson, Ivy Sloan and Professor James Haire) had resigned – 'we need some new stout-hearted members to fill the gaps and give us fresh impetus and energy'. In compensation the Council's President, Charles Kinahan, was persuaded to return to the Executive Committee and Eric McDowell – beginning a long and fruitful association with NIMGC – was co-opted. Both these men were later to receive knighthoods.

'Now that we have spring cleaned and re-organised ourselves', the report continued, 'we feel that next year we may be able to encourage our Chief Officer in cautious expansion in the fields of training and education'. The Council also bade farewell to the office manager, Margaret Gordon, who had been with the organisation for eleven years – 'Her quiet efficiency, good sense and good humour have maintained the core of NIMGC. We feel that her leaving will be as traumatic as a heart transplant operation'. The Council was also without an Honorary Treasurer for many months. Ansley Tolland, a member of the Executive Committee, stepped in temporarily and took part in crucial discussions and interviews with the Department of Health and Social Services and the Area Boards.

Dr Edith Cunningham took over from the exceptionally long-serving Derick Woods as Chairman in 1980. Her 'Chairman's Message' in the 1980/81 Annual Report indicated, first, that the role of the NIMGC was widening and, also by implication, that the organisation was still feeling the fall-out from the departure of John Phillips and Anna Hyland. 'Looking back', she recalled, 'two things have surprised me. I was quite unprepared for the dividends I have received personally from my modest investment of time and effort'. She valued 'the wealth of experience that has been shared with me' and appreciated 'the very special talents possessed by trained and dedicated counsellors'. However,

I was also surprised by the almost total lack of support from the Council. This body who represents the public whom we serve, who elected the Executive to expedite their wishes seems to melt into thin air between each Annual General Meeting. It was

discouraging to find, when we called a Special Meeting to discuss the proposed changes in the Constitution, so few members of Council bothered to attend that a quorum for the meeting was only just reached. We need a larger and more active Council; your Executive cannot fulfil its potential without positive support and help from its Council. The vitality of an organisation such as ours depends upon the interest and activity of its members. If we are convinced of the need for a marriage guidance council in Northern Ireland then we should not find it difficult to convince our friends, and encourage them to show their concern by joining the Council.

She appealed to 'old Friends' to join the Council: 'we need you desperately to help in so many ways for groups throughout the Province, for discussion, education and fund raising – to be a bridge between the public and the counsellors'. 'If we neglect our friends we lose them', Dr Cunningham observed ruefully, 'and I am afraid that this has happened to that wonderful group of Friends who supported us so ably in the past'.

The Chairman was able to convey good news: Roy Simpson, a Presbyterian minister from Derry/Londonderry, was appointed the new Director. Taking up his post in October 1980, Roy Simpson quickly proved that he had been well chosen, being particularly adept at using the media to the Council's advantage.[5]

'They throw their net far beyond the matrimonial bed'

In May 1980 the veteran *Belfast Telegraph* journalist, Betty Lowry, talked to Dr Ethna O'Gorman, consultant psychiatrist to the Council's sexual function clinic. She began by remarking that 'to most people in this part of the world the phrase "mixed marriage" means one thing – a marriage between a Protestant and a Roman Catholic. But when Dr Ethna O'Gorman speaks on mixed marriages at a public meeting organised by the Northern Ireland Marriage Guidance Council tomorrow night she will be talking about the problems faced by couples where one partner is a homosexual'.

Dr O'Gorman was due to address an audience largely consisting of people involved in counselling in various organisations – social workers, doctors, and interested laymen and women. She would talk about what can happen 'when a heterosexual and a homosexual are married'. 'The discovery that one of the partners in a marriage is homosexual need not mean divorce', she said, pointing out that sex is only one aspect of marriage. 'Married couples have so many other bonds – they enjoy the comfort of the same home, the same interests, and frequently children as well'. Dr O'Gorman felt very strongly about the law in Northern Ireland which still regarded homosexuality as a criminal offence.

Dr O'Gorman gave her services without payment as an 'honorary consultant' to NIMGC's Sexual Function Clinic. The Galway-born psychiatrist was a consultant in Belfast City Hospital and a lecturer in the Department of Psychology at Queen's University, as well as being 'a full-time wife and a full-time mother'. Betty Lowry hastened to add that the 'vast majority of the couples who seek help from the sexual function clinic are, of course, heterosexual'.[6]

It was at that meeting that the Council chairman, Derick Woods, announced that the new director of NIMGC would be Roy Simpson. In January 1981, having completed his first six months in the post, the distinguished journalist, Carmel McQuaid, interviewed Simpson about the work of the Council in a large feature, entitled 'Love on the Rocks', in the *Sunday News*. She began:

For all who are burdened by the stresses and strains of daily living, a band of 34 caring men and women, based mainly in Belfast and Bangor, hold out a soothing oasis – in the shape of a shoulder to cry on, a sympathetic ear, or thoughtful advice that will tide them through the rough patch. Though known as the Marriage Guidance Council, they throw their net far beyond the matrimonial bed – to anyone between 12 and 80 who feels let down, left out, hurt, abandoned or unable to go on; to widows, unmarried mothers, adolescents and anyone in need of help with relationships.

Well versed in the variations of human happiness, in the facets of the flesh and sore places of the spirit, they do not undertake to make problems go away; instead, by exploring the territory that has led to the present impasse, they help the client to cope better and to see the situation in a fresh light.

The counsellors, she understood, were specially equipped to deal with a whole list of losses, 'from the loss of personal prestige which a mastectomy or hysterectomy can bring, to the loss of a job and subsequent lack of income, to the loss of a physical presence that follows a divorce, or the loss of image that requires a new identity'. The counsellors worked from the premise that every human being has within himself or herself the resources to solve problems – but help may be needed. 'Their aim', she continued, 'is to convince clients of their ability to grow, and to get them to view themselves in a more exalted light.'

After the appointment had been arranged, 'the very procedure of sitting down and sharing the problem with another human being, often after months of bottling it up alone, has an automatic therapeutic effect'. The new Director explained:

In counselling we are dealing with feeling, and no problem is too trivial to be aired, no wound too personal for us to treat. We have something to offer to anyone who has any kind of communication difficulty. We are not claiming to be psychiatrists or psychologists, but we think we are good at what we do.

We're essentially human beings, not Superman or Superwoman, and the relationship between client and counsellor only works where there's trust and understanding. The success depends on what the individual wants and on how open he or she is to change. At the end of the day a client may not be prepared to change, or may not be able to open themselves to growth, but coming to us the first day requires an immense amount of courage.

Roy Simpson did not believe that love conquers all, that love is enough. 'You have to break love down to what it means, and at the end of the day it means caring, and sharing and making sacrifices – being able to grow and change and open yourself to another. Emotional strength is the ability to cope with the rough as well as the smooth, and no marriage ever keeps steadily on an even keel'. He identified 'unreasonable expectations' as the root decay accountable for an overwhelming number of marriage difficulties. 'Such a starry-eyed attitude', Carmel McQuaid observed, 'has spawned an astronomical disaster rate among teenage marriages in the under-18 group'.

The Director highlighted lack of communication or faulty communication as a 'formidable culprit in the marriage stakes'. Resentment built up in partners who refused to air their ambiguous feelings about in-laws, money, their roles in running the house, and the like. Faulty communication, he felt, frequently caused problems 'related to sex with partners remaining reticent about what particular touches or activities bring most pleasure'. 'At the end of the day', he said, 'how does a man know what a woman wants unless she tells him. Of course you need to be in a trusting relationship and to take the risk of saying "That's how I like it". But often both want to experiment and yet don't dare ask'.

In short Roy Simpson was prepared to discuss intimate details of relationship problems (without, of course, identifying any clients) to a greater extent than had previously been the case with NIMGC interviewees – with, perhaps, the exception of Dr Ethna O'Gorman. The Director concluded that many couples were victims of the traditional culture where it was more normal to talk about what you think rather than what you feel. This predominantly male attitude 'has traditionally shown a negative attitude to sex'. These 'throwbacks to less informed times' could militate against 'the sexual routine starting off with ease'. 'In later life', he added, 'the old notion that sexual athletics were only for the young, coupled with the female outlook towards men and sex can put an appalling dampner on displays of love. The physical and mental foreplay built up during courtship can diminish during the early years of marriage – and gradually warmth and tenderness fade away altogether'. Once demonstrations of affection stop, it could be hard to start them again.

The Director often found that sexual problems stemmed from 'some other circumstance…conversation soon reveals that the walls of their bedroom are paper-thin, leaving them in suspense that their movements will be heard, or that someone will walk in'. 'If they get their own place, the sex life sorts itself out', he explained. Childhood indoctrination could lead to ambivalent attitudes to sex in women who want marital relationships on the one hand, yet on the other feel unclean afterwards. In such cases talk was the ideal tonic. He said:

Permission to talk freely about sexual behaviour is therapeutic and all many people need. Once the counsellor feels she's comfortable with the subject, and once she uses sexual terminology without inhibition, the barriers are down and the client is able to talk about fears or sexual shortcomings.

Where sexual performance posed genuine problems the blame usually rested with strain, stress and physical tiredness. Policemen and prison officers in such circumstances could become impotent with serious consequences for the partner. On this issue he concluded:

Some adjustment is always needed, but I reckon sexually we get better all the time. If people from childhood are given good messages about themselves, emotionally and sexually, if they have healthy feelings about their own bodies and the bodies of the opposite sex, if they understand their own sexual responses and are educated emotionally – then relationships should pose no serious difficulties. They should learn to relate sexually.

The Director then moved to what was described as the 'Power Game' which could have 'a most pernicious effect on a partnership and any shift in who controls what can result in terrific strain'. Sometimes 'the Lord Provider' found his position threatened if his wife got a job – 'he's suddenly required to adjust to sharing the housework or to playing second fiddle salary-wise, so that his self-esteem, his expectations of himself, fostered by the culture here, take a sound blow'. 'All men find it hard to accept a woman's inherent right to freedom', he concluded.

The balance of power in a relationship could 'also teeter threateningly' after release from prison, retirement, unemployment or any circumstance which would throw a couple together for longer spells than were customary. The wife could find her husband knocking about her feet all day 'or attempting to usurp the little roles that have made up her daily routine'. This was very likely to happen when sailors ended their long sea voyages for good or when long-term prisoners were released.

Simpson also identified contraception as a 'fresh hornet's nest in the Power Game'. It left women with total responsibility. Contraception 'has been a tremendous boon to both men and women as it has allowed them to explore their own sexuality to its full depth…But it has also created tensions…A woman may desperately want a son and her husband feels he's being used as a stud, or a performing bear, and be nonplussed in this role'. Alcohol abuse could stem from a facet of the marriage which, once corrected, could induce sobriety. Or, indeed, it could be a symptom of personality disorder.

With the encouragement of his interviewer, Roy Simpson continued to reel off reasons why some marriages ran onto the rocks. They included: 'polygamous tendencies' resulting in adultery (a 'relationship flaw' which 'need not shipwreck the marriage'); shotgun marriages ('imperilled from the start and have a huge casualty rate'); and mixed marriages ('while suffering a higher breakdown rate, such marriages afford opportunities for enrichment'). Finally, the Director pinpointed certain phases of wedlock as 'Definite Danger' zones, 'amid pools of constant flux'. Most marriages broke up in the first four years, 'with the next shallow spot occurring after 20 years, when one in every five divorces take place'. His view was that:

"The reason would appear to be linked with man's higher point in his career. He suddenly sees he is not going to go any further and may very well seek his comforts elsewhere"…he also advances the hypothesis that 20 years of marriage leaves a couple emotionally very close – so that unresolved conflicts cropping up from the early years are transferred to the spouse. Conflicts with a mother or father may suddenly get foisted on to him and the debacle ruins the relationship.

His parting comment was that divorcees should come along for counselling before remarrying, 'so that any stumbling block to good relationships in their personal make-up can be identified and hopefully eliminated'.[7]

On Tuesday 4 January 1981 the *Irish News* published what was almost certainly its first feature on the Northern Ireland Marriage Guidance Council. This took the form of an interview in depth with Roy Simpson. He covered much the same ground as he had with Carmel McQuaid but, clearly, he was at pains to inform readers who were discovering the existence of the organisation for the first time. Simpson summarised the aims and objectives of NIMGC as follows:

- To increase public understanding of the significance of the marriage relationship in fostering personal growth and fulfilment.
- To promote awareness of the complexities of social adjustment and of personal stress involved.
- And to help couples and individuals in the development of mature relationships.

The Director once more stressed the importance of communication, 'both talking and listening'. 'A common fault is that people often think they are listening when they are not. We often hear what we want to hear', he said. This lack of communication and commitment between husband and wife could often lead to separation and divorce:

In Northern Ireland it leads many people to seek help from the Council. Between April 1979 and March 1980 the Council's volunteers had 3,878 interviews with clients, with 549 clients taking advantage of the new service…Many people go into marriage with false ideas and expectations; they don't realise that a couple must work every day at their relationship to have a successful marriage.

The silver screen image of love and marriage which always has a "happy-ever-after" ending is unrealistic and a marriage based on this idea will be doomed to failure unless the couple wake up to the realities.

Having outlined the service provided by the Council, Roy Simpson said that 'the majority of clients who visit 76, Dublin Road for counselling have problems with communication, and lack of affection from their partners'. Many came for counselling with bereavement problems and with personal relationship problems. One of the growing problems was in the changing role of women in society. He explained:

'Many men now feel themselves threatened. Men are no longer the masters of the household. This feeling of insecurity can grow and present a real problem and a danger to the security of a marriage…

In the case of a man who has just been made redundant, or a man who has finished a prison sentence there could be a strain in the marital relationship,' he said. 'They are about the house more than usual and are "in the way" of the wife who has her routine knocked about by their presence. It also affects the image and morale of a man if he is no longer the provider and the boss…

Bereaved people need encouragement and hope; it's often very hard for someone to live alone when their partner dies.'

The Director detailed how counsellors were recruited and rigorously trained, noting that there was no set limit to a counsellor's knowledge – a counsellor 'must keep learning and reading'. 'The Council looks for people who are warm, caring human beings who have been able to overcome major conflicts in their life, who are free from prejudice and who accept people as people', he said. It was not a case of advising people; it was a case of helping people to listen to themselves. 'It means you eventually find your own answers to the difficulty based on your own nature and needs, instead of having someone else's answers handed over to you like a doctor's prescription', he continued. 'In short, you find out what choices are open to you and the resources within yourself and your marriage to find your own way'.[8] Just how counsellors were recruited became a hotly debated issue in the spring of 1981.

'The love menders'
In April 1981 the *Sunday Times* 'Look' feature was devoted to a report by Clive Graham-Ranger on how the National Marriage Guidance Council selected its counsellors. The National Council at that time had 500 centres 'where 1,750 unpaid counsellors advise more than 35,000 cases every year, and in 1979 there were 527 new volunteers from which 243 counsellors were chosen'. 'From time to time', it was explained in the opening paragraph, 'disappointed volunteers, turned down at the gruelling one-day selection conferences, have written hurt letters to Look'.

Since the selection procedure in Northern Ireland in 1981 hardly differed from that in the rest of the United Kingdom, the report by Graham-Ranger is revealing. It is worth pointing out at the start that one of the candidates reported on, complained later: 'Throughout, the article is full of cheap sneering psychologising "knees-clamped-together-nonsense".' Graham-Ranger continued:

The Convener, Ruth Drury, ushered us into an upstairs room overlooking a new-cut croquet lawn. A small rounded woman with a voice straight out of Mrs Dale's Diary, Convener Drury has been a marriage guidance counsellor since 1974. Her job today, she said, was to direct group discussions. She handed out name tags. The candidates' badges also had letters from A to H corresponding to the order in which they would be interviewed privately by Selectors One and Two during the course of the day. I had a badge labelled "Observer".

Selector One, Ena McGeorge, was a sharp-eyed woman in her forties who could be mistaken for Shirley Williams, marriage council tutor since 1972. Selector Two, Mike Lavelle, a one-time counsellor, was a local government employee, used to testing job applicants. As a pair, the Selectors were like TV-cop interrogators, Hard Man, Soft Man. Two was gentle and keen to offer tea; One, aggressive and quick to snatch back such comforts.

The candidates were a cross-section from any High Street – two men and six women aged from 31 to mid-40s; most from state schools, one from public school. There were three divorced, one on a second marriage, the other four happily married. They were all turned out in practical, earnest, social worker attire, shoes polished, hair neatly trimmed.

In the first round each in turn had to give his or her name and tell how they felt about it. In the second round each candidate had to write a description of himself or herself as each thought those who liked, and those who disliked, would see him or her. The selectors said afterwards that these descriptions revealed a great deal about each candidate. The third round was a series of fifteen-minute discussions, which candidates left in pairs at half-hourly intervals for interviews with the two selectors. The remaining six took it in turn to draw cards from the table and discuss the topics on them.

The feature writer gave nicknames to the candidates. 'Eyes' picked up the first question card. 'As she stumbled over the word "heterosexual" her shocked eyes pleaded through big spectacles for someone to explain what the question meant'. 'Matron' was disturbed to think that her teenage daughter would be prescribed the Pill by a GP who had not consulted her – 'Arguments raged over sex before 16'. 'Public School Man' related his own heterosexual experiences at 14, 'and how he fought the "homosexual environment" of his public school'. He also favoured legalising cannabis, 'though as a non-smoker he insisted that he ate it rather than smoked it'. 'Self-made man', who inclined to the right, clashed with 'Public School Man' over political marches. 'Doctor's Wife' – 'Jewish, young, nervous, a mother' – had no idea what the Nazis had done to the Jews, 'an admission at which the group went silent. Birdsong drifted in'. 'Trouser Suit' intimated 'that although she could not say whether sex without love was immoral, it was most definitely painful'. 'The Nurse' remarked 'that it was odd how soliciting was illegal, prostitution wasn't'. 'Moon Face' gazed around 'in blank bewilderment as the discussion gradually revealed fragments of each person's beliefs and background, hardships and prejudices'.

The nervous tension in the room was growing and growing. It was heightened by the pairs of candidates coming and going for their one-to-one interviews with Selectors One and Two. Half returned to the room obviously shocked; half quickly regained their composure and dived back into the general discussion…By lunchtime there was a feeling of panic in the room. Convenor Drury attempted to bring everyone back to the reason they were there; the selectors were looking for "genuineness, non-possessive warmth, and accurate empathy…" she said. "This is not a question of acceptance or rejection"…The selectors ate separately.

When the group reassembled, the convenor explained that she was about to play a cassette of actors role-playing a typical guidance case. 'Self-Made Man used his sharpened analytical scalpel on several problems in a way which would have killed real patients'.

There were casualties. Eyes returned from her interview with Selector Two dabbing at tears. In the middle of a discussion about a woman whose husband was having an affair, Trouser Suit clasped her hands tightly and said, hysteria barely contained: "Sex…sex…that's all we seem to be talking about." Moon Face was wringing her hands.

After seven hours locked in mental and emotional conflict, the candidates were given 15 minutes in which to review how they felt about the day. The two men instantly launched into personal attacks on Selectors One and Two. They were not among the three selected to train as counsellors. The chosen three: Matron, Nurse and Doctor's Wife.

Graham-Ranger thought that the convenor and the selectors looked drained at the end of the day. The Convenor, Ruth Drury, explained to him: 'We're as thorough as time will allow. But always at the back of your mind is the fear that you might let someone through the net who may do more harm than good'.[9]

The Sunday Times was inundated with correspondence and telephone calls following the publication of this Look feature. The letters were edited by Bill Cater who observed that they 'all make painful reading'. He reminded readers that 'stepping forward as a volunteer counsellor demands self-sacrifice – the job is unpaid and takes a lot of time – and courage'. At the end fifty per cent or more of the candidates would be rejected, 'and however that rejection is wrapped up, it will hurt'. 'Public School Man' complained: 'How would you like to be described as "Moon Face"?' 'Self-made Man' asked: 'To what extent are selection and training procedures examined by independent researchers?' A National Council organising secretary from Leicester wrote:

All our 28 counsellors have been through the same process of selection and each found much that was familiar in Mr Graham-Ranger's observations. The very stringent selection process is designed not only to prevent those who might do more harm than good being let loose on clients, but also to prevent those who might be damaged by the pressure of clients being exposed to that risk. It takes people of strong, stable, mature understanding.

She had enclosed a Council survey which showed that four out of five clients who answered a questionnaire thought the counsellor did a good job.

However, another reader was less enthusiastic about the 'harrowing process' of the selection procedure. A person who wanted to be accepted needed 'to project yourself as someone with no strong convictions'. 'You will be severely tested by group discussions on subjects like abortion, homosexuality, race, education, penal policy, feminism, industrial relations, religion – all subjects about which people normally hold strong views. Do not however be tempted to express your views strongly'. In short, 'your reasons for wishing to become a counsellor should be fairly orthodox'. This correspondent concluded by reminding readers that the Marriage Guidance Council itself warned that the motives of those wishing to become counsellors 'are listed in one of their publications as love of power, sexual curiosity, unresolved personal problems, reparative drive (i.e. mending your parents' marriage) and inability to make social relationships on equal terms'.[10]

'More couples cite adultery'

The Northern Ireland Marriage Guidance Council directors had both predicted a rise in the divorce rate as a result of changes in the law. On 1 April 1982 the *News*

Letter had as its front-page headline: 'Divorce rate soars in Ulster: More couples cite adultery'. It reported that divorces in the region had doubled inside two years – 'and one in six is due to adultery'. In some areas one couple in three was breaking up. Among the groups whose marriages were most at risk were professionals and members of the security forces.

Courts in Northern Ireland had granted 1,497 separation orders, 300 more than in 1980. Twice as many marriages had ended in divorce as in 1979. The report continued: 'The family division of the Northern Ireland High Court filed 700 divorce petitions in 1979 – compared to 1,507 filed last year. Separation orders soared by 333 last year from 1,164 in 1980. Provisional statistics also show that adultery is an increasing cause of separation and that more wives begin divorce proceedings than husbands'. When interviewed, Roy Simpson said that the Marital Causes Order of 1978 had caused 'a massive influx of couples wanting divorce'. Six out of ten couples who split decided to live apart to have their marriages dissolved. 'Together, both the two-year and five-year separation methods accounted for 911 (or 61 per cent) of all couples granted the decree nisi last year'. More than 250 husbands or wives – or one case in six – cited adultery in court. During the previous year 973 women instituted divorce actions against their husbands, compared with 524 men who started proceedings against their wives. Other main reasons cited for the increase in separation orders were desertion (one case in fourteen), or 'behaviour' (one case in thirteen). Newtownards, Coleraine and Craigavon were the places mentioned where one in every three marriages were splitting up. Roy Simpson provided some explanations for the reporter, Noel McAdam:

Marriages are most at risk during the first nine years. Unfortunately it is couples with children, rather than childless couples, who tend to break up...We are beginning to realise that unemployment is an increasing factor involved in marital break-ups, with the loss of pride and the change in the roles of both partners. It would seem that the group which is least able to cope with unemployment is the middle classes, the professionals – the business executive and the teacher, for example – who have never been used to the dole. There is also a very high risk of marital break-ups in the security forces. There is evidence that wife-battering and violence towards children in the marriage is increasing also.

NIMGC had supported the 1978 change in the law, but it was now pressing for the Department of Health and Social Services to implement the provision for a conciliation service for couples who had decided to end their marriage. The Director added:

The legal machinery for divorce should be as simple as possible. The old laws caused antagonism and severe emotional and physical strain on the partners of a dead marriage...It is very important that the couple maintain some sort of relationship, especially where there are children. Marriage may not be forever, but parents are.

There is a provision in the law for a conciliation service for couples, but no move has been made to set it up. Under this, a couple seeking divorce talk to a conciliator to see what areas – such as financial – they are in agreement on. All this helps to reduce the bitterness which divorce can cause.[11]

Reminding readers that NIMGC's Flag Day was imminent, the *Lisburn Star* had its own news report with the headline 'Shock statistics on broken marriages'. It pointed out that 'the young are quite wrongly made the scapegoats, for it is interesting that 21 per cent of all divorces take place after 20 years of marriage'. It quoted an estimate that marital breakdown costs for the United Kingdom as a whole were at least £1,000 million. After providing much detail on the services provided by the Council, the report added: 'It is a fact that 40 per cent of people who re-marry after divorce actually get divorced again. It is a fact that children of a broken home are more likely to have a broken home themselves than children from a stable background'.[12]

In the spring of 1982 *The Sunday Times* commissioned a major opinion survey, on the 'place of women in today's world', conducted by MORI among a representative sample of 1,069 adults. Though the interviewees were spread through 51 constituencies, Northern Ireland does not seem to have been included in the survey. Nevertheless, the results did give some indication of changes in attitudes. Peter Wilsher, commenting on the poll results for *The Sunday Times*, began: 'Far and away the most important ingredient in a good marriage is the ability of husband and wife to talk freely to each other about their feelings. Being "in love" and maintaining a good sex relationship take a distinctly secondary place – in fact, women rate a shared sense of humour higher than either of them'.

There was a sharp drop – since a similar poll by George Gallup in 1947 – in the number of women who said they would prefer, if given the choice, to be men: 37 per cent in 1947, 20 per cent in 1982. The real variations came with age, and to a lesser extent with class, rather than with region. 'People over 65, brought up in a different time-warp, still think, three-to-one, that kitchen and nursery are the only fit place for the exercise of femininity'. He continued:

So, too and this is perhaps the saddest single statistic in the whole survey – are those of both sexes who now find themselves separated or divorced. Fully 46 per cent of them show nostalgia for the domestic hearth, presumably feeling that they, or their lost partners, would have been better off had they never thought of deserting it.

On sex life the poll revealed that 'the picture was less than roseate'. Just 52 per cent felt that sex life had improved, but 'then, only 5 per cent are prepared to grumble that it has actually got worse'. Interviewers met with 'distinct coyness' when they attempted to find out what, specifically, constituted 'a satisfactory sexual life for this supposedly sky's-the-limit generation'. Asked about 'frequency of sexual intercourse', 21 per cent responded once or more a week – 'after that the figures trailed rather dismally away…14 per cent never (including 12 per cent of the 18-24 year olds, which hardly sounds like permissiveness run mad)'.

'What hardly anyone, male or female, seems to bother much about any more is the blossoming of visual titillation' on Page 3 in the *Sun* and in soft-porn magazines, advertisements showing under-dressed ladies, garage calendars and poster hoardings. 'The big puzzle', Wilsher continued, 'putting together the "morality" answers and the choice of ingredients for a "good marriage", is just what to make of the adultery item'. Right across the spectrum at least two people in three 'deplore the notion of married people sleeping with anyone other than their proper, legal partner'. However, 'the little matter of sexual fidelity seems to rate very low indeed. In the overall list of 13 items it counts no better than eleventh and women seem marginally less concerned about it than men'.

Looking at the figures on household responsibilities, Wilsher concludes: 'Germaine Greer may wax and wane, multiple orgasm may cause the earth to move twice a week, general morality may tilt in favour of bare breasts in family newspapers and pre-marital cohabitation in the Communal super-squat. But some things, it seems, never change'. Only two per cent of men did the housework – 'Perhaps that is the sort of thing they talk about in all those deep discussions about the state of their shared feelings'.[13]

'Demand for our counselling services…continues to be greater than our resources to respond quickly'

The Annual Report for 1979/80, while it reflected (however indirectly) the problems created by the departure of the first Director and the Training Officer, contained much good news. 'Despite the difficulties which the counsellors have faced recently', it noted, 'for the first time the number of interviews given has topped the 2500 mark, reaching 2530'. The total number of interviews offered was actually 3,878 – 'this discrepancy between "offered" and "given" which mainly occurs in outlying centres, seems to point to the need for more effective publicity in these areas'. There were now thirty-four counsellors – 'a new record total' – and the Council's services had been extended with the opening of new centres in Rathcoole, Newry and Limavady.

Barbara Mitchell, a tutor with the Marriage Counselling Service in Dublin, joined the Council to fill the position left vacant by the resignation of Anna Hyland as Training Officer. The following year the Council lost the service of no fewer than eight counsellors (two of them due to maternity leave) but managed to give the same number of interviews, 'give or take a handful', as in 1979/80. There was an oblique reference to recent disruption: 'it is probably fair to say that the past year has tested out – and proven to the full – the resilience of the Council (especially of the office staff) and the commitment of the counsellors'. NIMGC looked forward to 'a less stretched and more settled year' in 1981/82.[14] Indeed, the Council was able to open new centres in Magherafelt and Lisburn and to extend its work in Bangor. More counselling hours per client were being given. Dr Clare Adams, Consultant Psychiatrist, agreed to become a consultant to NIMGC. She had been involved frequently in counsellor selection – 'her genuine interest, concern and advice have already proved invaluable to us'.

All training and supervision of counsellors remained under the control of the National Council through its tutors, Barbara Mitchell and Flora Taylor, who 'have no hesitation in being firm about maintaining standards'. In 1982/83 the number of clients fell from 617 in the previous year to 589 but the number of interviews increased from 2,657 to 2,678. The year 1983/84 saw a substantial rise to 616 clients and 3,431 interviews given. The report for that year observed that the Council's 'marital counselling service is highly respected for its professionalism and more than ever the service is becoming increasingly better known by the general public'. It continued:

Our advertising and public relations programmes have kept Marriage Guidance in a high profile to the community...While the primary focus of our counselling service is marital counselling we actively encourage people with all kinds of personal problems to come for skilled help. Thus we see the married, the unmarried, husbands and wives separately and together, the separated, the divorced, the remarried and many other people who need help for personal and relationship problems.

Client contacts rose from 8,778 in 1984/85 to 11,861 in 1985/86, though the number of interviews given fell slightly from 3,265 to 3,057 (1,265 to women, 575 to men, and 1,217 to couples). The report explained:

The demand for our counselling services in Antrim, Belfast, Bangor, Ballymena, Coleraine, Craigavon, Carrickfergus, Dungannon, Lisburn, Londonderry, Magherafelt and Omagh continues to be greater than our resources to respond quickly. For most of the year we have been working with waiting lists. A reduction in our counselling strength meant that slightly less hours of counselling were available than the previous year.

Our clients come from all walks of life...They present a wide variety of problems, but this year there has been a considerable increase in the number of clients who have presented problems related to having been the victims of incest in their childhood. We also continue to see a large number of security force marriages.

In 1986/87 the number of client contacts rose to 12,374 leading to 4,084 one-hour interviews being offered. The NIMGC decided that most of its counsellors should be trained in Dublin. In that financial year, as George Walker, the Honorary Treasurer reported, 'some two thirds of the training will now take place in Ireland and the remainder will be as usual at the National Marriage Guidance training centre in Rugby'. This, he continued, 'has helped to offset the considerable increases in training costs levied by Rugby and enabled the increase in our costs to be maintained within the budget'.[15]

It should be remembered that in the 1980s the relative cost of airfares, even within the United Kingdom, was much higher than they would be in the second decade of the twenty-first century. When this cost was added to the fees levied by Rugby, it was little wonder that NIMGC realised the savings in time and money which could be made by diverting as much training as was practicable to Dublin. John Chambers, appointed the Council's CEO in 1984, later recalled an extreme and very exceptional example of costs which could be incurred:

Around 1986 we chartered a small plane to send candidates for selection to a selection conference in the Isle of Man. I think we were the only local Relate service to charter a plane![16]

Julia Greer was a member of the first cohort to be sent for training in Dublin in 1986. This was in partnership with the Church of Ireland organisation, the Marriage and Relationship Counselling Service. As a cross-border initiative it was able to attract additional funding. Eight counsellors were sent from Northern Ireland to join eight counsellors from the Republic in Dublin, there to receive training provided by staff from Relate National in Rugby. Julia found that the two organisations cooperated most effectively in this stimulating, challenging, cross-cultural and very helpful course. It included role plays, working with couples. At one stage this residential course was located in the premises and grounds of a silent order of religious near Dún Laoghaire. This training was closely supervised and involved monthly meetings with representatives of NIMGC and MRCS and supervisors coming together alternatively in Dublin and Belfast. Then, in the true spirit of the enterprise, they met overnight in a hostel on the Border.[17]

Buying 76 Dublin Road

Keeping costs down to stay within the budget is a constant concern of every voluntary organisation. The Northern Ireland Marriage Guidance Council was, indeed, a voluntary organisation: while it had paid staff, it depended heavily on volunteers rendering their services for no financial return. However, like a growing number of similar bodies, it was dependent on the financial support of the tax payer and the rate payer. In its early years NIMGC obtained some funding from charitable trusts and grants from the Northern Ireland government, Belfast Corporation and some other local councils. After the imposition of direct rule and the reorganisation of local government (which included the setting up of area boards), the Department of Health and Social Services and the area boards became the principal funders. In his Treasurer's Report for the year ending 31 March 1980, J A L Tolland explained that the DHSS and the area boards 'jointly contribute grant-aid of 75 per cent of total expenditure'. 'This leaves 25 per cent to be raised by our own efforts,' he continued, 'thus, this year to break even we had to generate £10,577 and, in fact, the actual amount raised was only £8,417'. This shortfall was 'further exacerbated insofar as the Carnegie Grant of £2,500 received for the past two years has now come to an end'. In an attempt to improve the situation a professional fund-raiser had been appointed 'with, unfortunately, little success and this arrangement has now been terminated'.

In the category of money raised by NIMGC's own efforts by far the most regular significant item was clients' donations. Churches and a few firms made modest contributions; individual and covenanted subscriptions raised £626 in 1980/81; and other sums came in from the sale of books, 'lunches and teas', and fund-raising events such as coffee mornings and designated flag days – for example, the Craigavon Counselling Centre had 'a very successful flag day' in 1980 which 'raised the handsome sum of £277'. The flag days in 1985/86 in Belfast, Carrickfergus, Ballymena and Stormont 'brought in the record sum of £764'. Adrian Hazelden, a student of the College of Business Studies, ran in the Belfast Marathon in 1985, raising £715 for the Council. The Carnegie foundation's grants had ceased but some other trusts stepped in including the Esme Mitchell trust (which gave £1,000 in 1984) and the Sir Thomas McClure fund.

The steady widening of the scope of NIMGC's activities in the 1980s inevitably required greater expenditure. The opening of new centres outside Belfast and the provision of new services had to be accommodated in financial planning. That, however, did not include the unexpected. In the 1981/82 Annual Report, Dr Edith Cunningham included this item in her Chairman's Message:

In the near future we may have to face a change of premises. Harris Marrian has put 76 up for sale and although our tenancy lease does not expire until 1985 a sub-committee of the Executive is already investigating possible alternatives.

The Treasurer's Report stated that 'one further fact not directly reflected in the Accounts is that property housing our Headquarters and Counselling centre has been placed on the market to be sold as one or two units'. 'The financial and other considerations and implications are complex', he continued, 'and I would only reflect that we have already made some provision to cover such a contingency, the sum provided to the 31st March 1982 amounts to £24, 257'.

The 1982/83 Annual Report duly informed readers that the 'major activity during the past few months has been the purchase of 74/76 Dublin Road as our permanent Headquarters in Northern Ireland. It is our intention to refurbish 76 Dublin Road in addition to ensuring a secure and permanent home to assist us in financing our services for the future'. The Director, Roy Simpson, added that not only did this provide the organisation with a firm permanent base but also with room for expansion. The planning and refurbishment absorbed much energy in the ensuing year. The Executive set up a Building Sub-committee which liaised with Building Design Partners, the contractors and the DHSS. The Director believed that the purchase and refurbishment of the headquarters – 'a significant milestone in the history of the Northern Ireland Marriage Guidance Council…an act of faith' – was due very much to the Chairman, Sam Johnston, 'with his entrepreneurial skill and ably supported by an Executive committee full of enthusiasm and professional expertise'.

John Chambers became Chief Officer (this term now replaced that of Director) in 1984, following the resignation of Roy Simpson. A major duty for the new chief executive was to organise the official opening of the NIMGC headquarters. An 'open day' was held on 19 June 1985 to mark 'the completion of the purchase, renovation and decoration of our premises at 76 Dublin Road, Belfast'. This was the first official engagement for the council's new President, Sir Peter Froggatt. The formal opening was conducted by Chris Patten, Under-Secretary of State with responsibility for the Department of Health and Social Services. Nicholas Tyndall, Chief Officer of the National Marriage Guidance Council, and NIMGC's Patron, Lady Dunleith, were also present.

A selection of posters, designed and produced by pupils in secondary schools, was on display. This was a competition, judged by the cartoonist Rowel Friers and the journalist Alf McCreary, and sponsored by the Northern Bank. The prizes were presented by Sidney McClurg, General Manager (Administration). The winning poster by Finlay Kilpatrick of Comber High School was subsequently printed and used as a publicity poster by NIMGC. It was also purchased by a number of Marriage Guidance Councils in England and Wales.[18]

Relate Northern Ireland

In September 1987 the Northern Ireland Marriage Guidance Council had been in existence for forty years. Several events were arranged to mark this anniversary. The Ulster Museum allowed the Council to hold an exhibition of wedding dresses (including the one worn by Sally in ITV's soap, *Coronation Street*). This was opened by Esme Gilmore, Belfast's Lady Mayoress on 1 September and ran for six weeks. A thanksgiving service followed in St Anne's Cathedral on 6 September. Richard Needham, Under-Secretary of State in charge of Health and Social Services, was the principal guest at an open day at 76 Dublin Road on 14 September. The fortieth anniversary celebrations concluded with a celebration dinner at Queen's University on 25 September.[19]

The most important development of the anniversary year was undoubtedly the opening of Family Mediation Service on 2 November. It had taken more than nine years to put into partial effect a clause included (at the behest of NIMGC) in the Matrimonial Causes (NI) Order to provide such a service – this service, however, was an optional one and not compulsory in every case as envisaged in the 1978 Order. This was yet another indication that the Council had been widening the scope of its operations over the previous decade. This would continue in the years to come. The National Marriage Guidance Council had been ever more aware that the organisation's title was becoming more inappropriate with the passing of very year. The core business remained marital counselling but the listening, counselling and professional training provided by marriage guidance councils across the United Kingdom went far beyond that service provision. Even the word 'guidance' could be regarded as being rather too directive. The NIMGC Chief Officer, John Chambers, stated that 'I have been involved in the plans for changing the name to RELATE and all the other ways in which the organisation is meeting the challenge of the future. This has taken up a great deal of time, but I feel it is important for us to have someone involved as deeply as possible during this period of major change and development'.[20]

The name Relate Northern Ireland was duly adopted in 1988, a visible indicator that the organisation would continue to widen its reach in response to changing times.

Notes

1   David McKittrick, Seamus Kelters, Brian Feeney, Chris Thornton and David McVea, *Lost Lives*, 2007, p.774, p.813, p.847, p.892, p.933, p.973, p.1006, p.1029, p.1058, p.1106, p.1156 and p.1189; *Guardian*, 26 July 1989; Jonathan Bardon, *A History of Ulster*, 1992, pp.782-9
2   *Belfast News-Letter*, 9 June 1978
3   *Belfast News-Letter*, 8 September 1978 iv NIMGC Annual Report, 1980/81
4   NIMGC Annual Report, 1979/80
5   NIMGC Annual Report, 1980/81
6   *Belfast Telegraph*, 26 May 1980
7   *Sunday News*, 4 January 1981
8   *Irish News*, 4 January 1981
9   *The Sunday Times*, 26 April 1961
10 *The Sunday Times*, 24 May 1981
11 *News Letter*, 1 April 1982
12 *Lisburn Star*, 19 March 1969
13 *The Sunday Times*, 2 May 1982
14 NIMGC Annual Report, 1979/80 and 1980/81
15 NIMGC Annual Report, 1981/82, 1982/3, 1983/84, 1984/85, 1985/86 and 1987
16 Letter from John Chambers to Dave Murphy, 28 October 2013
17 Interview with Julia Greer 14 August 2013
18 NIMGC Annual Report, 1985/86
19 NIMGC Annual Report, 1987 and 1988
20 NIMGC Annual Report, 1988

CHAPTER SIX

'More than Marriage Guidance': Relate 1988-98

At 12.20 am on Saturday 20 August 1988 in the open countryside, on the main road midway between Ballygawley and Omagh, the Provisional IRA detonated a large bomb placed on a parked trailer. An unmarked military bus travelling from Aldergrove airport was blown off the road, eight soldiers were killed and twenty-eight others were injured. Alan Rainey, a dairy farmer, one of the first on the scene, told a *Belfast Telegraph* reporter: 'There were bodies strewn all over the road and others were caught inside the bus and under it…people were running around stunned, screaming and bleeding and shouting for someone to come to their aid…one of the soldiers – he was no more than a youngster – had somehow crawled into a calf-shed, six inches deep in muck, and as we arrived he gasped his last, bent over a bale of hay'.

So far that year, twenty-one soldiers had been killed in Northern Ireland. The year 1988 witnessed the untimely deaths of 105 in the region. The Troubles, described by some as low-intensity warfare, seemed as if they would never end. Another 81 were killed in 1989 and, in the new decade, the death toll between 1990 and the end of 1994 was 436. Yet the talks between SDLP leader John Hume and Sinn Féin leader Gerry Adams, bitterly criticised at the time, had begun in January 1988. By the autumn of 1994 they had borne fruit in the republican and loyalist ceasefires. In 1995, for the first time since 1968, the death toll was down to single figures, nine.[1] Northern Ireland very quickly became a much safer place than before.

Being housed less than a mile south of Belfast city centre, Relate Northern Ireland was – effectively – in a war zone. It bore the physical scars of the conflict once again in the spring of 1992. On 24 March the Provisionals detonated a 500lb bomb near Donegall Pass RUC station. Shock waves from the blast inflicted extensive damage on Relate's premises at 74-76 Dublin Road, just round the corner from the station. Many months passed before the offices were back in full use. The psychological scars of the conflict could not be repaired so easily. Relate's counsellors were still constantly brought face-to-face with the searing impact of past violence and current trauma, fears, suspicions, hatreds and bitter memories thrown up by a deeply fractured society.

The Family Mediation Service: 'the only opportunity to sit down together and talk about the children'

Before it was to suffer the impact of the Donegall Pass bomb, the headquarters of Relate NI were extensively upgraded. '"76" now looks very much brighter, more welcoming and very different from the not-so-distant days when we had a bucket on the first landing to catch drips from the ceiling when it rained!' the Chairman, Joan Wilson, reported. Peter Brooke, Northern Ireland Secretary of State, visited Relate to declare open the renovations. The building got new counselling rooms, a ramp at the front door for disabled clients, a downstairs toilet and a new office for Kate Lewis, the organiser of the Family Mediation Service.

Kate Lewis had been appointed in April 1987. By June eight women and two men had been selected to undertake mediation training and all had successfully completed their basic training by the end of the year. This new service offered by Relate NI was given a lunchtime launch on 2 November 1987. The principal task at first was to publicise the Family Mediation Service to members of the public and in particular to professionals involved in the area of separation and divorce such as solicitors, social workers and Citizens Advice Bureaux. Information sessions were given to interested groups and organisations. Lisa Parkinson, Training Officer of the National Family Conciliation Council, came over to address solicitors of the Law Society on 1 October 1987.

The steering committee, chaired by Michael Davey, Secretary of the Law Society, presented its final report to the Relate NI executive in January 1988. Between 1 April 1987 and 31 March 1988 the service had 103 enquiries, 60 clients (singly or jointly) attending appointments and 43 two-hour mediation interviews given. Joan Wilson observed that the Family Mediation Service 'fills a much needed gap for those whose marriages have broken down and are in need of help and support to continue parenting their children'.[2]

'Publicity about our work continues to be a priority', Kate Lewis reported in the spring of 1989. She gave eighteen talks and information evenings to 'a wide variety of groups including Citizen Advice Bureaux, Social Workers, Health Care workers and church groups', in addition to circulating information leaflets and posters to solicitors and advice groups. She found that around one in five of those making enquiries went on to attend mediation. Solicitors and social workers were most likely to make appropriate referrals which most often resulted in mediation meetings. Mediators were given the opportunity to enhance their skills and meet other practitioners at training events in Scotland and other parts of Ireland. In 1989 the total number of enquiries was 177 and 97 mediation appointments were given.[3]

The 1990-91 Annual Report succinctly explained the purpose of the Mediation Service and what was being provided:

Mediation is for couples who are separating or divorcing. Meeting with a Mediator helps the couple to resolve disputes between them, especially those concerning their children. It is helpful for the children to know what is happening and mediation can help couples deal with their children in such a way that they will suffer as little as possible from their parents' separation or divorce. Mediators do not give legal advice but work in co-operation with solicitors.

The DHSS approved funding for the service on the basis of 75 per cent of expenditure. The intake system was reviewed and subsequently revised. Four additional trainee mediators were selected in June 1990 and began their training in September. Mediation was now being offered in the Foyle office. By the spring of 1991 Kate Lewis had contributed to seven radio programmes and two television programmes including the network show, *The Time, The Place* on divorce. Her talks included a six-week course in the Institute of Continuing Education at Queen's University and two training days for lay magistrates. At a national level she was involved with Relate's Working Party on the proposed divorce reforms for England and Wales. At the Academy of Family Mediators annual conference in Boston in July, Kate Lewis led a workshop entitled 'Techniques for managing religious, racial and cultural diversity in family disputes'.[4] In May 1991, at the National Family Conciliation Courts Conference in Pittsburg, 'I found myself as a surprise contributor to a session on international developments in mediation'. 'There was great interest in the development of family mediation in Northern Ireland', she reported, '– sadly our world-wide reputation is for more violent means of dispute resolution'. The following year she organised an interdisciplinary day, in co-operation with the Family Law Association and sponsored by the Nuffield Foundation, for individuals (primarily solicitors) involved in family proceedings.

In 1991-92 the number of enquiries rose to 232 resulting in 178 intake appointments, 138 mediation appointments and 70 mediation cases. Clients referred either directly by Relate counsellors or from information given by reception staff tended to be clear that they were not seeking counselling but did want mediation. Many self-referred clients first heard about mediation from their solicitor or social worker. 71 per cent of clients were concerned with access; 44 per cent with the termination of the relationship; and 37 per cent had property and finance as an issue. The sheer volume of demand had become formidable. The Family Mediation Service that financial year had 140 parents working together in mediation, responsible for 130 children. Help and advice was offered to an additional hundred parents who were responsible for 215 children. 'Many parents', Kate Lewis reported, 'have said that mediation has provided the only opportunity to sit down together and talk about the children'. The Family Mediation Service became affiliated to the National Family Conciliation Council, which Kate said, 'will give us access to a national training programme for trainee mediators, and will plug us into a network of similar services'.[5]

Julia Greer, starting out as a volunteer counsellor in 1986 and later becoming a trainer and supervisor with Relate, found mediation an exceptionally difficult and demanding service to deliver. This was primarily because it required the attendance of both partners and because one partner was likely to be reluctant to be involved, there were many false starts.[6]

Training mediators was an expensive business. It involved basic training in England over four separate weekends. The Tudor Trust gave a substantial grant towards the costs of travel and accommodation but the organisation could not be sure that such generosity could be relied upon in future. Kate Lewis reported in 1993:

One difficulty experienced was in providing appropriate cases for trainees to co-work with an experienced mediator. This was particularly so for the Foyle trainees…New mediators bring with them enthusiasm, a quest for knowledge and lots of questions about present practice. The existing mediators found themselves challenged both to pass on knowledge and to re-think our ways of dealing with couples. This was refreshing for all concerned.

She added that the Department of Health and Social Services provided funding for a three-year evaluation of the service.[7]

Training

Training was assuming a much more central role in Relate's work. In 1988-89 Mari Fitzduff acted as supervisor of Relate's education and training team. This team worked with young people including those in the Northern Ireland Association of Youth Clubs, Ashfield Girls' High School, Ballynafeigh Methodist Church and Castlereagh Venture Scouts. It also worked with engaged couples, predominantly in Presbyterian churches. Training courses were provided for post-graduate trainee General Practitioners in Belfast, Bangor, Craigavon and Derry. Social workers, clergy and probation officers were given six-day courses in Basic Marital Counselling. The range of support groups and organisations obtaining education and training was very wide. They included: Northern Ireland Council on Alcohol; Journal Club Windsor House (Psychiatric staff); medical students in the City Hospital's Department of Mental Health; the Care Course at RUC Garnerville; staff who worked with mentally handicapped adults and staff from residential children's homes in the Eastern Health & Social Services Board; Crumlin Road Prison; the Corrymeela Community; the Post Ordination Training Group in the Down & Connor diocese; RAF Aldergrove; and Action MS.[8]

In 1990 the organisation, having decided it needed a member of staff dedicated to this task, appointed Judith Loder as its Training Officer. Observing that Relate was able to draw on forty-three years of experience in Northern Ireland and how important it was 'to share this unique experience with many other people in the community', Judith Loder explained in her first report:

The skills and knowledge of Relate counsellors, sex therapists and mediators are relevant to many other people. The Training Department uses experienced Relate workers to take these skills out into the community. Social Workers can benefit greatly from Relate insights into working with couples. General Practitioners can learn from Relate counselling skills and the experience of sex therapists. Teachers can improve their ability to work with the developing relationships of children. Clergy can experience the Relate style of working with couples who are preparing for marriage or who are having problems in their relationship.

She added that in 1990-91, with the opening of the Foyle District office, Relate now had adequate space for training purposes and that a 'Surviving the Breakup' course was being made available in the north-west. In Belfast the course, 'Marriage Breakdown – A Family in Crisis' had generated so much interest that it was being extended. Extensive work had been done with all the health boards, including one on sexual issues to train staff working in residential child care in the WHSSB. She quoted some comments made anonymously by participants, including:

Training in Aids Awareness: "Information frightening but factual – many thanks".
Introduction to Counselling for Trainee GPs: "Helpful in that it showed the difference between holding consultation and counselling".
Surviving the Break-Up: "I have taken many small and major steps in the 6 weeks".

Altogether in that year 1,557 training hours had been worked and 127 groups and organisations had been involved.[9]

Relate National's report, 'The Organisation and Delivery of Education and Training Services in Relate', published in January 1992, identified Northern Ireland as the top centre in terms of the total number of courses provided (45 courses and media events totalling 471.5 hours between 1 April and 30 September 1992). This was a considerable achievement in view of the disruption caused by the bomb detonated close to the organisation's premises in March 1992. In addition to training programmes Judith Loder was often asked by voluntary bodies and churches to provide a speaker to talk about Relate's work. Naming those who had responded, she added that the 'giving of their time voluntarily is very much appreciated'. Among the training courses Relate was contracted to deliver were: 'Understanding Human Sexuality, Sexual Identity and Sexual Relationships', a six-day course for the eastern and western health boards and the Probation Board for Northern Ireland; 'Sexual Awareness for General Practitioners' (one day); 'Working with Divorced Partners' provided for Northern Ireland Civil Service Welfare Officers; and 'Assessing the Strengths in a Marriage', a three-day course provided specifically for social workers specialising in adoption and foster care.[10]

Sue Clements-Jewery in 1991-92 commuted regularly from Liverpool to act as Relate NI's education work supervisor. In June 1992 'six very experienced trainers effectively left the training team', mainly to concentrate on other work and in Rosemary Dunlop's case to take a year's sabbatical. Sue Clements-Jewery also withdrew in order to work solely for the Relate Federation North West Region based in Warrington. These losses were balanced by the selection of Julia Greer and Rita Glover as Relate Trainers for the organisation's education department which delivered external training courses in Northern Ireland. Hours worked in 1992-93 had contracted, due principally to financial constraints and the damage inflicted by the bomb explosion of March 1992, to around 800 but in 1993-94 they rose again to just under 1,600. Contract courses accounted for slightly more than half of the training work provided.[11]

Feedback on some of the training courses appeared in the 1994-95 Annual Report. One participant on a three-day training course for caring professionals on counselling skills, accredited by the Associated Examining Board, commented that 'it demonstrated a structured approach to counselling and highlighted possible pitfalls and ways to avoid them; it was action packed and work related'. A participant on the course entitled 'Working with Young People and their Relationships' commented:

I felt the one main thought that stayed with me since our talk was the need to be relaxed and at ease when talking and dealing with sexual topics otherwise it becomes very difficult for a teenager or young person to be willing to "open up" and talk freely.

A person who came along to a 'Surviving the Break Up' workshop observed that 'to be told it was completely normal to have these feelings, (ie grief, loss, guilt, fear of coping alone) and knowing you weren't alone did wonders for my self esteem and confidence'.[12]

In January 1995 Judith Loder moved from the role of Training Officer with responsibility for external training to the role of Training Manager with additional responsibility for the basic counsellor training programme and continuous professional development for all staff and practitioners. 'Fortunately', it was reported, 'Lynn Davidson was appointed Personal Assistant to the Training Manager in February 1995. Her expertise has been invaluable and together with other Relate staff and trainers and some external expertise when appropriate, we have provided a comprehensive range of training, both within our own organisation and in response to customer's requirements'. Most in-service training was supplied by the organisation's own in-service supervisors, Julia Greer, Rita Glover, Val Kohner and, on occasion, by Isobel Reilly, Professional Services Consultant.[13]

The impact of legislation on working practice in Relate NI became a major theme in in-service training provision in 1995-96. The Children Order (Northern Ireland), a once in a generation reform of public and private law relating to children, came into force in November 1995; the implications of the Order for the organisation's work were duly communicated to all staff and practitioners, along with Child Protection Awareness training. Then, in December 1996, the Disability Discrimination Act became law and a working party made up of managers, staff and practitioners was set up to explore the implications of the legislation. In 1997-98 the Training Department received a grant of £37,000 from the Lottery Fund to provide, over a two-year period, a range of client courses including 'Surviving the Break Up', 'Taking Charge of My Life' and parenting courses. In that year Judith Loder resigned in order to pursue her career elsewhere.[14]

'The damage to dear old "76" by the bomb which exploded in the early hours of March 24th, 1992'

Early in 1992 John Chambers, Chief Officer of the organisation since 1984, learned that the Lord Chancellor, Lord Mackay of Clashfern, would be visiting Northern Ireland. The opportunity to bring him up to date on Relate NI's activities could not be missed. John Kennedy, Clerk of the Assembly and now a member of Relate NI's Executive, arranged a meeting in the Senate room of Parliament Buildings at Stormont on 28 February. The Lord Chancellor discussed the organisation's work with Chairman Joan Wilson and other members of the Executive and he delivered an address to the executive committee, saying:

I am aware that Relate in Northern Ireland offer a very appropriate and imaginative range of services, available within one building which means that the Counsellors and Mediators can co-operate and respond more easily to the need to cross-refer clients. By bringing together the preventative and support services in this way couples and their children are given an opportunity to find sensitive workable solutions to difficult interpersonal problems.

He said that marriage remained an extremely popular institution, which was essentially a social, psychological and legal rite of passage – 'It is also a very public recognition of a specific level and form of commitment, it involves mutual legal obligations of support and sharing which other relationships do not'. John Chambers, Kate Lewis and Bruce Stewart gave a presentation on the work of Relate.

Less than one month later that 'one building' suffered an unexpected dislocation. 'Starting with the bad news, we were all devastated by the damage to dear old "76" by the bomb which exploded in the early hours of March 24th, 1992'. So wrote Joan Wilson in her Chairman's Report for 1991-92. She continued:

However, it was truly typical of the team spirit in Relate to see how many people turned up with brushes and pans and offered help and by lunch time at least two counselling rooms were ready for clients and the following day it was "business as usual". The clients also took everything in their stride and uncomplainingly through rubble and glass. I particularly want to pay a tribute to the office staff who, with a smile on their faces, coped with really terrible conditions and went on with the work.[15]

Sir Eric McDowell, who succeeded Joan Wilson as Chairman in June 1992, reported in the spring of 1993:

It was September before the repairs, following the bomb in March, were completed. So for six months the normal working environment in Dublin Road was disrupted, and I would like to pay tribute to the cheerfulness of all who carried on so wonderfully during that period. Coping with the arrangements for repairs and compensation threw additional burdens on our Chief Officer, and inevitably lessened his time on more productive matters.

In the same Annual Report, Chief Officer John Chambers, added this observation:

This has been the most challenging year that I can remember in the history of Northern Ireland Relate. The serious damage to our headquarters by the bomb last March came at a time when everyone was already overstretched. It is a great tribute to all concerned that despite the difficulties we still managed to increase the number of counselling sessions by 14 per cent. The training department was most seriously affected by the bomb and that has resulted in a reduction in the number of courses we were able to offer.[16]

Lady Jean Mayhew, wife of the Northern Ireland Secretary of State, Sir Patrick Mayhew, paid a visit to 76 Dublin Road in November 1992. Relate NI's premises were now looking well but the building stood apart from others in the area, neighbouring Shaftesbury Square in particular. Beginning with an IRA bomb in a fish shop on the Shankill Road on 23 October 1993, killing ten people, and concluding with the Ulster Freedom Fighters' firearms attack on the Rising Sun bar in Greysteel, Co. Derry/Londonderry, twenty-six people died violently in just a week. Indeed, this was the greatest number of deaths as a result of the Troubles in any month since October 1976. The author was asked by Brian Cathcart (later chief executive of the Hacked Off pressure group) to contribute an article on the situation in Belfast for the *Independent on Sunday*, 31 October:

During break I sit with colleagues at Millfield, part of the city's further education institute. "If I could go, I'd go now, to Spain or somewhere – my wife and I like the sun," says a lecturer, calculating whether an early retirement package would enable him to live abroad. He has been teaching here since 1969, when rioting raged in the streets outside. Now, he says, the atmosphere is as tense as it was 20 years ago. Another stabs her finger at the Sun's picture of Gerry Adams carrying the IRA man's coffin. She is outraged, and though we're from all parts of the city, no one disagrees. If anyone thinks John Hume should still be talking to Adams, they do not say so.

I seem to be the only one who does not know someone immediately affected by the killings of the past ten days. One told of a neighbour in his eighties who rushed to help in the Shankill last Saturday: in his mind he was on campaign once more against Rommel, digging his mates out of the rubble, shouting warnings of a fresh German attack…

Now, at 6.30 pm on Thursday 28 October 1993, I drive into the city centre with my driving licence on the dashboard ready to hand to the police at the checkpoint by the City Hospital. I go through Bradbury Place and Shaftesbury Square, still bearing the scars of an IRA bomb 18 months ago; I pass the Europa Hotel, dozens of its windows boarded up, and the Grand Opera House, covered in scaffolding after a car bomb last May; and I park beside Windsor House, Belfast's tallest building, just back to normal after an 800 lb bomb in January 1992.

And yet we are not back to where we were in the 1970s…[17]

More than twenty years later, astonishingly, the tallest building in Shaftesbury Square which had been leased by the Department of Health and Social Services, still bears the scars of the Donegall Pass bomb of 24 March 1992 and has remained largely derelict ever since. No wonder that the staff, trustees and committee members of Relate NI, just round the corner from this building, began to think that a search for new premises should begin.

International dialogue and mixed marriages

Northern Ireland Relate organised a seminar for employers held in Malone House in Belfast in October 1990. The guest speaker was Nancy Paul of Excel International. She had researched the impact of divorce on men and women both in England and the USA. She told delegates that she had found that men's work performance dipped as a result of divorce but that women as a whole did better at work. She also discovered that, although many people worked longer hours when they were going through a divorce, their effectiveness was reduced and they were more likely to be absent from work. The Relate presentation at the seminar suggested that employers needed to:

- Recognise the problems caused by divorce and relationship problems
- Encourage employees to attend counselling and allow time off during the day if necessary

- Use Relate's services for training personnel managers
- Consider using Relate to provide a counselling service for employees on a contractual basis.[18]

John Chambers had accompanied Kate Lewis to attend the annual international conference of the International Union of Family Organisations Commission on Marriage and Interpersonal Relations held in Pittsburgh in May 1991. A major overall conclusion was that 'interventions which promote co-operative working relations with both parents after divorce rather than encourage adversarial contests will be in the long term interests of the community as a whole'. This type of international dialogue was to be continued at the 1992 conference with the theme 'Marriage across Frontiers'.[19]

This International Union conference was hosted jointly by Northern Ireland Relate and the Catholic Marriage Advisory Council in Northern Ireland – that such a collaboration was no longer a ground-breaking event demonstrated how attitudes were fast changing (at least in the voluntary sector). The 'Marriage Across the Frontiers' conference met in May in the Slieve Donard Hotel in Newcastle, Co. Down. Its aim was to discuss 'national, ethnic and religious differences in partnership'. Thirty-seven organisations from eighteen countries attended – predominantly from European States and America, with the delegate from the General Federation of Iraqi Women unable to attend for very obvious reasons that year.

The main paper at this 1992 conference was presented by Professor Peter Stringer from Queen's University Belfast. He reported on the findings of a major piece of research carried out for this conference by Gillian Robinson, entitled, 'Cross-community Marriage in Northern Ireland: Social Support and Social Constraints'. This topic was closely related to the other key address, 'Mixed Marriages – Some Key Questions', presented by Professor Augustin Barbara, University of Nantes, France. Professor Stringer's paper, in John Chamber's view, 'is still probably the best piece of research ever done in this difficult field'.

Mixed marriages (which in Ireland always meant legal unions between Protestants and Catholics) inevitably caused tension in a society riven by opposing religious and cultural affiliations. Many still recalled the 1908 *Ne Temere* papal decree which had declared that marriages between Catholics and Protestants not solemnised according to the rites of the Catholic Church were null and void. In particular they remembered the application of this decree in an especially distressing case in Belfast in 1910: Alexander McCann, instigated it was alleged by his priest, had suddenly left his Protestant wife and taken away her children. A case in the Irish Republic made international headlines in the summer of 1957. The Protestant wife of a Catholic farmer in Fethard-on-Sea, a village in Co. Wexford, left home with her two children following a row over the religion in which the children were to be brought up. As a result the businesses of local Protestants were boycotted, with the encouragement of senior Catholic clergy. Though Taoiseach Éamon de Valera declared in Dáil Éireann that 'I regard this boycott as ill-conceived, ill-considered, and futile', it continued for more than a year.[20]

Of course it was in Northern Ireland, rather than in the rest of Ireland and in other regions of the United Kingdom, that mixed marriages were particularly fraught, even more so with the onset of the Troubles. Members of the Orange Order still risked being expelled for attending Catholic funerals right to the end of the twentieth century. Back in 1974 the Northern Ireland Mixed Marriage Association (NIMMA) had been founded as a result of a conference held in Corrymeela in north Antrim. Its mission: 'Supporting couples who are united in love across traditional Christian divisions and promoting acceptance of these relationships within Northern Ireland society'. This organisation continues to provide support and information to couples either in or contemplating mixed marriage. 'In a society where sectarianism is institutionalised', it lobbied for the acceptance of mixed marriage, increased integrated education and wider availability of shared social housing. In 2013 NIMMA reported:

Much has changed since those early days and NIMMA has played a major role in influencing landmark changes in clerical attitudes and regulations toward mixed marriage to such an extent that it has never been easier to make a mixed marriage. NIMMA strives for changes to baptismal restrictions imposed by all the major denominations, for Eucharistic sharing for interchurch couples, true reconciliation and a shared future for all.[21]

Restructuring

'There is no doubt about the demand for our services', John Chambers observed in the spring of 1992. The statistics bore him out. In 1991-92 the total number of interviews offered – 7,516 in 1990-91 – was 9,930; the total number of interviews given – 5,428 in 1990-91 – was 7,813; and the total number of new clients – 1,271 in 1990-91 – was 1,544. 'Our target of 10,000 hours of counselling during the past year was almost met', he reported. 'This represents the largest increase in output in one year in the history of Relate in Northern Ireland'. He continued:

Indeed we have had to hold back in the amount of publicity we engage in, because we know we will be swamped by the number of people looking for help. There is also no shortage of people wanting to train as counsellors, sex therapists, trainers and mediators. What we lack is the necessary finance to train and support more practitioners.

The organisation had changed its name from the Northern Ireland Marriage Guidance Council to Relate Northern Ireland, indicating a widening of the scope of services offered. This, together with the inexorable expansion of its work, inevitably led to thinking about whether or not some restructuring was necessary. Jack Hamilton of JH Consultancy Services was asked to make suggestions and his report was duly submitted in March 1992, only days before the detonation of the IRA bomb in Donegall Pass. This report provided NI Relate with a 'framework for action' for discussion in the ensuing year.[22]

A day of consultation was set aside for everyone in the organisation to consider *A Framework for Action*. The Executive established a working party to consider the report further and to make recommendations. Twelve meetings ensued and the recommendations made by the working party were approved by the Executive. These recommendations were circulated to staff and practitioners and passed on for consideration to the National Executive in Rugby.[23]

As a distinguished company director and accountant, Relate's Chairman, Sir Eric McDowell was well placed to preside over the structural changes being agreed. Agreement had been arrived at with the National Executive Sir Eric set out the key features of the new working relationship:

1) Northern Ireland will cease to belong to the North West Region and will have a direct relationship with Rugby, primarily through the Director of Field Services there.
2) Supervisors will be employed directly by Northern Ireland.
3) A Professional Services Consultant, employed by National, will be based in Northern Ireland, on secondment. The consultant will also provide services to the Marriage Guidance Counselling Service in Dublin [the Marriage and Relationship Counselling Service], previously undertaken by the North West Region.
4) A membership agreement will commit Northern Ireland to complying with the National Standards for Constituent Status and to periodic review of the operation of the relationship with National.

The maintenance of a close relationship between the two organisations was emphasised by the continuance of a representative of Northern Ireland on the National Executive. John Chambers served for many years on the National Executive, including the time that it was decided to adopt the name Relate. It was Sir Eric who succeeded him, and John Chambers later recalled that 'Sir Eric McDowell made a major contribution to the National organisation during a few very difficult years – his contribution to the organisation locally and nationally was very significant.'[24]

Some job titles and duties changed. John Chambers was now designated 'Chief Executive'; Kate Lewis became 'Head of Professional Services'; Judith Loder was now 'Training Manager'; Joan Dunlop was 'Office Manager'; and Sheena Bell was in charge of mediation intake. John Chambers explained that the re-organisation 'will enable me, as the Chief Executive, to have more time to spend on a variety of matters including strategic planning, income generation and the external networking that is vital to our future development'. Kate Lewis's new post was, he believed, 'a new, challenging and vital role for her and NI Relate and one for which she has already shown herself to be well able'. She was to be assisted by Isobel Reilly, the new Professional Services consultant and 'an excellent team' of supervisors employed from 1 April 1994 by NI Relate and 'thus much more available to all the rest of the staff and two part time coordinators for the Mediation Service'.[25]

International Year of the Family, 1994

Northern Ireland Relate clearly was an organisation which would involve itself wholeheartedly in the International Year of the Family, 1994. Kate Lewis, in her new role as Head of Professional Services, took responsibility for organising two events. The first was a competition, 'Recipe for a Happy Family Life', sponsored by the Nationwide Building Society. Over a thousand entries were received from children and adults. The prizes were presented by Lynda Jayne of Downtown Radio. Mrs Margaret Wilson won the adult prize, an engraved decanter donated by Tyrone Crystal. Rosalind Kenney was the winner in the 4-10 years section and the winning entry in the 10-16 years category, by Helen McCoy, began:

For The Pastry:
Take ½lb of listening and add a little respect, some grated kindness and a dash of Trust. Sprinkle in a family outing and add a family meal, stir in an ounce of honesty and a kilo of peace. Mix in a ¼ pint of forgive and forget and a lot of praise.
For The Sauce:
Start off with a big heart and some creamed patience, mix until you reach tranquillity add ½ ounce of sweetened understanding, bring it to the boil, then count to ten so as it doesn't let off steam.
For The Filling:
Collect 1 oz of Thanks and weigh out some love, toss in some compassion and co-operation. Whip up some gentleness and pour in some laughs. Bake with a helpful Prayer until it's golden brown, not olden frown…

The major event, also sponsored by Nationwide, was the NI Relate conference with the subject, 'The Effects of Separation and Divorce on Children and Young People'. It was attended by people representing most of the professions involved with children and young people. There were four main speakers. The key points made by Dr Joan B Kelly, Executive Director of the Northern California Mediation Centre, were:

- Simplistic statements are not useful as no single factor is predictive of children's post-divorce adjustment.
- Problems experienced by children in divorced families include: more aggressive, impulsive and anti-social behaviours, more difficulties in social relationships, including those where parents have lower academic achievement.
- The children who suffer most are those where parents had a high level of conflict when they were still married.
- When children feel caught in the middle of their parents' discord they suffer more.
- Contact between fathers and children diminishes dramatically after divorce.
- Children benefit when their parents work out their disputes through mediation or counselling and avoid placing their children in the middle of their struggles.

Among the key points made by Janet Walker, Director of Research at Relate Centre for Family Studies, Newcastle-upon-Tyne, were: 'A relatively small percentage of divorcing parents use family mediation services…Most families become financially worse off after divorce…Fathers who were well off financially were more able to keep contact with their children…We need to reconsider our expectations of parents who do not live together.' Lynn Peyton, Assistant Director of Social Services, Southern Health & Social Services Board, believed that there was a need in Northern Ireland to address the needs of children from divorced and separated families in a more structured way. She said that a 'quality service for families experiencing disharmony and breakdown should meet the following criteria:'

- *be accessible to all who need it*
- *be provided by specially trained staff in agencies which are best placed to provide the service*
- *be linked to a range of specialist services which can respond to children with specific difficulties*
- *offer choice, as many people are reluctant to use statutory services*
  evaluate service outcomes

Margaret Fawcett, Lecturer in Social Work at Queen's University Belfast and RelateTeen Counsellor, concluded that 'Young people need: to be listened to; to be given information; permission to maintain relationships with both parents; to know they can't "stitch" their parents back together; to be kept clear of conflict between their parents; to be able to express their feelings, and to talk about what troubles them'.[26]

RelateTeen: 'Bruce's baby…a pioneering venture for the National organisation'
RelateTeen was set up in response to research evidence on the effects of divorce on young people 'and in recognition of the lack of independent resources to help young people adjust to separation and divorce'. In 1993 in the United Kingdom four out of ten new marriages were ending in divorce, making Britain the country with the second highest divorce rate in the European Union. 'In personal terms it means that each year over 160,000 dependent children will experience the removal of one parent from their daily lives'. The overall divorce rate in Northern Ireland was lower than in the rest of the United Kingdom: 2,213 divorces took place there in 1993 and this represented around 3,500 children (almost half of them aged between 5 and 15) who had to adjust to parental separation and divorce.[27]

The driving force behind this initiative was Bruce Stewart, the RelateTeen Co-ordinator. Funding came from charitable trusts, Children in Need primarily. Led by Bruce Stewart, eight counsellors were selected for training. Four were recruited from within Relate and the other four 'appointed on the basis of relevant experience in teaching, youth work and social work'. Basic training included sessions on the social and legal context of marital breakdown, adolescent development and counselling methods as well as the impact of separation and divorce on young people. Experts from outside agencies provided additional training on skills and techniques, focusing particularly on working with anger and loss.

A counselling room at 76 Dublin Road was set aside specifically for RelateTeen, furnished with rugs, a settee, beanbags and posters. On a table books, leaflets and other appropriate resource materials were set out. Another table with chairs was provided to facilitate paper exercises. 'The aim was to create an informal and relaxed atmosphere in which young people could meet and talk with their counsellor'. One-hour appointments with counsellors were offered, generally in the late afternoon and early evenings to fit round school activities.[28]

In 1991-92 RelateTeen received 25 enquiries, of which 15 developed into full counselling cases. The team of counsellors, acquiring experience in the problems faced by young people in the wake of their parents' separation or divorce, encountered the following 'main reactions':

- A deep sense of loss of the family unit they once had
- Confusion about their feelings and loyalties
- A disproportionate sense of responsibility for what has happened

The following year, 1992-93, was described as 'a demanding and exciting year for RelateTeen'. Bruce Stewart reported that 'despite not advertising our service widely, there is an increasing awareness of our service and a willingness to refer young people to it'. That year RelateTeen got 32 referrals and offered a counselling service to 24 of these. Another six counsellors were recruited and trained. It was felt that, at this stage, there was a need to evaluate the service more objectively. A research project was being designed intended to highlight the particular problems experienced by young people when their parents separated or divorced.[29]

In 1993-94 the number of RelateTeen enquiries rose to 54:

The most commonly reported problems are difficulties in talking with parents, feelings of anger, sadness and confusion, difficulties in sleeping, concentrating and problems at school. Alice (not her real name) at 17 took on an adult role in the family, looking after younger children and managing the home. She had great difficulty struggling with her own feelings of hurt and upset. In her own words, "it really helped to have someone non-biased to talk to…I had always been told to look after my Mum. No-one ever told me to look after myself or asked me how I felt about my parents' split-up." Alice's story could be repeated by many of the young people attending the service.[30]

In her visits to Northern Ireland, Princess Diana, the National Patron of Relate, displayed a particular interest in RelateTeen. In November 1991 she attended a lunch at Hillsborough for Relate, Help the Aged, the Northern Ireland Pre-School Playgroup Association and the Leprosy Mission. December 1993 saw the Princess's last public engagements in Northern Ireland when, after opening a new child development unit at the Ulster Hospital, she attended a reception at Hillsborough for Relate and Homestart.[31] As Sir Eric McDowell recorded:

The occasion was the formal launch of the RelateTeen project in Hillsborough Castle on 8th December. Bruce Stewart, the project leader introduced privately to Princess Diana some of the young teenagers who had experienced the counselling. The Princess also met David French, the National director of Relate over from Rugby, Lady Bloomfield and members of the Appeal Committee, counsellors, trainers, mediators and staff members of Relate Northern Ireland. We were delighted to welcome the Princess who was very knowledgeable about, and most interested in, our work here.

But the Chairman also had this to report: 'Our pleasure in the visit was shattered a fortnight later by the tragic news of the sudden death of our friend and colleague, Bruce Stewart'. He was only in his mid-forties when he died. John Chambers gave this tribute:

Bruce came to us in 1989 with a reputation for skilled work, professionalism and a great sense of humour. He built on those skills within Relate and shared with us many ideas and insights honed over twenty years in social work.

RelateTeen was very much Bruce's baby. He put tremendous energy into the project which was a pioneering venture for the National organisation. Bruce brought to RelateTeen skills of the highest calibre in dealing with troubled teenagers and their families.[32]

'Helping Young People Affected by Parental Separation'

During the Troubles 'an essential coping strategy for most people has been to carry on with everyday life as though everything were normal', Margaret Fawcett of Queen's University Belfast and Isobel Reilly of NI Relate observed in an article they wrote for *Child Care in Practice* in 1995. They continued: 'this remarkable determination to keep going has been shown in both individual and family life. It has also been amply demonstrated by the business community and by health and social service agencies'. This included some local initiatives 'which have been often overshadowed by the more negative images of the Province'. One such initiative was the unique counselling service established by NI Relate in 1990 'for young people adversely affected by the break-up of their parents' marriage' – RelateTeen.

Isobel Reilly had been recommended by the national organisation to be appointed Professional Services Consultant to NI Relate. In 1995-96 she collaborated with Margaret Fawcett, Lecturer in the Department of Social Work at Queen's University Belfast, to prepare a detailed study of RelateTeen. RelateTeen, after all, was a Northern Ireland initiative. They found that until around fifteen years earlier 'there was a paucity of information about the experiences of children and teenagers' in divorcing families. Since then there had been 'substantive studies' on this subject in the United States and the United Kingdom. Margaret Fawcett and Isobel Reilly identified four key themes from these contemporary studies 'which have informed the developmental work of RelateTeen' – the divorce process; the risk factors; the impact on adolescent development; and the lack of support services.

Divorce was now understood to be a process rather than an event, in which the nature and severity of effects on children vary from one stage to the next and from one child to the next. They quoted a study by Ann Mitchell of a cross section of divorced families in Edinburgh:

Pre-school children tend to regress when their parents split up. Some children, and especially those under eight blame themselves for the break-up and have fantasies about reconciliation: aged six to eight they feel a great sadness; nine to 12 an intense anger, and in their teens they have a profound sense of loss.

An examination of divorce petitions by K McCoy and M Nelson for the DHSS in Belfast in 1983 'showed that children in over half of those families sampled had lost contact with the non-custodial parent'.[33] The removal of one parent from the child's home life often led to a drop in living standards and therefore poorer housing. Some children had to change school and leave behind former friends.

The authors then considered the risk factors. Following the acute adjustment phase immediately after separation, 'most children have adjusted and are coping well at the two year stage'. However, up to 25 per cent 'will continue to experience adverse long term effects as a result of their parents' divorce'. These included lower educational attainment and continued emotional disruption. Three factors appeared to correlate with serious adjustment problems for children. One was unresolved conflict between parents: if children became involved in 'high parental discord, and feel caught in the middle, it is deleterious to adjustment'. Another was desertion by the non-custodial parent – 'Children consistently describe the loss of contact with a parent as the most negative aspect of divorce'. The third was 'poor adjustment of the custodial parent'. The quality of parenting could be diminished by depression and anxiety in mothers in particular, impacting therefore on the emotional and social adjustment of children at the two year stage. The authors pointed out that, nevertheless, 'for some children their problems start, not at the divorce stage, but in a conflictual and unhappy marriage'.

Writing about the impact on adolescent development, the authors observed that divorce and the changes it brings to family circumstances 'coincides with changes in their own development – physical maturation, intellectual growth, emotional independence and transitions in social roles'. Adolescents have the cognitive skills to piece together the reason for their parents' separation and can draw on their peers and friendships outside the family for support. However, 'it would be wrong to assume that adolescents are grown up enough to understand what is happening in the family and old enough to simply get on with their own lives'. Quality of communication was crucial and studies of divorce had shown an extremely poor 'level of communication in circumstances of family breakdown'. The authors continued:

Parents are also important role models and if one parent is absent or has been devalued in the divorce process then it is much harder for the young person of the same gender to develop appropriate adult behaviour. Young people also have a need for clear and consistent boundaries, but inevitably parents are in emotional turmoil when a marriage breaks up, making the provision of such boundaries very difficult indeed. Negotiating independence may be further impeded if the adolescent becomes overburdened with adult responsibilities and feels it is their job to stay at home, protect and take care of the deserted or rejected parent.

Clearly, there was an urgent need for a support service. A study of the experiences of a hundred children in 1994 by Y Walczak and S Burns found that one-third of the sample were given no explanation for the separation, and that 48 per cent of mothers and 78 per cent of fathers did not talk directly with their children about the marriage break-up. Children could feel 'caught in the middle' and become 'adept at bottling and hiding their own feelings rather than upsetting their parents further'. They can be left with no one available to listen to their side of the story.

Adults have access to counselling and mediation services, but it was being revealed that few independent resources were in existence to help children adjust to separation, divorce and stepfamilies. 'It was against this background that in 1991 Relate (NI) decided to develop a counselling service for young people aged 12-18 adversely affected by their parents' separation and divorce':

The decision to establish RelateTeen was in many ways a logical development to work already undertaken by Relate (NI) in the areas of couple counselling and mediation practice. The focus on older children represented a coherent starting point and one which fitted most closely with the skills, expertise and resources within the agency.[34]

The three-year pilot phase of RelateTeen was ended formally by the reception with Princess Diana at Hillsborough in 1993. 'In keeping with the low key approach to the start of the project', information posters and leaflet were circulated round schools in Belfast, social service agencies and GP surgeries for the launch of the permanent service. Young people were being referred in rising numbers by professionals and families and so 'the team began the challenging process of applying their training and expertise to a new area of work'.

Between 1991 and 1994 there were 140 enquiries and of these 43 girls and 21 boys came in for counselling. The first surprise was that at the enquiry stage contact was generally initiated by a concerned adult on behalf of a teenager. In 60 per cent of cases the concerned adult was a mother and in about a quarter of cases the adult was a professional such as a GP, a teacher, a social worker, a probation officer or a family mediator. The majority of young people came forward for counselling immediately following their parents' separation. Striking gender differences were apparent:

Girls' difficulties were most commonly described in terms of changes in mood and attitude such as depression, tearfulness, moodiness at home and poor concentration at school. In a few referrals there was reference to incidence of self-injury and drug overdoses. By contrast, boys' difficulties were consistently described in terms of changes in behaviour. Expulsions from school, drug abuse, fighting, poor concentration at school, mitching, aggression and out of control behaviour were the concerns most commonly identified in the referral to counselling.

These findings were in line with those made elsewhere, that boys were found to be more vulnerable to the separation/divorce experience than girls. Twenty-five of the sixty-three referrals concerned teenagers coming forward for counselling some years after their parents' separation (nineteen of them more than five years after). 'This highlights the long-term difficulties (noted in research evidence) for young people in adjusting to family circumstances'.[35]

Jayne's story

When Jayne, aged 14, came to RelateTeen she brought with her many strong feelings of confusion, anger, helplessness and fear. Her parents were separating and it was a process that included a good deal of conflict and occasionally some violence. As the eldest girl at home she felt she should be coping much better than she was. She also believed that she should somehow have been able to stop the fighting and ensure that neither her sister nor her brothers were frightened or hurt in any way. It was to get help with this that she came to RelateTeen.

At the beginning, time was spent helping Jayne to see that this goal was not an achievable one. The second step was to help her to see that she was not responsible for her parents' separation, nor was it her responsibility to 'make it better' for her sister and her brothers. This took a little time but when she truly grasped the truth of it she felt a weight had been lifted from her. She then developed some coping strategies to help her with her parents' separation. We spent some time looking at how she could feel less vulnerable and also ways in which she could express her anger in a constructive and safe way. This enabled Jayne to speak to her parents in a clear manner that was non-threatening for them to hear. The case study report continued:

Most parents, in our experience, are often grateful for some guidance from their teenager as to what would help them during what is an extremely difficult and painful time for everyone. Jayne's parents were, in fact, unaware how frightened she was until she told them. Once she had coping strategies in place she felt that she no longer needed to come to RelateTeen. As always, it was left that should she need someone to talk to at any time in the future we would be delighted to hear from her.[36]

Four years later RelateTeen heard from her again. She rang up wanting to come and have a talk. When she arrived she was very tearful and distressed. The reason for this was that her parents, who hadn't spoken to each other for some years had started to get friendly again. This brought back all her feelings she had when she was fourteen years old – mainly fear and vulnerability. The work this time was to help Jayne to get a greater understanding of where she was in her life and also to help her to move emotionally and practically from a helpless fourteen year old with limited options, to a reasonably assertive and confident eighteen year old:

Somehow, seeing her parents again, Jayne had got "stuck" in the old feelings she had when she was fourteen. She moved through this process with an astonishing speed as all she needed was a little space and a safe environment to "move on". Some of the work we did was to help her to get a greater understanding of her parents. She was able to acknowledge her mum and dad as individuals who had choices to make in their lives. She could step back and see that they had their lives to lead and she had hers. She loved them both but now knew that she could not control or protect them. When she finished counselling for the second time she said she now felt "free".[37]

Patricia Donnelly, who became a Relate NI Trustee in 2002, is certain that RelateTeen provides a vital service. Marital conflict 'is a time of great emotion for them and they've got a lot of challenges'. A separate service provision was necessary 'because teenagers do have absolute beliefs about things – they think it's right or it is wrong – and all the evidence from very good researchers like Mabel Hetherington and others will tell us that teenagers do least well' during a time of parental separation:

They're very responsive to any marital conflict. They get triangulated by it: you've got Parent A, Parent B and that child will be more allied to one of those parents. And so, should there be a conflict, that teenager will ally himself or herself and often become the target, unnecessarily, and getting in the way of a resolution. They act in a beneficial way, they think to protect, but actually they are also preventing those two adults from more directly dealing with each other – so it is to try to stop them rescuing their parents, stopping them feeling responsible; and also to let them have a childhood.

The service provided should not be too disruptive. Communication 'doesn't always have to be face-to-face' and, following the initial assessment, contact could be maintained by email or mobile phone texting.[38]

Colin's story
Working out how best to counsel troubled teenagers involved a close study of best practice. There was a great diversity in youth counselling both in terms of service delivery and methods of work. This was due in part to the variety of organisations involved which ranged from schools and youth services to health and welfare agencies. However, it also reflected a variety of approaches to counselling itself. In their research on RelateTeen, published in 1995-96, Margaret Fawcett and Isobel Reilly, after acknowledging this variety of approaches, set about clarifying RelateTeen's use of the term 'counselling'. They drew a distinction between *informal* personal help which (in a teaching setting, for example) could range from 'crisis conversations' to 'career guidance' and 'discipline linked interviews' and *formal* counselling which was the approach used by RelateTeen. According to the Open University academics J Mabey and B Sorensen, formal counselling could be said to exist where 'there is a contracted relationship between counsellor and client and where the two parties meet at an agreed time and place for the sole purpose of the counselling interview'.[39] In formal counselling the contractual relationship between worker and young person exists for the sole purpose of enabling the young person (in the words of the British Association of Counselling 1992 Code of Ethics) to 'clarify ways of living more resourcefully and towards greater wellbeing'.

The counselling model used by RelateTeen was a three-stage problem solving approach. In Stage 1, the teenagers were encouraged 'to explore their current situation and identify problematic areas'. Then they work with their counsellor in

Stage 2 'to determine what they would like to do differently'. Since young people often do not know what they want or how to manage their situation, 'an essential feature of this helping model is enabling young people to learn how to open "new doors" for themselves'. In Stage 3, 'the young people are encouraged to go on to develop action plans and strategies to achieve the goals they have set themselves in Stage 2.'

In practice the phases of helping were not always sequential – 'flexibility is essential and the literature emphasises that workers will find themselves moving back and forth during the counselling process'. Other features of this three-stage problem solving model had a particular application to the needs of RelateTeen clients. They included the incorporation of 'core values of respect, genuineness and client self-responsibility' – values considered 'an essential basis for effective relationship building with young people whose trust in adults has often been broken and whose voices have often been lost in the middle of marital conflict'. This model also promoted a problem solving approach to young people's difficulties in which 'the counsellor has an active role in modelling and teaching new skills in problem solving'. This approach was intended to acknowledge teenagers' capacity to grow, develop and exercise power in their lives 'at a time when they often feel powerless to influence their changing family circumstances'.[40]

Margaret Fawcett and Isobel Reilly then presented a case study to demonstrate this creative approach at work. The focus of this study was a thirteen year old boy referred because of concerns about his behaviour and breakdown in family relationships. Counselling took place over eight one-hour sessions which were preceded by an information appointment and concluded with a joint meeting involving the resident parent. Names and personal details were changed to ensure anonymity:

Thirteen year old Colin was referred to RelateTeen by his mother. His parents had separated five years ago and he lived with his mother and eight year old sister. Colin had weekly contact with his Dad who lived near-by, but after a row he had not visited his father in two months. His mother was concerned at the breakdown in relationship between father and son and by changes in Colin's behaviour at home and at school. He had become moody and withdrawn at home while at school his work was deteriorating. Colin refused to discuss the situation with his mother, and so she approached RelateTeen as she felt he needed someone to talk to.

Colin responded promptly to a letter and a leaflet sent by Relate. He and his mother attended an information appointment. Over coffee and biscuits the worker explained the service using a flip chart and drawings, while Colin's mother outlined her concerns. Colin was the eldest child in a violent and abusive marriage. After separation she had made every effort to facilitate contact between the father and the children. The breakdown in relationship between father and son had caused her concern. Colin, appearing quiet and shy, listened attentively, 'contributing once or twice to guess the meaning of some of the drawings, and nodding or shrugging his shoulders at intervals during the mother's conversation'. 'I was all into myself', Colin said later. 'I was worried in case I didn't like the person I was going to meet, and I felt nervous in case I didn't know what to say'. Before leaving, when alone with the worker in the RelateTeen room, Colin agreed to come again but only on condition that his father was not to know that he was attending.

It was clear that Colin wanted a 'safe' place to talk to someone, a place where he could explore his fears in greater detail and find a way forward. In the ensuing one hour weekly sessions Colin was taken through the three-stage counselling model described above. In the first stage the worker used creative techniques that involved writing and drawing. 'In the first session Colin mapped out his family and social network using shells and stones which he then transferred to flipchart paper as a colourful ecomap'. Since he seemed to enjoy this active approach, in the second and third sessions he explored the story of his parents' separation through drawings of the houses he had lived in:

This proved a very powerful tool in recalling the painful memories of his parents' marriage. He talked of witnessing scenes of his father beating and kicking his mother, and vividly recalled when as an eight year old he had been beaten by his father in a drunken temper. This had been the last straw for his mother who had walked out with Colin and his young sister. In Colin's eyes this scene had particular significance, because in the ensuing five years he saw it as "his fault" that the marriage had ended.

Through further creative drawing work, Colin in cartoons told of the recent incident which led to the breakdown in the relationship with his father – his father had lost control of his temper over a minor disagreement and grabbed Colin as if to hit him. He stopped visiting his father and 'in response to his mother's insistence that he should see his Dad again, his way of protesting had been to stop talking to her'.

In the next stage Colin explored how he would like things in his current situation to be different. He did want to see his father again, provided violence was not threatened, and he wanted his mother to 'back off' to allow him more space to have his own feelings. At this stage it was important to help Colin recognise that he had choices: to manage his own feelings appropriately; to refuse to be drawn into parental arguments; and to negotiate his needs with adults in his life.

Using discussion and role play, Colin looked at constructive ways of dealing with his own anger, and 'an assertiveness skills approach of extracting himself from parental conflict'. A joint meeting with Colin and his mother revealed that she had not recognised the link between what had seemed like a minor tiff and her son's previous experience of violence in the family. After two final follow-up sessions, Colin re-established contact with his father with no further repeat of the incident. 'The tension between Colin and his Mum eased considerably and Colin's overall mood and sense of coping with his life appeared to improve his ability to cope with school and the daily hassles of life'.

Three months after counselling Colin had this to say about the benefits of RelateTeen:

It was great having someone who listened, someone who was neutral and who didn't take sides. It made me realise I wasn't the only one. I was able to talk about being angry with my Dad and get things out in the open. RelateTeen showed me how to cope with my parents rowing and with being angry. Now I feel strong and happier, I feel good about myself.

In her own reflection his mother said it was 'such a relief knowing that someone else was interested in Colin…The first day he went it was if the weight of the world had been lifted off his shoulders. I think it was having somebody who had no axe to grind, who was just prepared to listen…The change was almost tangible. He walked straighter, he was a different person'.

Feedback from other RelateTeen young people drew attention to similar positive outcomes:

Girl aged 18: caught in the middle of high conflict separation. Referred after suicide attempt
"Having someone to listen and give an unbiased point of view was invaluable. It felt like a weight off my shoulders. It helped clear things in my mind and the counsellor suggested practical ways of coping with stress. Now I am much calmer and friendlier and people have told me I am a nicer person."

Boy aged 15: referred after parents separated. Concerns re aggressive behaviour at home
"When my parents broke up I lost everything. It was like I was dead at the time. I felt I was going crazy, picking fights with everyone in the family. I told the counsellor everything. I spoke my heart out to her. It wasn't anything she did. She just listened and the talking cleared everything out of me. I have calmed down. I'm back to my normal self and that's all I wanted."

Margaret Fawcett and Isobel Reilly concluded by identifying good practice issues. The first was Informed Consent because most RelateTeen young people did not self refer. Contact with the service was usually initiated by a concerned adult, usually a parent. It was vital, therefore to emphasise that it was the young person's choice as to whether or not they wished to come and to provide explicit information about what was expected to happen during the sessions. The second issue was confidentiality – not as straightforward as many might assume. For example, Colin's distress at his father's behaviour was eventually shared with his mother in a joint session.

This need to share information outside the one to one counselling relationship can occur around issues such as child abuse, general concerns re parenting, at risk adolescent behaviour, and re-referral to other agencies. In order to ensure that the process is handled ethically and sensitively the limitations of confidentiality are spelt out at the first information appointment, specifically with respect to alleged child abuse and knowledge of an arrestable offence. This is in line with Relate procedures on confidentiality which adhere to the British Association of Counselling Code of ethics.

Balancing competing interests and rights in this area was always challenging. Supervision of the counsellor was therefore an essential support mechanism.

RelateTeen was a service specifically for children of parents who were separating. However, there were many other young people in school who were in need of counselling who did not fall into this category. Soon after he had been appointed as Chief Executive, Gerald Clark had been joined by Robin McRoberts as Director of Services. Robin was particularly interested in supporting teachers involved in pastoral care in schools. Julia Greer, for example, in her role as supervisor provided a support service at Rathmore Catholic grammar school in Dunmurry, and Wallace High School and Friends School in Lisburn. Such provision was rapidly becoming specialised; as a result it was increasingly supplied by organisations, other than Relate, specifically focussed on counselling school pupils.[41]

Another issue was Parental Consent and Parental Involvement. Colin made it clear at the outset and in later sessions that he did not want his father to know that he was attending RelateTeen. However, taking into account the Children (NI) Order 1995, the normal stance was to encourage the family to advise the other parent of RelateTeen's involvement. The first information appointment included liaison time with the referrer. 'The overall counselling plan can include family/step family meetings, joint work with parent and child, or even conjoint work with sibling groups'.

Finally, good practice included RelateTeen developing links with other professional groups and youth services. Where possible the aim was to prevent inappropriate intervention. Inevitably, however, some issues only emerged once counselling was under way. It could become necessary to refer the young people on for more specialist help. Occasions where this happened had involved concerns regarding anorexia and bulimia, high-risk suicidal behaviour, drug abuse, sexual abuse and mental health issues.[42]

Funding

Neither the Northern Ireland Marriage Guidance Council, nor its successor Relate NI, were government bodies but even at a very early stage, from 1950 onwards, NIMGC had depended to a considerable degree on grants from the Northern Ireland government, Belfast Corporation and, at times, other local authorities. Was the organisation a charity? An agency? An 'arms-length-body'? Since it had not been set up by government initiative, it was not strictly speaking a quango. Later, in 1998, Sir Eric McDowell described it as 'a company limited by guarantee and exempted from using the word "Limited" in its name'.[43] The organisation was also registered as a charity. Relate was one of a growing number of voluntary bodies which were obtaining funding from government. For the year ending 31 March 1988, Relate received £61,895 in government and area board grants, £7,835 from trusts, £11,762 in donations (£9,332 from clients), £1,482 from subscriptions, and £11,899 from 'sundries' (ranging from bank interest to media fees).

To maintain a respectable level of independence and to extend and develop its services, Relate needed to raise more of its own funds. This need was signalled by chairmen and honorary treasurers in successive annual reports. An appeal was launched during the fortieth anniversary in 1987; this, according to Joan Wilson, 'raised some money, but I see this as just the beginning of major fundraising in our efforts to raise £100,000'. The following year the Honorary Treasurer, Alan Walker warned that as 'the national organisation has been facing a critical year financially, considerably more of the training and supervision costs are being passed on to the local centres. Our expenditure in this area is set to double in the coming year...' In 1991 John Chambers, referring to the lengthening of waiting lists for counselling, announced that one full-time counsellor had been appointed 'and we are hoping to appoint 2 more half time salaried counsellors this year'. He warned: 'This is a major step forward, but it also has financial implications'. He had 'faith that the community in Northern Ireland will support us financially'.[44] But was that faith misplaced? Previous fund-raising appeals had often produced an underwhelming response.

In his report for 1991-92 John Chambers bleakly observed that 'this is the first year since I became Chief Officer in which we have finished the year with a significant deficit'.[45] In his Chairman's Report for 1992-93, Sir Eric McDowell wrote: 'We have been concerned for some time at the inadequacy of our finances to fund the developments in our work which the situation in our province requires'. In November 1992 the Executive decided to appoint Derek McVitty as consultant for a fundraising campaign, and Lady Elizabeth Bloomfield agreed to chair an appeal committee being formed for that purpose.[46]

An appeal committee of thirty of the great and the good (including one knight, five CBEs and seven OBEs) was duly formed. The Relate appeal was launched on 5 November 1993 in Belfast City Hall by the GMTV presenter, Eamonn Holmes. 'His willing support for the Appeal was much appreciated' as was that of Lady Jean Mayhew 'whose presence was a great encouragement'. The target set was £250,000 before the end of 1994.

The reasons for the appeal were outlined. The most obvious one was the continuing increase in the demand for Relate's services – 'for many people, the waiting time for counselling is just too long so that any help we might eventually offer is too late to prevent another separation or divorce'. Another was the introduction of new services – for example 'RelateTeen...recently endorsed by our National Patron, Her Royal Highness, The Princess of Wales'. Changes in government policy needed a response:

Imminent change in the principal existing source of funding – most of our funding comes from public sector grants but government policy towards voluntary organisations is changing. Grant aid is being reduced, to be replaced by payment for specific services in a contractual arrangement between providers and purchasers. The services which Relate provides are consistent with the new statutory policy of care in the community and the range of our services is not matched by any other provider in Northern Ireland.

To respond to these changing needs Relate had to be ready to assemble a larger complement of fully trained professional staff. 'We estimate that we shall need some seventy new practitioners at a training cost of £250,000 over the next two years' – the appeal target.

By the end of March 1994 £87,000 had been raised, allowing staff recruitment to begin. Most of the donors were private individuals but the region's business community was reasonably well represented. Several trusts contributed, along with nine Presbyterian congregations and five Church of Ireland parish churches. Three Catholic churches became donors the following year. David Clements, the Honorary Treasurer, was able to report a comfortable surplus. More regular and traditional fund-raising continued. The annual Relate Ball at Belfast Castle raised £1,757; £362 came from Co-operation North Maracycle; and flag days (with Sir Eric McDowell as an exceptionally enthusiastic collector) produced £1,037 in Belfast, £835 in Foyle, and £404 from a collection at Stormont and Rosepark. The Dean of St Anne's Cathedral contributed £1,000 from the funds he raised during his annual Christmas 'sitout'; BBC Children in Need contributed a substantial £8,500; the Enkalon Foundation gave £1,500; TSB Foundation gave £2,500; and Nationwide Building Society for International Year of the family provided £1,750.[47]

The target of £250,000 was not reached but by 1996 'as the Appeal reaches its closing stages it is good to report a gross income of over £165,000'. The major funding event had been a lunch on 31 May 1995 addressed by Sir Kenneth Bloomfield in the Culloden Hotel, Cultra, hosted by the Chamber of Commerce and Industry Northern Ireland. 'This has been our most successful fundraising event ever' which enabled NI Relate to recruit and train more practitioners and was largely responsible for the 13 per cent growth in the organisation's services over the year. 'Unfortunately we finished the year with a financial deficit which will need to be eliminated in the coming year', John Chambers observed in the 1995-96 Annual Report but on the same page Chairman Sir Eric McDowell added some perspective: 'It is interesting to note that our income and expenditure for the year has been over £550,000 compared with £250,000 in 1992 – an increase of about 120% in 4 years'.[48]

Evaluation of remedial counselling: 'Like couples in middle life, we in Relate have to "take stock" of where we are'.
Counselling for couples and individuals with a relationship problem remained the central core activity of Relate. It was a constant struggle to meet the demand for this service despite a steady increase in the number of counselling hours. For a while in 1988-89, for example, no counsellors were available in Craigavon, Magherafelt and Carrickfergus.

In 1994-95 sixty counsellors worked 7,736 sessions with clients in twelve different locations in Northern Ireland. The couples seen had a total of 3,270 children under the age of sixteen. Women attending on their own predominated, 3,293 making up 43 per cent of sessions worked. Men attending numbered 1,301 (17 per cent) and 3,142 men and women came as couples (41 per cent). With a more managed system of initial reception appointments, a carefully maintained waiting list and additional recruitment of practitioners, Relate was able to offer reception appointments within two weeks of enquiry, most day time appointments within 4-6 weeks, and evening appointments within 8-12 weeks. Changes made in recent years were listed:

We have –

- Increased the proportion of fully trained counsellors. We now have 60 counsellors – 44 trained and 16 in training.
- We have more male practitioners than ever before – 8 in counselling, 2 in mediation and 8 in RelateTeen.
- Better recruitment and equal opportunities policies which attract a range of practitioners who reflect the community in Northern Ireland.
- A better choice of appointment times for clients – including evening appointments.
- A greater geographical spread of out centres.
- A considerable increase in the proportion of income generated by client donations.
- Small touches that make us more user friendly – name badges worn by staff and practitioners, tea/coffee in the waiting room and a regular programme of redecoration of the rooms used by the public.

And yet we need to do more

Both the staff and the executive felt that the time had come for a thorough evaluation of its counselling work: 'Like couples in middle life, we in Relate have to "take stock" of where we are'. In 1994 Relate Northern Ireland, with the financial support of the DHSS, commissioned the Relate Centre for Family Studies in Newcastle-on-Tyne to undertake the study. Attempting to answer the question, 'Why did we do it?' the 1996-97 Annual Report explained:

Relate counselling exists for the users of our services. It is also important for funders to measure how their money is being spent…Evaluating counselling is no easy task and very many problems have had to be overcome. For years Relate resisted doing this because we felt that clients who come to us are already distressed enough and to ask them to complete questionnaires might be to add to their burdens. There was also the concern about what to ask and how you could evaluate something as difficult to measure as counselling…

In January 1994 a proposal was sent from Price Waterhouse to send brief questionnaires to Relate clients as part of their formal evaluation of Relate Northern Ireland as required by the DHSS. After discussion it was agreed that a more in-depth research programme was preferable and, to take account of the sensitivities required, it was decided to use the instrumentation already tested in an earlier Relate pilot in England, with some refinements in the light of that experience.

The evaluation sought to include more information about the people who approached Relate for help. Why did some clients choose not to enter counselling following a reception interview? Why did some clients not complete the process having embarked on it? The evaluation also sought to: ascertain the effectiveness of the organisation's services from a consumer perspective, looking specifically at process and outcome; look more carefully at the interaction and match between counsellors and their clients; provide data relevant to the needs of Relate (managers and practitioners), funders, government departments and policy makers; and develop measures for accountability internally and externally.

A series of questionnaires was devised to be used pre-counselling, in-counselling, and post counselling, and a follow-up after six and twelve months. The study focused on clients attending Reception Interviews at the Belfast and Foyle centres between 1 December 1994 and 3 March 1995. Completed questionnaires were returned weekly to the centre in Newcastle-on-Tyne.

In summary, the evaluation revealed that most clients, irrespective of the degree of their involvement, were satisfied with the service they received and felt that many of their needs had been met. Most would go back again in the event of further problems.

Clients going to an initial interview displayed high levels of distress. Around one third of them had visited their GP during the two weeks prior to visiting Relate – 14 per cent of them had come at the suggestion of their GPs. Clients sought counselling to enhance their understanding of the relationship with their partner, but men and women wanted to achieve this through different routes. 'Men were likely to want to focus on practical concerns about preserving the relationship, while women were more likely to attach a high level of importance to their own feelings'. Eleven per cent of clients were going to Relate because they had recently separated, and four per cent were seeking counselling because they wanted help to extricate themselves from relationships.

Thirty-eight per cent of clients terminated their involvement with Relate after an initial interview, the evaluation revealed. More than half this number had decided that counselling was not 'an appropriate intervention'. Others indicated that they did not attend for a second time because of 'a partner's unwillingness to attend, or the help on offer was not what they needed, or the counsellor did not adequately focus on the marital relationship, or there were problems getting appointments or because they were in work and/or had child care commitments and had difficulty in arranging appointments. A few clients indicated that they were put off by the financial cost involved'. One in four of those not returning for a second interview felt that the relationship had improved anyway. Over one in three of these felt that the improvement was due to the help they had received at the first interview. The following comment was thought to be typical:

I'd just like to say, I feel if my partner and I had not gone to Relate when we did we would not be living together now.

However, one in five who opted out after the first interview did so because they had decided to separate. The data did indicate that 16 per cent of separated clients who had only attended one interview had got back together with their partner.

Sixty per cent of those clients who went through counselling to an ending planned with their counsellor had most or all of their needs met – indeed, 45 per cent of clients wished they had gone sooner. More than two thirds of clients were satisfied with the services they had received. One commented:

I found it helpful that blame was not discussed. Whose fault it was became irrelevant. This gave me confidence to move on and build on the more positive elements of my relationship.

Most clients, including nine in ten of those who attended a single interview or did not complete the process, indicated that they would willingly recommend Relate to other people seeking help with relationship problems.

How was the service to be bettered? Relate Northern Ireland declared its intention to introduce: an assessment system as a pilot project in Foyle starting in September 1997; drop-ins for a quicker, more accessible service; telephone counselling; crèche facility to tie in with drop-in and offered twice weekly; offer longer sessions for shift workers and others; a clear system on client donations. 'Behind these ideas lies the belief that we need to spend more time assessing client need at first interview'. This would create the need for additional training for practitioners and profiling the worker to make a better match with client need.[49]

The final report was presented by Professor Janet Walker and Peter McCarthy from Newcastle University at a special seminar in Belfast Castle on Friday 13 March 1998. Sixty invited guests, mainly from existing statutory and other voluntary organisations, attended. The report included the findings of questionnaires completed by clients six months and twelve months after completing counselling. The results reinforced the conclusions of the interim report. The final percentages were: a year after Relate counselling 65 per cent of those who completed the process felt their relationship had improved compared with 27 per cent of those who attended only a reception interview.

Relate staff reported on some initiatives already developed following the publication of the interim report. These included a new introductory appointments system piloted in Foyle, a telephone help line and the training of all counsellors in 'Solution Focused Counselling'.[50]

Planning the 50th Anniversary

In the autumn of 1997 the Northern Ireland Marriage Guidance Council – now Relate Northern Ireland – was due to celebrate its fiftieth anniversary. A series of events stretching over twelve months was planned to mark this golden moment. The Chief Executive, John Chambers, signalled the approaching anniversary a week before Valentine's Day. 'Cupid is not ageist', he warned in a press release, saying that the open expression of romantic affection should not be left just to younger couples. He continued by reflecting on a half century of change:

In 1997 there are many more couples who have been together for a very long time than there were in 1947 when the Marriage Guidance Council was founded because people are living longer. Valentine's Day is a good opportunity to celebrate a relationship no matter how long it has been.

When Relate was formed as the Marriage Guidance Council 50 years ago it was responding to severe marriage problems largely arising from the strain on relationships during World War Two. Since then an ageing population has seen some remarkable changes in attitudes to love and marriage. For instance in 1947 there were only 196 divorce petitions and on our first year we dealt with 103 cases. This year there are likely to be about 2,500 divorces and Relate will have over 2,000 new cases to deal with.

The same 50 year period has also seen a significant fall-off in the number of marriages per year and an increase in the number of people who choose to live together rather than marry. The word "partner", in the context of a loving relationship, was probably unheard of in 1947. In 1947 half of the couples who came to Marriage Guidance had their problems described as medical which really meant sexual and it is reported that almost all of those cases were a complete success although what criteria defined success in those days is unknown.

That first week in February 1997 Relate was providing counselling in Newry for the first time. John Chambers concluded that, as it moved towards its Golden Anniversary year, Relate was positive about its achievements – 'Most people come to Relate in deep despair, but many go away with their anxieties reduced and with hope for the future'. After outlining the services offered, he announced that plans for the Golden Anniversary included: a major Conference in April in the Waterfront Hall, Belfast on the subject of 'Teenagers and Divorce'; participation in the Second World Congress on Family Law and the Rights of Children and Youth in San Francisco in June; an attempt to produce the largest wedding cake in the world for 4 September, the 50th anniversary; and a celebration in Belfast City Hall.[51] Indeed, a Relate NI 50th Anniversary committee had been busy making plans over the previous months, holding its first meeting on 18 September 1996. A pivotal event to mark a half century of marriage guidance would be a major conference on how separation of parents impacted on their teenage children.

'Teenagers and Divorce': the Relate Conference

On Friday 18 April Relate hosted its most significant conference so far in Belfast's newest and most prestigious venue, the Waterfront Hall. Entitled 'Teenagers and Divorce' it was designed to examine how divorce affected teenagers in Northern Ireland and to hear what could be done to help them through the break-up of their parents' relationship. Margaret Fawcett from Queen's University and also a RelateTeen counsellor and family mediator, reported to an audience of around two hundred the preliminary findings of a study of the needs of teenagers when parents separate and divorce.

Relate, increasingly aware of the lack of relevant research, had approached the Department of Health and Social Services in 1994 to seek funding for a research project. This was to explore the needs of teenagers when parents separate and divorce. The funding was provided and undertaken by Margaret Fawcett and Relate's professional services consultant, Isobel Reilly. The findings, published in 1995-6, are discussed in detail earlier in this chapter. The conference gave the opportunity to publicise the research results to a wider audience. Dr Martin Richards, the keynote speaker, set the scene by emphasising how little research had been done in this area:

With a few honourable exceptions (eg Mitchell, 1985; Walzak and Burns, 1984), the research that has been described does not investigate children's views and experiences directly. This gap becomes particularly crucial if it is acknowledged – as the Children Act 1989 does, for example – that children should be consulted about important decisions concerning their lives. I want to make the point that the lack of relevant research makes discussion of how children could or should be involved in decision making at divorce much more difficult than it should be.

The audience heard that young people had to deal with wide-ranging changes as a result of their parents' break-up. These included changes of house, school, living arrangements and altered roles and responsibilities in their homes – all at a time when they were already undergoing the physical and emotional changes of adolescence. The level of cooperation between separated parents on parenting issues was low. Domestic violence was reported by 30 per cent of families. Alcohol abuse by parents was also reported by 30 per cent. A significant number of young people were in contact with a range of support services outside home and school.

'Many of the young people had a sense of utter confusion about what was happening and of being unable to cope', the audience heard. Comments such as 'I thought I was going crazy' and 'I felt I was cracking up, losing it, going insane' were typical. Many teenagers were not aware of any source of help and, actually, were not very sure what they wanted. They were ambivalent about how much they wanted other people to know about their parents' separation. This was mirrored by over half the parents in the study. One young girl said that 'she knew her parents wouldn't have liked anyone outside the family to know their business'.

Ninety-five per cent of parents interviewed reported health problems during the separation. This impaired their ability to provide support for their children. One mother said: 'I wasn't able to cope. I was a nervous wreck. I had a new baby, my relationship with my husband was rocky, there was no money and my daughter had to step in and do more than her fair share'. The report on the conference continued:

In working with young people the critical factor in the help given to teenagers by adults outside of the family, was the personal approach of the adult concerned. They needed someone who was easy to talk to, who took the time to listen to their story, who was trustworthy and who wasn't judgmental.

Celebrating the golden moment

A particularly memorable celebration of Relate's golden anniversary was held in Derry/Londonderry. On Friday 27 June 1997, following a wine reception courtesy of Derry City Council, there was a performance of 'Pleasure & Repentance', described as 'A Miscellany of Poetry, Prose and Music on the theme of love and marriage'. This was produced and directed by Nevin Harris, a senior civil servant in the Department of Education, now based in the city and much involved with the Foyle Centre, who had also been for long the driving force of, and leading actor in, the Osborne Players in Belfast. This 'light hearted look at love and marriage', compiled by Terry Hands, was staged in the Foyle Arts Centre, Lawrence Hill. The performers were Sheila Dixon, Desmond Shaw and Nevin Harris who read three dozen items ranging from *A Description of Love* by Sir Walter Raleigh, to *Fain would I wed* by Thomas Campion, *The Flea* by John Donne, *The Mess of Love* by D H Lawrence, *Cupid's Nightcap* by S J Sharpless, and *The Arrow in the Heart* by William Hazlitt. Maurice Leyden sang ten songs, including: *The Last Rose of Summer*; *We'll go no more a'roving* (by Lord Byron); *She moved through the fair*; …and *Satisfaction* by The Rolling Stones.

On the actual anniversary date, 4 September, Robert and Sarah Wylie from Derry/Londonderry – celebrating their own golden wedding anniversary – were invited to share their day with Relate. 'It actually began last Thursday when the couple awakened to a day which they'll never forget', the television personality and journalist Anne Hailes wrote in her *Irish News* column. 'It was going to be a very special time with family and friends gathering to drink a glass of good cheer but then Relate Marriage Guidance came into the picture'. She explained:

You might wonder why! After all, if a couple have made it to their golden wedding they must have something going for each other! As it happened Relate was celebrating its own 50th anniversary. On September 4 1947 as the Wylies were tying the knot in Derry, a group of men and women gathered in Belfast to form a local branch of the National Marriage Guidance Council and since then they've been helping couples come to terms with difficulties within their relationships. But last Thursday it was a case of success toasting success when the Wylies accepted an invitation from John Chambers of Relate to join a luncheon party in Belfast's Europa Hotel.

The couple were given a grand send-off from the city. Anne Hailes continued:

Before he retired Robert was a bus driver originally with the Ulster Transport Authority and when he heard of the jollifications, Ulsterbus PR Roger Hope insisted in being involved and brought the pair, their doctor son Alastair and bridesmaid Nan Crown and her husband Ernie by express Ulsterbus from Derry to the Europa bus station. From there they were whisked off on an open top bus round Belfast.

Naturally the bus stopped at 76 Dublin Road where, after meeting the Relate staff and receiving gifts, they travelled on to the Europa Hotel where Billy Hastings of Hastings Hotel Group welcomed them for a champagne lunch in the Gallery Restaurant. 'It's been unbelievable, a day to remember' was how Robert summed it up to Anne Hailes over a four-course meal. After speeches, and press and television interviews, the couple set off for home and family celebrations.

Then on 18 September, couples celebrating their golden anniversaries travelled from all over Northern Ireland for afternoon tea at Government House, Hillsborough. In full dress uniform, Bill Hall, the Queen's representative, the Lord Lieutenant for Co. Down, took tea with the guests of honour who all had one thing in common: each couple was married in 1947. Anne Hailes (for long closely involved in Relate's activities) presided over the afternoon's entertainment. Stanley Fitzgerald, not only a retired senior History Inspector but also an award-winning amateur actor in the Osborne Players, had the audience in the palm of his hand as he read poems and told rib-tickling stories of married life. A record of the occasion continued:

Young musicians from Wallace High School played for the audience of 150. There wasn't a dry eye in the house when Anne told the story of a young English woman who fell in love with the son of the house as they walked in the gardens. She hadn't the courage to tell him of her feelings; instead, when she returned home, she wrote of her love in a song which soon afterwards he heard at a house party in London. He immediately realised the significance and he invited her back to Hillsborough and soon wedding bells rang out. Hankies were in evidence amongst the audience in the Throne Room when Lianne McCauley sang the lovely ballad, "In the Gloaming".

During the afternoon couples spoke about their wedding day, the cost of receptions and the difficulty of getting a pretty dress so soon after the war. 'One lady caused great laughter when she told of standing on the steps of the church, a young bride of 10 minutes, only to see her milkman husband kidnapped by his colleagues and driven off on a milk cart drawn by a lusty horse.' Albert and Betty McCracken, a couple invited to Hillsborough, returned from the event only to be swept into a surprise dinner party in the Strangford Arms Hotel in Newtownards attended by seventy guests. The Wylies had already posted to Relate a cheque for £100 and many of the couples invited to Hillsborough Castle subsequently sent donations 'ranging from £10-£100'. [52]

The year 1997 was 'rounded off' with a concert at the Rialto in Derry given by the Londonderry Amateur Operatic Society and Britannia Brass & Reed Band who presented *Showstoppers '97* on 6 November. For nine years the Operatic Society (conductor, Jim Goodman) and the Britannia Band (conductor, Ken Goodman), with Charlie Wilson as accompanist, had been giving a series of charity concerts. Relate was chosen as one of the four good causes to benefit in 1997. The twenty-nine items at the Rialto included: *Kiss me Kate* (Cole Porter); *Me and My Girl* (Noel Gay); *Bourée* (M Praetorius); *Showboat* (J Kern); and, very suitably, *The Londonderry Air*. [53]

A celebratory event in Belfast City Hall had been long in preparation. Alban Maginness, the first nationalist Lord Mayor of Belfast, ensured that the Banqueting Hall was made available on 24 April 1998. The City Hall was, of course, an appropriate venue as NIMGC had been founded in the Lord Mayor's Parlour in 1947. Sponsors were persuaded to support the event by donating prizes for a light-hearted quiz and glasses of Black Velvet (a combination of stout and champagne said to have been invented by the German Chancellor, Otto von Bismarck). John Chambers introduced the proceedings; Anne Hailes acted as compere; Stephen Burnside was Quiz Master; music was provided by a harpist and two young students of the Ulster College of Music; and Sir Eric McDowell closed the proceedings. A raffle raised £875. The event 'was full of laughter and conversation as Relate said thank you to their staff and their partners and to the many invited guests, people who had been associated with the organisation through 50 years of service'.

Notes

1   David McKittrick, Seamus Kelters, Brian Feeney, Chris Thornton and David McVea, *Lost Lives*, Belfast, 2008, pp.1106, 1156, 1189, 1224, 1266, 1307, 1344 and 1381; *Belfast Telegraph*, 20 August 1988
2   NI Relate Annual Report, 1988 and 1988-89
3   NI Relate Annual Report, 1988-89
4   NI Relate Annual Report, 1990-91
5   NI Relate Annual Report, 1991-92
6   Interview with Julia Greer, 14 August 2013
7   NI Relate Annual Report, 1992-93
8   NI Relate Annual Report, 1988-89
9   NI Relate Annual Report, 1990-91
10 NI Relate Annual Report, 1991-92
11 NI Relate Annual Report, 1993-94
12 NI Relate Annual Report, 1994-95
13 NI Relate Annual Report, 1995-96
14 NI Relate Annual Report, 1996-97 and 1997-98
15 NI Relate Annual Report, 1991-92
16 NI Relate Annual Report, 1992-93
17 Jonathan Bardon in the *Independent on Sunday*, 31 October 1993, reprinted in *The Belfast Anthology*, edited by Patricia Craig, Belfast, 1999, pp. 110-112
18 NI Relate Annual Report, 1990-91
19 NI Relate Annual Report, 1991-92
20 NI Relate Annual Report, 1992-93; ATQ Stewart, *The Ulster Crisis*, London, 1967, pp. 43-44; Dermot Keogh, *Twentieth-Century Ireland*, Dublin, 1994, pp. 240-241; Letter from John Chambers to Dave Murphy, 28 October 2013
21 http://www.nimma.org.uk/; *Celebrating The Work, Evaluating The Impact*, NIMMA, 2008; Mixed Emotions: *Real stories of mixed marriage*, NIMMA, 2012
22 NI Relate Annual Report, 1991-92
23 NI Relate Annual Report, 1992-93
24 Letter from John Chambers to Dave Murphy, 28 October 2013
25 NI Relate Annual Report, 1993-94
26 NI Relate Annual Report, 1994-95
27 Margaret Fawcett and Isobel Reilly, 'RelateTeen – Helping Young People affected by Parental Separation and Divorce – Part 1' in *Child Care in Practice*, Vol. 2, Issue 2, 1995, p. 48
28 Fawcett and Reilly, 1995, pp. 51-53
29 NI Relate Annual Report, 1991-92 and 1992-93
30 NI Relate Annual Report, 1993-94
31 *Down Spectator*, 4 September 1997
32 NI Relate Annual Report, 1993-94
33 Margaret Fawcett and Isobel Reilly, 'RelateTeen – Helping Young People affected by Parental Separation and Divorce – Part 1' in *Child Care in Practice*, Vol. 2, Issue 2, 1995, pp. 48-52
34 Margaret Fawcett and Isobel Reilly, 'RelateTeen – Helping Young People affected by Parental Separation and Divorce – Part 1' in *Child Care in Practice*, Vol. 2, Issue 2, 1995, pp. 48-52
35 Relate NI Annual Report, 1990-91
36 Relate NI Annual Report, 1994-95, p. 4
37 Relate NI Annual Report, 1994-95, p. 4
38 Interview with Patricia Donnelly, 2 March 2009
39 Margaret Fawcett and Isobel Reilly, 'RelateTeen – Helping Young People Affected by Parental Separation and Divorce', *Child Care in Practice*, Vol. 2, Issue 3, March 1996, p. 67
40 Fawcett and Reilly, 1996, p. 68
41 Interview with Julia Greer, 14 August 2013
42 Fawcett and Reilly, 996, pp. 68-75
43 NI Relate Annual Report, 1997-98
44 NI Relate Annual Report, 1990-91
45 NI Relate Annual Report, 1991-92
46 NI Relate Annual Report, 1992-93
47 NI Relate Annual Report, 1993-94
48 NI Relate Annual Report, 1995-96
49 NI Relate Annual Report, 1996-97, pp. 3-7
50 NI Relate Annual Report, 1997-98
51 Burnside-Citigate News Release, 7 February 1997
52 *Irish News*, 8 September 1997; NI Relate Annual Report, 1997-98; Minutes of the Golden Anniversary Committee, 9 October 1997; Letter from Susan Robinson to relate, 4 October 1997
53 *Showstoppers '97* programme

CHAPTER SEVEN

The challenge of peace: forging partnerships 1998-2013

A new era

Political and sectarian violence did not end completely with the paramilitary ceasefires of 1994, but Northern Ireland had turned a corner. Certainly hatred remained, and the deep divisions in society were periodically demonstrated by confrontations at Drumcree, outside Holycross School in Belfast, at Harryville in Ballymena, and by further killings and paramilitary violence. Nevertheless, the 'peace process' was under way. Eventually, in 1998 a honed version of William Whitelaw's power-sharing solution of 1973 was accepted by a majority in Northern Ireland – with much truth the SDLP deputy leader, Séamus Mallon, described the Good Friday Agreement that year as 'Sunningdale for slow learners'.

The DUP, which had opposed the 1998 accord, was persuaded in time to work alongside nationalists in a devolved administration. With the terrible exception of the Omagh bomb, planted by dissident republicans on 15 August 1998 and which claimed 29 lives, the era of terrorism and sectarian murders seemed to be over. After repeated false political starts, finally, in May 2007, a power-sharing government was in place with a realistic prospect of functioning for more than just a few months. By then a whole generation had at last grown up with little or no direct experience of political violence. The comparative peace of the new millennium did not reduce Relate NI's case load. Quite the contrary: the number of clients coming forward was increasing inexorably. Sir Kenneth Bloomfield's 1998 victims report, *We Will Remember Them*, and the Social Services Inspectorate report, *Living with the trauma of the "Troubles"*, published in the same year, both called for counselling as part of a long-term recovery process. It had been some years past that Relate had declared that it was 'not just a marriage guidance council'; now it was broadening its reach still further, particularly by strengthening partnerships with other agencies.

As the demand for Relate's services continued to outstrip the organisation's ability to respond, it was becoming ever more obvious that its headquarters in Belfast's Dublin Road was no longer fit for purpose.

Gerald Clark at the helm: new contracts, accreditation and deficit elimination
In 1998 John Chambers, an ordained Presbyterian minister, made the decision to return to a pastoral ministry and departed for Inverness in the autumn. In 1994 he had been appointed chair of the International Commission on Couple and Family Relations. The following year, when he was also honoured by being awarded an OBE, he chaired a conference in Fribourg, Switzerland. In 1997 he was in San Francisco as a delegate to the Second World Congress on the Rights of Children and Youth,

and brought with him Kate Lewis and Margaret Fawcett to conduct a workshop on RelateTeen research. His last conference as chair of the International Commission was in Oxford. In his final address he summed up the conference in four lines, based on the style of Kahlil Gibran in his book *The Prophet*:

Let us be stimulated and challenged by our differences
Let us feel safe in our similarities
But let us not be too different or we will fall apart
And let us not be too similar or we will wither with boredom

Those four lines have since been quoted on all the International Commission's documents.

In his last Chief Executive's Report for NI Relate, he reminded readers that he had spent almost fourteen years in that post and a further five years before that as a voluntary counsellor – 'it has been a large part of my life and around 40 per cent of the life of Relate Northern Ireland'. Judith Loder, the Training Manager, and Kate Lewis, Head of Professional Services, also moved on to posts in other organisations in the same year. Joan Wilson had been appointed the first Chairman of the Trustees, but illness had prevented her from fulfilling those duties after June 1997. Sir Eric McDowell took over as Acting Chairman and he was right to observe: 'Much of the growth and development in Relate's services to clients has been due to the vision, enthusiasm and sheer hard work of those people who are moving on'.

The new Chief Executive was Gerald Clark who was to serve even longer than his predecessor in this post. He took over during the autumn of 1998, a time of returned uncertainty when it was proving ever more difficult to implement the provisions of the Good Friday Agreement. This and other 'changes in the environment in which we operate', Gerald Clark wrote in his first Chief Executive's report, '…have further contributed to the general sense of uncertainty and insecurity that many voluntary organisations have experienced'.[1]

Gerald Clark had trained as an engineer and had become a senior manager in Shorts Bros. & Harland aircraft factory in Belfast, managing engineering projects. One of those projects involved the development of a missile system, which troubled his conscience – so much so that he stepped aside, resigned, and travelled to Paraguay, South America to work for the (Anglican Church) South America Missionary Society. He returned after seven years to become the Director of the YMCA in Belfast. After ten years he moved to Geneva, Switzerland to work for the World Alliance of YMCAs. This involved almost continuous long-distance travelling, in particular to direct development work in USA, Canada, Eastern Europe and Africa. After six years, when all four of his children had left home for University, leaving his wife too often on her own, Gerald decided to return to his native city: he applied for and was appointed to the post of Chief Executive in Relate NI. The management skills he had acquired in Shorts and overseas were to serve him well.

John Chambers had moved to Scotland a couple of months before Gerald arrived to begin work in the autumn of 1998. The absence of an overlap meant that the new Chief Executive was left to discover much on his own. As he first came up to 76 Dublin Road, he found that all arriving there had to stand in a porch and ring a bell, waiting to be let in. As he rang the bell, he noticed that a bus stop was directly outside: immediately he realised that clients – not wishing to announce to the world that they were in need of relationship counselling – could be seen waiting awkwardly, being stared at by passengers on buses drawing to a halt. 'This is dreadful', he thought. Almost his first decision as CEO was to change the door of Relate's premises, allowing clients to enter without waiting and being exposed to view. Then he negotiated with Translink, explaining the situation and, without any hesitation, the transport company moved the bus stop down the street.

The most urgent problem was finance. With a substantial deficit, Relate NI was staring into a financial crisis. How had this situation arisen? Relate NI was now a charity limited by guarantee, but the trustees were divided into two committees, the Financial Services sub committee and the Professional Services sub committee. The two groups met separately before each Board meeting to begin with: although the trustees all met together immediately afterwards, with each sub committee reporting to the Board, there was always the risk that, when projects were being discussed by the Professional Services sub committee, inevitably at times insufficient attention was being paid to the financial implications of the decisions being made. When, several months before the end of a financial year, the funds were close to running out, the CEO had toured trusts and other potential funders – this action produced some money, but never enough. Annual shortfalls therefore accumulated to become a significant deficit.

Anxiety about the organisation's debts might have been greater but for the high standing Relate NI had not only in society as a whole but also in the eyes of senior civil servants. In addition, captains of industry were on occasion persuaded to join the board and some became chairman. Bob Jordan – Chief Executive of the Northern Ireland Chamber of Commerce, CEO of Esso in Northern Ireland for twenty-seven years, Chairman of the Belfast Institute for ten years, Chairman of the Fisheries Board – served as Chairman of Relate during this time. He had been invited to involve himself in Relate's affairs by Sir Eric McDowell, then serving as chairman. He recalled John Chambers going round the health area boards promoting the work of marriage guidance. This was in the hope of getting a share of what was universally described as 'slippage', money remaining at the end of a financial year. Bob Jordan thought that the boards proved to be 'very helpful' on such begging rounds with the result that Relate NI 'almost seemed to just manage'.

The financial pressure on Relate became particularly great because of the provision of new services, such as RelateTeen, and because salaries were increasing just as it had been agreed to pay counsellors. Bob Jordan was delighted that Gerald Clark accepted the Relate NI CEO post because he arrived with 'great expertise' while at the same time acknowledging that he was being thrown in 'at the deep end' at a time when what he called 'tail-end funding' still prevailed.[2]

Bob Jordan was Chairman when Gerald Clark took up his post. As he revealed in his Chairman's Report, this coincided not only with 'an increase in demand for our services' and 'changes of personnel' but also 'a reduction in financial support'.

He continued:

Although we managed to limit the increase in our expenditure to 0.1%, our income from grants was reduced by 12%. Unfortunately, notification of the reduced grants was not received in time to enable management to take corrective action, and we finished the year with a deficit. In financial terms this has been a serious setback and presents us with a real challenge for the year ahead.[3]

New contracts for counsellors

One major reason why the organisation's costs had also risen sharply was because counsellors were now being paid (however modestly). The problem was that the volunteering ethos was still there: counsellors tended to give their services only for three or four hours a week and nearly always during mornings and afternoons. Relate NI simply was not getting a sufficiently good return on expensive training and, in addition, a high proportion of potential clients could only come for counselling in the evenings. Gerald Clark also discovered that there were too many managers. When money had been obtained for a specific project a manager would be appointed, but when the time-limited funding ended, that manager would be retained to undertake other duties within the organisation.

The new Chief Executive had to 'rethink the whole package' and hammer out a new strategy with the Board. Too many counsellors were working too few hours and often at times of the day when they were least needed by clients. It was agreed that counsellors should be asked to work a minimum of six hours a week and also be willing to work in the evenings. The Relate Certificate in Couple Counselling was now well established as a national qualification, alongside the brand name of Relate, but it was also important to have National recognition across the counselling profession. In recognition of this, and in line with best practice, supervision provision was increased for all counsellors to enable them to apply for accreditation with the professional body for counsellors, The British Association of Counselling and Psychotherapy (BACP).

The only way in which this new strategy could be implemented was to declare all current counsellors redundant and to ask them to re-apply, provided they accepted the new conditions. Many counsellors were shocked and bewildered at this change – it was 'a very difficult time', Gerald Clark recalled.[4] Many counsellors welcomed the changes in supervision provision which enabled them to gain accreditation. However, the organisation was losing half its counselling workforce – valued colleagues who could not now give the hours required by Relate because of other career or family commitments. Those who could not guarantee to work at least six hours a week and in the evenings, those who had undertaken rigorous and time-consuming training and – until recently – given their time for no pay could be forgiven for feeling slighted, rejected and deeply hurt. More flexibility could have been shown, many felt. For decades these low-volume counsellors had been the mainstay of the organisation and it is difficult to avoid the conclusion that their contribution was under-valued. The shock waves of this sea change were to be felt for many years to come. However, for others, the new conditions offered new opportunities within the organisation. 'It was a time of loss but also of opportunity', Julia Greer recalled. She continued:

Relate lost some highly valued counsellors who had worked for many years for a few hours each week but were unable to commit to a higher volume of work or to the specific hours required by the organisation. It was a time of change and if there is one thing that counsellors know about it is change and so the loss was mourned and everyone moved on.[5]

 The outcome of the Board's decision was that, in a very short time, Relate NI's workforce was cut by 50 per cent. However, some benefits came with the changes. Clients were now getting a service which suited them better: they had more opportunities to come in the evening; and since those they were talking to were becoming more experienced (working a minimum of six hours a week) and increasingly better trained and qualified, the quality of the relationship counselling they were receiving was of a high standard.

One casualty of these organisational changes was Relate's mediation service. It was not seen as financially viable. Rather than being formally closed down, it 'withered on the vine', Julia Greer recalled, as counsellors were made redundant. This was 'not good', she added, especially as many solicitors appreciated the service and, indeed, undertook training in this area. The mediation service was 'let slip out under the door' to be continued in south Belfast by Sheena Bell who set up Northern Ireland Family Mediation – an organisation which continues to flourish.[6]

The next step was to secure a reliable flow of income. Instead of seeking funding well into the financial year, the plan was to have agreements in place at the start of each financial year. This was not following a lead given by the national organisation: Relate NI was acting on its own initiative. Gerald Clark set up meetings with the Department of Health and the four area health boards. Here he explained how Relate NI had been revamped and how it could be seen to offer a professional service. The area boards in turn needed the external validation of national accreditation and gave funding to ensure that provision.

Relate had always asked their clients for donations to help cover costs. These were entirely voluntary. The outcome was that those in straitened circumstances would often give generously while some who were comfortably off would feel it quite appropriate to contribute a mere £5 an hour. It was decided to charge a standard rate of £35 an hour but to have bursaries set aside for those who were unemployed or otherwise on benefits. Actually the cost of relationship counselling was around £60 an hour and those asked for £35 an hour had this explained to them.[7]

Bob Jordan recalled that Sir Eric McDowell was exceptionally keen on rattling a collection box on designated appeal days, regarding it as an opportunity to tell passers-by about the work being done by Relate. He would stand at Sprucefield twice a year on a Thursday, a Friday and a Saturday. Sir Eric said to Bob, 'when people come to you, communicate'. Bob Jordan found that those prepared to put coins in the box did not really want to chat, nor did he feel comfortable with this way of addressing strangers – 'Well, that's not me', he said. Collections were phased out. 'This represents the more professional shift', Patricia Donnelly observed. 'We don't have the same box-rattling – though there is always the place for the public to give'. Relate, she felt, could not have the same immediate attraction that some other charities possessed.[8]

Both the Chief Executive and the Board of Trustees were agreed that the management structure was top heavy. Fortunately, this was a time when Northern Ireland's economy appeared to be remarkably buoyant, with a regional unemployment rate actually lower than the UK average. This boom subsequently proved not to be a miracle but a mirage – according to Graham Brownlow, an economist analysing these years, the revival of 1998-2008 was characterised by 'a bloated public sector and a weak R&D', 'excessive reliance on the UK taxpayer for the prosperity of NI', and 'a public sector spending spree', the regional economy overheated further by the spillover effects of the 'Celtic Tiger phenomenon' in the Irish Republic.[9] In the short term, however, it meant that those in management positions in Relate had no difficulty finding rewarding employment elsewhere and soon the organisation's management was reduced, without the need to make anyone redundant, to two: the CEO and his deputy. These decisions made in time did much to ensure financial health – henceforth Relate NI was not in deficit, even after the international implosions of 2008.[10]

Responding to social needs

Relate Northern Ireland for long had a deserved reputation for providing a thoroughly professional service. The new Chief Executive was determined not only to maintain this professionalism but also to ensure that the organisation would rapidly tailor its services to react to changing conditions and respond appropriately to societal need. These services had to take account of changing patterns and trends within families, communities and society as a whole. In 1999, under the heading 'What are the needs?', Relate summarised them in so far as they were relevant to the services it could be expected to provide.[11]

The pattern of Northern Ireland's social need, relatively speaking, was largely as it had been since the 1920s, with a high level of social disadvantage: unemployment rates were persistently higher and more long term than elsewhere in the UK; Northern Ireland had the lowest level of disposable weekly income in the UK; and at the close of the old millennium social security benefits made up 22 per cent of gross weekly household income, compared with a UK average of 14 per cent. A relevant conclusion for Relate was that those 'most in need of counselling support are those who can often least afford to pay for the service'.

Under the heading of 'Marriage', the following facts were noted. The marriage rate was falling in Northern Ireland; people were marrying at an older age; one in four marriages were secular; 'more and more couples co-habiting'; 12 per cent of those who married in 1999 were divorcees; and 'people's expectations of marriage are changing'. Statistics concerned with children included: 28 per cent of births in the region were outside marriage; each year in Northern Ireland around 2,400 children under the age of 16 'are affected by their parents' splitting up'; 17 per cent of children here lived in one-parent families; more than one third of children in Northern Ireland were living in poverty; and at least one in four children suffered some form of abuse.

The impact of relationship breakdown on individuals 'is usually painful and stressful, leading to strong feelings and a sense of loss'. It impacted on the mental, physical and emotional health of those directly and indirectly involved. The social and economic cost of relationship breakdown on society could be seen in terms of:

- Pressure on health and personal social services
- Days lost to industry
- Family and societal instability
- Poverty and financial hardship
- Pressure on the courts
- Policing
- Disaffection

Relate was becoming ever more aware of the prevalence of domestic violence. It featured in 28 per cent of the organisation's counselling casework. Each year there were over 10,000 reported incidents in Northern Ireland. And domestic violence 'tends to increase at the point of separation'. As the new millennium was about to dawn in Northern Ireland there were almost 5,000 legal separations or divorces each year, a 44 per cent increase on ten years earlier. In the region 27 per cent of marriages ended in divorce – divorce being the 'second most stressful life event (after the death of a spouse)'.

Under the heading 'Our response to the needs', Relate outlined its 'full range of services…provided to all sections of the community, irrespective of social class, religion, gender, disability, colour, creed or ethnicity', and which, by this stage, included sexual orientation. Relate's core service was relationship counselling which began with an introductory appointment – a consultation with a counsellor to determine whether individual or couple counselling was appropriate. Some clients found this initial session very helpful and sufficient while others avail of pre-marital or relationship counselling either on their own or with their partner. At this stage clients with a sexual difficulty may be appropriate for referral on to psychosexual therapy if they have a sexual dysfunction. A significant number of clients come to end their relationship and engage in separation or divorce counselling while others come to discuss issues in reconstituted (or step) families. RelateTeen, the service for young people caught in the crossfire of their parents' separation, continued to be offered in Northern Ireland and Relate National. The Marriage and Relationship Counselling Service in Ireland had also now adopted this initiative with support also available to parents and through peer education projects.

Other services, with the aim of 'building better relationships', included: family mediation, to help separating couples to resolve their disputes amicably (though this service would very soon after no longer be offered); and courses for churches, voluntary and statutory organisations, the private and business sectors, and schools and colleges – these included relationship education, counselling skills, personal and emotional development, and ones for pre-marriage and pre-retirement.

As the millennium was drawing to a close Relate NI was undergoing tectonic organisational change. A major drive to bring new blood into the organisation was decided on. Starting out in 1947 as, in practice, an overwhelmingly Protestant body, the Northern Ireland Marriage Guidance Council, well before it became Relate NI, had effortlessly crossed the region's notorious religious divide in recruiting those who delivered its services. However, it had not entirely shaken off the perception that its counsellors were comfortably-off middle class ladies with time on their hands.

The recruitment drive of 1999, 'the biggest ever', Julia Greer recalled, 'was a very deliberate attempt' to provide Relate with a 'more diverse workforce'. Information evenings were held to ensure that this would happen. In the past those selected for training in counselling had been recruited in cohorts of eight. In 1999 sixteen were selected and they included four male counsellors, three counsellors from ethnic minorities, a counsellor from the Lesbian Gay Bisexual and Transgender (LGBT) community and a counsellor who was visually impaired (and who would have her guide dog present in the counselling room). It was important that the counselling workforce attracted and reflected the diversity in the clients then coming to Relate particularly the increasing numbers of clients in same sex relationships and bisexual clients in heterosexual or homosexual relationships. While all counsellors were trained and sensitive to working with diversity in relation to gender, religion, ethnicity, age, ability/disability, culture and sexual orientation, it was appropriate that the ethos of diversity was reinforced and reflected in the counselling workforce.[12]

Meanwhile, those who had been with Relate for many years had acquired an expertise that needed to be shared with those new to counselling. Julia Greer remembered:

It felt like there was an opportunity when you were trained and experienced as a counsellor that there were things you could move on to in Relate. One of them was education; another was psychosexual therapy; and the other was supervision. And then there was mediation. So I trained as a mediator. I trained as a supervisor.

Those who passed on skills, knowledge and the results of their experience served as trainers. To be chosen to be trained as a trainer required rigorous selection since, at that time, this involved travelling to Relate National's headquarters in Rugby. New opportunities were emerging. Organisations, including private businesses, were becoming more familiar with professional counselling and discovering that counselling skills could be used in new areas. Those who had been trained, for example, in couple counselling could also apply their skills, knowledge and experience in fresh fields. There was a growing demand for short courses for those who wanted to learn counselling skills. Improving communication was often a priority, notably for newly-qualified GPs who came to these short courses on a regular basis on their professional development days. The courses covered such topics as listening skills and empathy – 'basic stuff really'. Julia also recalled the provision of courses for social workers on, principally, 'family dynamics and working with couples, not as counsellors but in the context of their work'. She delivered a course for a bank to improve bank officials' ability to ensure good customer relations. Most of this training, however, was 'for professionals involved with families at all sorts of different levels' including family support workers.

Judith Loder had a full-time post as training manager and managed a vibrant dynamic team of trainers. Alongside the external training they provided courses for clients including pre-marriage courses for couples and for separating couples a course entitled, 'Surviving the break-up'. There was a course on life transitions for individuals called 'Taking Charge of Your Life' as well as a pre-retirement course. There were workshops in schools and Further Education Colleges to promote discussion around healthy relationships and this training was often provided by trainers who worked as RelateTeen counsellors and who had a particular interest and expertise in working creatively with young people.

The continuing professional development of counsellors was also important and there was an ongoing programme of training after counsellors completed their basic training. An emerging area of concern was how to work with couples when there was domestic violence and whether to see them separately or jointly. This was challenging work which Relate had always engaged with but there was a lack of clarity about the best way to do this work and a need to develop clear policy and procedures to ensure client safety.

Rita Glover was the couples counselling manager at this time and was determined to get the best possible training in place so counsellors could learn to work proactively to promote safety within intimate relationships. She arranged for Dr Virginia Goldner, Co-Director of the Gender and Violence Project USA to share her considerable expertise on a visit to Relate Northern Ireland. In her model of working couples were initially seen individually and within the context of the relationship, the abused partner was encouraged to take responsibility for his/her safety while the perpetrator was encouraged to take responsibility for his/her abusive behaviours. A two-day training course for all counsellors focusing on domestic violence followed and this included assessment skills at the start of counselling and throughout the process as well as preventative strategies to raise awareness, aid communication, and reduce conflict.

Around the same time Relate was approached by Gerry Heery who had written and delivered a group programme working with male perpetrators of domestic abuse. The course called 'Preventing Violence in Relationships' (PVR) was in use for male perpetrators who had come to the attention of the courts. Relate adopted the course so male perpetrators could self refer before they reached this point. Marjorie Houston, a Relate counsellor and trainer, co-facilitated the course with Gerry Heery and over the next six years a small team continued to deliver this innovative preventative course alongside the enhanced counselling interventions provided by all Relate counsellors.

A striking feature of the services offered by Relate as it approached the new millennium was the development of partnership arrangements. Relate NI was working more closely than ever before with other voluntary and statutory organisations.

A growing range of inter-agency projects provided opportunities for collaborative working and sharing of expertise and resources. Relate NI by now had an impressive line-up of highly-qualified and trained staff and counsellors bristling with a wide range of hard-won accreditations. It was only natural that other organisations turned to 76 Dublin Road to seek the provision of consultancy services such as supervision, training needs analysis, service developments, and training to deal with child protection and domestic violence.[13]

However, 76 Dublin Road was fast becoming incapable of accommodating all the services Relate sought to provide.

Moving to the Glengall Exchange

For many decades the name of a comparatively insignificant thoroughfare near Belfast city centre had been – in public perception – used interchangeably with that of the long unbroken rule of Northern Ireland's main political party. The principal building in Glengall Street had been the power centre of the Ulster Unionist Party: here in the party's headquarters many a fiery speech had been made to galvanise activists and to castigate leaders pursuing policies considered too liberal; here there had often been passionate debates about how best to uphold the Union; and in its smoke-filled rooms cabinet ministers had striven to ensure the unswerving loyalty of independent-minded backbenchers and at election time canvassers were urged to get loyalists to vote early… and sometimes (since nationalists were likely to do the same) to vote often.

Glengall Street's power had been rapidly eroded from 1969 and then taken away completely by direct rule in the spring of 1972. The building remained a unionist party headquarters but its authority had all but gone particularly as supporters of the Union were now giving their backing to a variety of loyalist parties which, to add to the confusion, had a propensity to alter their titles. After the Good Friday Agreement of 1998 the DUP, with no base in Glengall Street, became in time Northern Ireland's largest party. The Ulster Unionist Party moved to premises in an east Belfast suburb and the building in Glengall Street, bereft of care and attention, was devoid of a tenant.

Meanwhile 76 Dublin Road in Belfast was becoming ever more unsuitable as a headquarters for Relate Northern Ireland. Not only was it in close proximity to decaying or neglected untenanted buildings but, due to its own structural defects, it faced spiralling maintenance costs. The premises occupied two Victorian houses, numbers 74 and 76 Dublin Road. Relate was in the process of computerising its appointments system and a large room in number 74 was set aside for the computers. One day Fran Raine, in charge of the computer system and Client Services Manager, approached Gerald Clark. Her opening words were: 'We have a problem'. A gap had appeared between the floor and the skirting – the whole floor had dropped by about two inches. A specialist was called in and he quickly demonstrated that wooden beams had rotted. He immediately condemned the building as being unsafe for public use.

Premises were rented in Adelaide Street principally to house the computerised appointments system and everything else was crammed into 76 Dublin Road. This state of affairs continued for two years and meanwhile Gerald Clark searched for a new home for Relate. He actually looked over the Unionist Party headquarters in Glengall

Street but decided that the building was unsuitable. Then, as part of a redevelopment scheme, that building was demolished and the purchaser of the site, the architect Patrick Coogan, began to prepare plans for a six-floor building, intending to occupy three floors with his own business (the Presbyterian Mutual Society would purchase one other floor). He asked Gerald Clark if Relate might be interested in purchasing some of the planned building. The Relate Board of Trustees decided to buy two floors: the city centre site was considered ideal; the price was reasonable, especially because, as part of a redevelopment scheme, the construction of the property was not liable for VAT; and, as plans had yet to be completed, Relate could specify exactly what the organisation needed to suit its clients, all its services and its staff. These decisions were made during a sustained (and, ultimately, unsustainable) property boom – their major defects notwithstanding, 74 and 76 Dublin Road fetched a very good price.[14]

Relate had to operate in neutral territory and this part of central Belfast could unhesitatingly be described as such. Not only was Glengall Street easily accessible from all parts of the city but it also was right beside Northern Ireland's largest bus terminal. As Glengall Exchange rose up from the ground, the trustees had no doubt but that this was going to be the ideal building in a perfect location.

On 26 May 2005 Nigel Hamilton, Head of the Northern Ireland Civil Service, officially opened Relate's new office. The organisation occupied the third and fourth floors – 5,700 square feet – of the new building, Glengall Exchange, 'conveniently located just behind the Grand Opera House, opposite Translink bus terminus'. In his opening address Nigel Hamilton, after paying tribute to the work of Relate and its staff, said:

I am impressed by the standard and location of these new facilities. The proximity to transport links is indicative of the thought and consideration given to how clients access the services provided. I have no doubt that these new premises are entirely appropriate for the vital role undertaken by Relate and will enable its committed, dedicated and professional staff to continue providing a first class relationship counselling service.

'Not only was Dublin Road becoming increasingly expensive to maintain,' the Chief Executive Gerald Clark said, 'but the facilities there were inadequate to meet the growing demand for our services'. 'As Northern Ireland's main provider of relationship counselling services, we deliver over 9,000 counselling hours per year by highly trained staff throughout the province'. He expressed his gratitude to the Relate trustees for their approval to sell the Dublin Road premises and 'to undertake the risk of borrowing £350,000 to enable us to purchase this superb new office in Glengall Street' and for the financial support from the Department of Health and the Area Health Boards.

Fran Raine, Client Services Manager at Relate, further explained:

This new office represents an investment of £1.2 million and provides a centrally located, modern, well equipped facility for delivering our professional services to clients. I am delighted to be able to offer our clients modern facilities which include a comfortable reception, 11 soundproofed counselling rooms and book shop sales. The office is convenient to public transport and city centre car parking and has special access facilities for the disabled.[15]

David Young of the *News Letter* interviewed Gerald Clark in September 2006, when more than a year had elapsed since he and his staff had moved into the Glengall Street offices. The occasion for the interview was the publication of statistics indicating that the divorce rate in the United Kingdom had started to fall. The Chief Executive said that he was not allowing himself to get complacent – he had seen 'too many Ulster families torn apart to start getting carried away by facts and figures'. 'It's good news', he said of the eight per cent fall in separations, 'but there's always more hard work to do'. He continued:

Hopefully, some of the credit for the reduction belongs to organisations like ourselves. Marriages are lasting a little longer than before – it was 10 years, now it's 11 and a half – but, when you think about it, most of the children affected are still under 10, and separation has a huge impact on them.

Gerald Clark was at pains to emphasise that Relate was involved in much more than marriage guidance counselling. Over the last eighteen years the service, which now employed 43 trained counsellors in seven centres across Northern Ireland, had steadily expanded its remit and now offered support and advice on any relationships, 'regardless of form'. He explained:

Relate was traditionally viewed as purely a marriage guidance service, working with married couples…Now we've moved on from that and are focusing and specialising on relationship issues in a broader sense. Whether a couple are married or cohabiting it doesn't matter, or it could be a gay or lesbian couple who are requiring counselling for their relationship.

It could be an individual, someone who has come through a number of relationships; the relationships have broken down and they want to understand them better. It could even be someone from a work situation having difficulty communicating with a colleague.

This 'broader focus', as he described it, was about to spread even further. Relate counsellors were now undergoing intensive training on the complex skill of counselling an entire family unit. Gerald Clark elaborated:

What we are trying to do is realise that working with the couple is only part of the picture because a couple's problems also have an impact on the children…We are doing the family counselling so that it takes the children into consideration in a separation. What we are trying to do is create a safe environment in which children can grow and develop. And to help create that safe environment we are providing counselling to the parents to try and help the parents stay together and provide a stable environment for the children or, if they have to separate, separate in such a way that the relationship continues in regard to parenting responsibilities – for the sake of the children.

He referred to the fact that with 50 per cent of couples who split, the father loses contact with the children after a very short period of time. Relate was therefore trying to maintain that parental contact with the children 'so that they can grow and develop in a healthier environment'.

Though Relate was a charity its work was partly funded by the government. Although this funding enabled the organisation to provide a comprehensive service, the Chief Executive said that this could also create a 'wrong impression of the work they do'. He explained:

Sometimes people think that if counselling doesn't cost much then they don't have high expectations of what service they'll receive. OK, we are a charity but what we really are is a not-for-profit organisation and our focus is on providing a professional service.

The counsellors are all paid for the work they do, receive training toward accreditation and are professionally supervised every month, some private counsellors wouldn't have that.

Counselling was no longer being viewed as the last and most extreme option. Relate was currently piloting a preventative counselling programme, 'where couples about to set out on a life together come for advice on how to avoid common pitfalls in the future'. This was a programme built upon courses delivered to church groups over many years. Gerald Clark said that more and more people in Northern Ireland were now prepared to give counselling a try before a relationship broke down irretrievably:

People are much more open about it now…They view it as an accepted therapy and realise the benefits in it. We realise it's often a daunting step through the door so our counsellors do a lot of work putting people at ease from the start. We'll do whatever we can to help.[16]

Getting into counselling
Becoming a counsellor in Relate required an extraordinary commitment – a commitment not just of time but also of emotion. Clients almost always displayed high levels of anxiety, particularly during initial interviews. The first task of a relationship counsellor was to put those coming in through the door at their ease. But counsellors, too, experienced anxiety. One of them anonymously wrote a record for the organisation entitled, 'Thoughts of a new counsellor':

The evening before I began my counselling career, I decided, (with a madness that only a very discerning female will understand) to dye my hair. "Pale Ash Blonde" said the box, "Dark Urine Orange" said my mirror! Change of plan, hairdressers before Relate!

Grey skirt, grey jumper, neat white collar. I could have kissed Margaret next day in the office when she said "your outfit is lovely – just right".

The Buzzer! She's here! I'm in! Hello, I'm Karen and that was the start of a fourteen week relationship with Jean and Peter.

Jean and Peter (not their real names) are married with three children. She is 40, he is 41. They live on a farm. Jean is fed up. She doesn't want to "plough and sow or reap and mow". She wants to take up a challenging post at her local university. Peter is not pleased. He is jealous, sexually demanding, occasionally violent and always on Jean's back about her "terrible housekeeping". Jean escapes into reading. She came alone to Relate. Peter came three weeks later.

We had good days and bad. Days when I felt incompetent, days when I felt we'd cracked it! They cried together, I cried with them. Jean wrote a poem for me. Peter bought Jean a dress. Jean began to wear make-up and perfume. The housework was shared. The locked door of communication opened just a little. They left after successfully taking a small step towards each other, they knew how to now. They were still at odds over Jean returning to work. It's a doddle this counselling stuff. Next![17]

Rosemary Dunlop has possibly served longer than anyone else as a counsellor for Relate NI She studied psychology at Queen's University Belfast and later discovered that Professor Seth, the Head of the Psychology Department, was a founder member of the Northern Ireland Marriage Guidance Council. He also taught the author. In the summer of her third year at Queen's she worked in Windsor House, the psychiatric unit attached to the Belfast City Hospital. The encouraging result was a warm endorsement by the staff of her positive interaction with patients. This helped to clarify her future direction towards counselling. Some years later, while living in Jamaica, she trained as a counsellor and worked with the United Church and also with the Government's Family Court, a far seeing enterprise where a number of support organisations, including family counselling were all housed in the same building.

After returning to Northern Ireland she applied and was selected to be a counsellor with the Northern Ireland Marriage Guidance Council in 1982. The fact that training and practice of counselling were carried out at the same time was an attraction. The training was spread over two years and was rigorous and challenging. It involved going to the National Marriage Guidance Training Centre in Rugby six times during the two years. The NIMGC paid for the training and travel expenses.

The system of starting counselling with one client per week, building up to three per week while working with the supervision of a tutor was supportive. In addition there was monthly group supervision. The commitment was considerable, reckoned to average ten hours work per week when note writing was added to counselling time, supervision and relevant reading.

By 1989 Rosemary was one of a small number of trainers working with school groups, Youth Training Programme groups, police, psychiatric nurses in training and other groups, providing courses on Relationships, An Introduction to Counselling, Basic Marital Counselling Skills, Sexuality and Preparation for Marriage.[18]

Julia Greer, who became a schools careers officer after graduating with a degree in psychology at Queen's University Belfast, was attracted to Relate, not at first because she was specifically interested in couple counselling, but because she was aware that this was the organisation which offered the best training in counselling in Northern Ireland. After spending ten years at home raising her children, Julia became involved in Quaker Cottage, a project working with children affected by the Troubles in north and west Belfast. This gave her a strong interest in becoming a properly trained counsellor.

Academic institutions offered counselling courses but without providing the practical experience she felt was so essential. She did a couple of courses at Queen's University but these left her searching for something less overwhelmingly theoretical. The University of Ulster offered a Masters degree in counselling but this, she recalled, provided only 'a purely theoretical experience, no practice was involved'. 'Relate had the only decent training that was practice based', she continued. She was accepted for training in 1986. 'This was really good training, and it was free, and it was done at the weekends'. She admitted that she first became involved with Relate 'at one level for very pragmatic reasons' without being then specifically focused on couple counselling. She was interested in decent professional secular training with no particular religious focus or bias and Relate had the reputation at the time of providing just that. Starting out as an unpaid volunteer doing three hours of counselling a week, and earning money doing other jobs, she gave her services to Relate for the next eighteen years. Julia constantly added to her academic qualifications (including a Masters in psychotherapy), became a paid counsellor and eventually had a full-time post with Relate as a supervisor. In 2004 she moved on to set up her own practice in Bangor but maintained her contacts with Relate and was elected to the Board of Trustees in 2011.[19]

Rosemary Dunlop and Julia Greer had devoted very many years of their lives to relationship counselling – and at the time of writing, continue to do so. But if Relate was to retain its vibrancy and expertise, it had to take care to recruit and retain fresh cohorts of able and well-trained counsellors. Elaine McCormick is one of the youngest counsellors working regularly for Relate. Interviewed in November 2013, she recalled that her initial interest in relationship counselling arose from studying for A Level Psychology at the Northern Regional College in Antrim. Elaine was a civil servant in Northern Ireland for a time and then went to the United States during which, after attending a two-year part-time course in a local college, she obtained a business qualification. When she returned to Northern Ireland, during maternity leave in 2004, she began study for her counselling diploma. She obtained this qualification in 2007 and first used it when employed by Cruse Bereavement Care. The nature of the counselling in that organisation was almost exclusively one-to-one and she was eager to widen her experience and become involved in relationship counselling as well. She then did a post-graduate qualification in relationship counselling at the University of Ulster campus in Jordanstown – a course she greatly enjoyed and was full of praise for one of her lecturers, Mary Jenkins.

For Elaine it was the name, the standing of Relate which made being engaged there an ambition she had long nurtured – 'Relate has a very good reputation and always has done…it fitted into the values I wanted to follow'. When she was employed by Relate she continued to do one-to-one counselling, and still does so when clients come to the organisation alone. However, 'when two people come into the room it completely changes the dynamic: as well as listening to one person's story, you're hearing both sides and there's a thing about maintaining neutrality, more challenging than just the one-to-one'. Her eyes sparkled as she described the nature of the challenges presented, always 'looking at the body language and how they're holding themselves'. In short 'it's quite exciting work because every couple is different'. 'You can come across a lot of anger and resentment', she continued, particularly when issues were raised that had not been talked through before. Sometimes all her skills are required to ensure that the atmosphere in the interview room remains 'nice and calm'.

Elaine McCormick, who generally does between three and six sessions a week, made it clear that this input demands far more than three to six hours of her time. In addition to travel and careful preparation before each meeting with clients, it is vital to follow up every session with a written record.

'Marriage is easy…it's living together that is difficult'

On occasion in its publications Relate NI would quote opinions given by clients on the service provided or, via case studies, illustrate the work done by the organisation. The identity of clients, of course, was not revealed and in this example of relationship counselling the names were changed.

David and Jean had been separated for two months when they came to counselling. Both were in their early thirties and had two teenage children. They had been married since they were teenagers themselves.

The early days of the marriage had easily settled into a pattern where Jean stayed at home looking after the housework, David and the children. David worked long hours to provide for the family. However, over the years, Jean began to feel trapped in a marriage where she felt her own needs were not recognised:

It was hard for her to tell David how she felt and her frustration grew, causing her to be angry with him for no apparent reason. David withdrew from the relationship, working as much overtime as he could manage. Eventually they could not talk, would not make love and the relationship broke down completely.

At first separation was a relief from this constant round of arguing. They discovered how much they missed each other and how much the children missed David. When the anger between them lessened they began to talk.

The couple wanted to resolve their differences but Jean was fearful that 'things would return to normal again'. And David was afraid of the effect another separation would have on the children. They turned to Relate. During the first four weeks of counselling the couple 'looked realistically at what had gone wrong between them'. For the first time, Jean was able to talk about the frustration of caring for everyone else and her own need for support from David as the children grew older and reached adolescence:

David had never seen Jean as vulnerable before, or needing any support for herself. In fact, he had felt quite inadequate by comparison with her, only feeling of use at work where he was well respected for his skill and dedication.

This case study concluded:

Counselling helped them to develop skills so that their frustrations could be nipped in the bud in future.

It is easy to slip back into the old familiar pattern at times. David and Jean are both aware of the conscious effort it will take to change and keep the marriage alive in the future.[20]

Patricia Donnelly, a highly-experienced clinical psychologist who became a Relate NI trustee and subsequently Chair of the organisation, reflected on the organisation's relationship counselling:

Sometimes it's mediation. Sometimes it's unhappiness. They come because they are unhappy...Part of the skill of our workforce is around helping a couple to understand the nature of that unhappiness, whether it is an actual conflict or an unspoken conflict or something unresolved, and help them come to a view of what they want from their relationship. Sometimes it's about not having realistic expectations, or no expectations, or about having a partnership that worked under certain conditions but not now that those conditions have changed.

Those changed conditions might be the appearance of children or of children growing up and moving on. She believed that there were two 'peaks of breakdown'. The first involved 'the young, married in their teens, never had a life, married because it was a way out of whatever/wherever you were at the time and it breaks down within the first seven years, often the first two or three years because it's hastily done'. Such young adults were experiencing rapid development but often in opposing directions.

The second peak involved couples who had been together for twenty to twenty-five years: 'your kids leave and you look at each other, there's nothing left; one or other or both decide that's not enough. You put your relationship on hold while you had all these other responsibilities, but it atrophied while you didn't pay enough attention – it isn't good enough'.

'I do think that most people come to keep their relationship together', Patricia continued. Relate did not strive to keep marriages together 'if that's not what people want'. However, if couples 'are very clear that the relationship is over, then they don't come, they walk away'. Of course separations were very often not mutually agreed. The partner wanting the relationship to survive but having to face the fact that the other did not, often came for counselling. 'So we will work with them and their grief around that and help them understand it and pick up the pieces with their children or whatever'. Others come for counselling, she continued, because the relationship 'is more finely balanced and they may be ambivalent'. Such people may be flirting with the idea of separation but 'I think it's probably still mostly about making the relationship work'. 'And there's the optimism of human beings…there are times in any relationship that, with internal as well as external pressures, you need a bit of a third-party referee or a time out to think through what you want'.

Patricia Donnelly worked in intensive care for fifteen years in the Children's Hospital. 'It would be very sad' because a couple who had been so close during their child's terminal illness, 'couldn't find comfort' after the child's death … 'it's all too painful, it's too sore'. The statistical record for relationship breakup in these cases was 'absolutely massive', that is, around 50 per cent.

Was she of the opinion that a same-sex relationship could provide a stable background for children? 'Absolutely. I think anyone can. It's like any partnership. Single parents can provide a stable background'. And, in the case of a same-sex relationship 'the burden of parenthood is easier if you share and it gives diversity as well'.

Patricia commented on statistics which showed that the number of divorce petitions filed by women had overtaken those filed by men:

I think you are seeing the change in women's role, in society as well…women are not prepared to put up with it, they are taking control, and I think some of the court settlements favour women, frankly, even where the woman is not the custodial parent… In the past there was so much to lose and a fear of what you would lose. I think it's showing that complete flip.

She continued: 'I think it's much more interesting that we've got a lot of couples who are not choosing to marry – this would have scandalised our parents in the past but they are no longer scandalised'. So many 'of our children aren't married and they're living with their partners and nobody bats an eyelid, including our mothers' – mothers who were delighted that their children and grandchildren were in stable relationships. Indeed, 'usually a wedding happens for another kind of reason – people just think, "Och, that would be a nice thing to do", and they don't legally see a difference in the commitment that they make to it'. She felt that, as a result 'the figures from the courts are only part of the picture given'.

Patricia Donnelly had become acutely aware of the great increase in the number of single parents. As in other parts of the United Kingdom, this was not evenly spread. She has a little map of Northern Ireland which shows all the pockets of deprivation – 'if you look at what goes along with those pockets of deprivation, it's teenage pregnancies'. Single parents rose high on the housing lists. These pockets were to be found especially in parts of Craigavon, estates around Brownlow, parts of Antrim and west Belfast.

'When I was a jobbing therapist I would go to estates in Dungannon or outside Craigavon or west Belfast', Patricia would go to a house to see someone to do an observation and 'what you would find was that they were still in their track suit or pyjamas; next door there was also someone known to us'. They were all single women with 'a big support network there'. She found 'kids with different fathers who were also fathers of other children – kids were going to school with half-brothers, half-sisters and cousins in this social network. She and her colleagues were trying to get over the message 'particularly to these younger women' that there were other ways out of 'the trap of deprivation than pregnancy'. Such teenage mothers became the thirty-year-olds 'who are coming back to you depressed but it's fine when your kids are very small but the burden of parenthood, when you haven't had a childhood, is very hard'. Becoming parents when they were still children, they missed out on their independent adulthood and 'spent fifteen years of parenting on top of that'.[21]

'Sex is perfectly natural but not naturally perfect'

Sex therapy at Relate was offered to couples who were experiencing difficulty in the act of lovemaking, or who had lost the desire for sexual contact. Individual clients could also be helped to become more at ease with their sexuality. With an appropriate change in names, this case study demonstrated psychosexual therapy in practice.

Mike and Anne, a young couple in their late twenties, had been married for five years. Although they were an attractive and likeable pair, they were both reserved and shy:

They were typical of many sex therapy cases, in that one partner felt sole responsibility for their inability to make love. Anne blamed herself, because although she wanted to have intercourse with Mike, and he was very gentle and patient, she had to stop him every time as it was so painful. Neither had ever heard of this happening to anyone else. They felt very isolated, until a visit to their GP led to them coming to see a Relate therapist.

It is important for the therapist to treat both clients, as often the "healthy" partner has a problem which only shows up as the treatment progresses. This was the case with Anne and Mike. He had erectile difficulties. Both their problems were worked into the treatment plan, and dealt with as therapy progressed. This helped to equalise the relationship between them.

This couple had apparently been brought up in families where sex was a taboo subject, and it was difficult for them to talk together. Treatment helped them to be comfortable with their own bodies and with each other. They were also given a programme of sex education and information, which helped them to communicate with each other more freely.

There were times when a lot of encouragement was necessary. They felt like giving up, but with persistence they eventually succeeded in making love. When they came back for an appointment three months later, they found it hard to believe that they ever had a problem. Their general relationship has improved, and they are both more confident in themselves and their marriage.[22]

Psychosexual therapy had been provided by the National Marriage Guidance Council in 1973 and brought to Northern Ireland soon after that. As noted in Chapter 3, it was Dr Ethna O'Gorman who was the leading advocate, trainer and provider of this service from the outset. Patricia Donnelly remembered her with particular affection:

I just remember when I was training all those years ago in the eighties there was a doctor called Ethna O'Gorman…a wonderful woman, never docile, a fantastic campaigner, one of life's campaigners…She ran a sexual function clinic in Fitzwilliam Street, just across the street from the City Hospital – it was part of Windsor House… she used to have people on rotation from Relate who were doing their training. That continued for a very long time.

When she described her as 'a fierce woman', Patricia Donnelly was doing so in admiration. Much opposition had to be overcome and it took persistent lobbying to persuade people with authority in Northern Ireland that such a service was required. After she had retired Dr O'Gorman could be certain that she had expertly trained a substantial cohort of practitioners who would carry on her ideals and work for very many years to come. Patricia certainly was convinced that counselling in this area was vital because 'at the heart of a poor relationship – either as a cause and mainly as an effect – there will be a poor sexual relationship'. Rather than having just one or two with specialist knowledge, 'most of our counsellors need to be able to do some of that: you need to be able to take a sexual history because sometimes simple things can make a big difference'.[23]

In 1995 it was reported that the number of appointments for Relate Psychosexual Therapy had declined by 26 per cent from the previous two years. This was attributed in part to the lack of publicity for the service. Previously the service had been advertised in the local newspapers – 'This led to a number of inappropriate calls and enquiries to the service'. Relate therefore 'revamped our publicity material and intend, over the next year, to increase the public awareness of the help that can be provided for sexual problems'. In particular, the plan was to target general practitioners who were often the first to hear about sexual difficulties in a relationship:

The good news is that psychosexual problems can be overcome with the right kind of help. We believe that our four highly trained therapists are the right people to provide this help.[24]

By 2003 Relate was spelling out more specifically what service was being offered: 'Difficulties in having sexual intercourse; failure to achieve orgasm; difficulties in getting or maintaining an erection; premature ejaculation; loss or lack of interest in sexual desire; pain during intercourse'.[25] The number of hours offered in what was simply being described now as 'sex therapy' rose from 395 in 1993-4 to 810 in 2002-3 but dropped back to 386 hours in 2010-11.[26] Counselling case studies continued to appear on occasion in Relate's publications, for example this one on sex therapy in the 2010-11 Annual Report:

A couple in their late twenties had been married for a few years but had recently been experiencing intimacy issues with their sexual relationship; the female client was experiencing painful sex and the male client was becoming annoyed with her and could not appreciate why they would be having this issue. The couple attended our sex therapy to explore these difficulties and after ten sessions were better able to recognise and express each other's needs and understand each other's ideas of intimacy.

Sex therapy was the second most demanded service, though it was dwarfed by the time absorbed by relationship counselling. The total hours offered by Relate NI in 2010-11 came to 9,316 (8,517 for relationship counselling) of which 386 hours were devoted to sex therapy.[27]

Family Counselling
The format of Relate NI's 2000-2001 Annual Report was entirely different from its predecessors. The whole report could be opened out to poster size; on one side there were the usual chairman and chief executive reports, financial statement, staff list and summaries of services offered. On the other, in a large font on a purple background and reinforced by photographic images of distress and comforting embrace, the following information was laid out:

FACTS AND STATISTICS
- There has been a 45% increase in the rate of separation/divorce over the last 10 years
- 1 in 3 marriages end in divorce
- 1 in 2 second marriages end in divorce
- Co-habiting relationships are even less stable
- Domestic violence is increasing alarmingly with 14,520 incidents in N Ireland
- Lone parents head up 21% of families with dependent children
- 28% of children have experienced the divorce/separation of their parents by the age of 16.

HUMAN COST:
- Marital separation/divorce is the second most stressful life event
- Divorced people are more likely to die of heart disease
- Three times as many divorced men as married men drink excessive amounts of alcohol
- Divorcees of both sexes are more likely to smoke than married people
- In GP practice, marital problems are the most common complaint from women
- Cancer survival rates are markedly poorer for divorced men and women
- Divorced men attempt suicide 5 times more often than married men (3 times more often for women)
- 25% per cent of divorced families fall into poverty within 5 years of the marriage ending
- One third of children in NI are living in poverty
- Young people are more likely to become parents at an early age

FINANCIAL COST:
- Relationship breakdown today costs the public purse an estimated £15 billion per year in the UK
- £73 million was spent in Northern Ireland in 1999/00 on children's services – family breakdown is cited as one of the main elements

'Building Better Relationships'
RELATE CAN HELP THROUGH:
- *Relationship Counselling*
- *Counselling for Young People*
- *Psychosexual Therapy*
- *Education and Training*[28]

Relate was finding that, increasingly, clients were coming not as couples but as individuals, a growing number of them teenagers. Relate National had been recognising this developing need for family counselling and had been delivering training in this area. Gerald Clark observed this and became convinced that Relate counsellors in Northern Ireland should be trained to deal with a broad range of clients – not just adults and not just teenagers. Gerald met with the Director of the institute of Family Counselling in England and after consultation with the Board of Trustees a major decision was taken to introduce a new service, Family Counselling to Relate Northern Ireland. Couple counsellors and RelateTeen counsellors were offered new systemic training to enable them to work in the new service which provided counselling for a family as a unit. When the training was completed it resulted in greater flexibility across referrals and a more comprehensive and integrated service for clients.[29]
This is how the service was summarised:

Family counselling is largely preventative work, dealing with life issues before they become serious problems requiring specialist interventions. Every family has arguments at some time. Usually they are easily resolved, but sometimes the problems just get worse and the longer they are left the more difficult it is to make up, creating tension and stress for everyone.

Family members can see a Relate trained family counsellor, individually, or as a small group, or as the whole family.

Outcomes:
- *increased understanding to make choices about how relationships are managed within the family setting*
- *more effective way of anticipating and managing areas of difficulty within the family*
- *improve capacity to communicate both within the couple relationships and across generations and in stepfamilies*
- *access to other forms of help as necessary, in order to improve relationships such as, parenting and family support resources*[30]

The 2010-11 Annual Report included this family counselling case study:

A mother had referred her 13 year old daughter to RelateTeen as the couple had recently separated and their daughter had withdrawn and had problems with her eating and sleeping. The 13 year old girl attended for 8 sessions and explored the impact her parent's separation was having on her and her siblings. Her parents and siblings also attended 2 of the sessions. By the end of the work the young girl's eating and sleeping had improved and she was better able to approach her mother about her concerns.

A total of 325 hours (286 in the previous year) were offered for family counselling and young people's work in 2010-11.[31]

Partnerships

The provision of family counselling by Relate NI's specially trained and accredited staff met a particular need identified by the Department of Health, Social Services and Public Safety and the four area health and social services boards. They had very large numbers of people, from diverse backgrounds with a host of problems, making very great demands on their staff – staff who often did not have the experience or qualifications to provide the support urgently needed. The Department and the area boards found it very much in their interest to assist Relate to fund the training and accreditation of counsellors in family counselling: this meant that there was a cohort of Relate counsellors trained to deal with children, teenagers, individual adults, couples, separated and divorced adults, LGBT couples and individuals, and whole families.

Relate NI now entered into contractual relationships with a kaleidoscope of boards, trusts, government bodies, arms-length bodies, agencies, voluntary organisations, charities, educational institutions and private firms. These partnerships also helped to give the organisation an assured level of financial independence – 60 per cent at least of Relate NI's expenditure did not depend on government grants.[32]

In his Chief Executive's Report for the year 2005-6, Gerald Clark began:

Relationships are part of every day life for all of us. These relationships take on various forms, from the most intimate personal relationships between a couple, to that between parents and children, brothers and sisters, grandparents and grandchildren, friends and colleagues. We are all in relationships of one sort or another and each one of them has the potential to influence our lives for good or ill and the level of impact depends upon the nature and intimacy of the relationships we enjoy.

These had a bearing on our physical and mental health and, 'when it comes to families', on the health and wellbeing and education of the children. The health of relationships impacted to a greater or lesser degree on productivity in the workplace, relationships within the community, the benefits to be gained from education and the state of our health:

It is therefore not an overstatement to say that the work of Relate NI as a specialist, not-for-profit organisation, offering a professional expert service on relationship issues, has the potential to enrich and enhance the wellbeing of our whole society in Northern Ireland.

Relate was constantly seeking to enhance and improve on the range, quality and extent of its services. This was to ensure these services were provided at the highest standards to achieve the best results and to ensure the safety and welfare of the organisation's clients. During 2005-6 a major counselling training programme was implemented. This set out to: increase Relate NI's workforce by 60 per cent; to train the organisation's counsellors in systemic practice; to facilitate the introduction of the new counselling service for families; and to enhance the skills of its counselling workforce on issues such as domestic violence, child protection and sexual issues. As the Chairman, Professor Norman Nevin, reported: 'Our training and life skills programme is being expanded in order to equip individuals and couples with awareness and the essential skills to build rich and lasting relationships that will weather the storms of life and to prevent relationship breakdown with its devastating consequences, particularly on the lives of children'. The organisation placed 'great emphasis on the protection of children and the creation of a safe environment within which children can grow and develop as healthy citizens for the future'. The CEO explained:

Our focus on the protection of children, mental health issues and building better relationships brings us into partnership with other voluntary and charitable organisations within Northern Ireland. We work in partnership with the NI council for the Homeless and the Simon Community in providing training to prevent homelessness and to improve the understanding and appreciation of relationships for those in hostels.

We work in partnership with the NI Prison Service in providing training to encourage better relationships and thus help prevent re-offending and we also work closely with the NI Chest Heart and Stroke Association in providing training for their staff and counselling for victims of strokes etc.

The close working relationship with the Department of Health, health boards and trusts and other charitable organisations, Professor Nevin observed, 'affords us valuable and unique opportunities to offer our specialist services to a wide cross-section of the public'.[33]

Just why an expertise in relationship counselling and an ability to deliver it should be in demand by such a wide range of organisations might not be immediately apparent. Why, for example, would Chest Heart and Stroke need Relate's counselling services? The answer was that when a husband, wife or partner suffered a stroke, statistics revealed that this placed an enormous strain on couple relationships. Expert help was sometimes badly and urgently needed. Both the Northern Ireland Housing Executive and the Simon Community were becoming ever more aware that every family split down the middle doubled the demand for accommodation. Pressure on publicly-owned housing stock and hostel places ensured that it made good business sense to call in Relate NI and avail of its family counselling service.

The determined efforts made by Relate to train and support counsellors working with perpetrators of domestic abuse continued. The twenty-six week Preventing Violent Relationships course described earlier was now well established with male perpetrators voluntarily signing up to the course as well as paying a substantial fee to do so.

Women were invited to attend a separate information evening so they could learn about the course. Many women also chose to attend individual sessions following the ending of an abusive relationship.

For counsellors the over-riding principles that informed the work was a zero tolerance of violence in intimate relationships and equipping both partners to establish healthy relationships into the future.

Relationships also included the relationship between employers and employees. Allied Bakeries engaged Relate's services, for example. If a staff manager became aware that an employee's work was suffering because of relationship difficulties, Relate could provide counselling help discreetly and with guaranteed confidentiality.

Other organisations which entered into partnership arrangements with Relate NI included Nexus NI, Cruse Bereavement Care, Barnardo's, Parents Advice Centre, the Northern Ireland Centre for Trauma and Transformation in Omagh, Christian Guidelines and ACCORD (the Catholic voluntary organisation offering marriage and relationship counselling and marriage preparation programmes). Gerald Clark, realising that so many charities and other voluntary bodies could learn more from each other, created a forum for them, the Regional Voluntary Counselling Organisations. This helped to increase the confidence of the newer and smaller organisations and led to the introduction of informal standards for such bodies in Northern Ireland – standards which facilitated referrals from one organisation to another by enhancing a feeling of trust between them and which gave the government more assurance of service provision quality.

The organisation had, and continues to have, an ongoing programme of professional development training days for all its staff. This means it can respond to emerging issues such as increasing numbers of clients presenting with issues such as the impact of depression on couple relationships or work with adult survivors of child sexual abuse and their partners. Relate NI was being regularly consulted by an expanding number of organisations. One of these was the Northern Ireland Prison Service (NIPS), following a meeting Gerald Clark had with the governor of Maghaberry prison. In the financial year when Gerald retired and handed over to Dave Murphy as CEO, 2010-11, the Annual Review reported:

Relate provides counselling and training in Maghaberry Prison for offenders, dealing with personal, relationship and family issues. This work is delivered in partnership with the Prison Family Welfare Services which evaluates the benefits of the services provided by Relate in the Prison. We also deliver training for offenders prior to release, dealing with their expectations and the realities of returning to society and how to prepare for this. This work with the NIPS has now been delivered over a four year period.[34]

Relate's work with the Probation Board for Northern Ireland 'focused on individual interventions with PBNI clients', assessing their needs in terms of personal issues, relationship issues with parents, children or partners and providing a service to address identified needs. In 2010-11 it was reported: 'There has been a high attendance rate for the counselling services provided and client feedback has been very positive'.

In September 2011 Relate was commissioned by the ACCESS (ARC Child Contact Emotional Support Service) Project based in the Healthy Living Centre in Irvinestown to deliver a counselling service to children (aged 5-16) in Co. Fermanagh 'where emotional wellbeing is being negatively impacted upon as a result of parental/family relationship breakdown'. In the Craigavon Youth Engagement Programme, Intense Mentoring Service for young people, Relate offered face-to-face individual sessions to young people 'who had difficulty fitting into their local communities and who may have had relationship issues with family and others'. These young people were identified by the Community Safety Partnership and referred to Relate. 'Five individuals completed the intense mentoring programme'. Despite the small number involved, this was judged to be 'a very successful piece of work and one we would hope to repeat in the future'.

Relate secured funding via the Northern and Southern Health and Social Care Trusts under the Big Lottery Fund's Impact of Alcohol Programme which aimed to reduce the harm caused to people, families and communities in Northern Ireland directly affected by alcohol misuse. In the NHSCT area Relate became the lead member of a consortium partnership with Ballymena CAB, Causeway CAB and Cookstown CAB to provide family counselling and benefit maximisation and debt advice services to families impacted by alcohol misuse. In the SHSCT area Relate works with health and social care professionals in the statutory and voluntary sectors to deliver family relationship counselling services where alcohol misuse was having a detrimental effect on family life.

Dealing with the fall-out from alcohol misuse became a significant part of Relate's work. During 2011-12 Relate teamed up with Extern and Citizens Advice NI to develop a project focused on providing relationship counselling, youth and family support services, 'benefit maximisation' and debt advice to families and young people 'impacted by alcohol misuse' in the Belfast, South Eastern, Southern and Western Health and Social Care Trust areas. Relate was the lead member of the consortium and the project 'Back on Track' was given development money from the Big Lottery Fund to develop a stage 2 funding proposal during the course of 2012.[35]

While this project did not ultimately receive longer term funding from the Big Lottery Fund in 2013, significant learning was derived from the project partnership and the consortium is continuing to explore alternative sources of funding for 'Back on Track'.

Relate's work with Health and Social Care agencies was usually with couples 'with challenging and complex presenting issues and needs'. The aim was to offer therapeutic engagement in helping to create an environment 'conducive to the developmental needs of children and young people'. The work ranged from communication issues, handling differences, to managing conflict with individuals, couples and families where there were children in need. During 2011-12 Relate developed a new service with the South and East Health and Social Care Trust through the Ards Sector Family Hub.

Schools on occasion called on Relate. This was to provide support to pupils identified by the school as possibly benefitting from counselling in respect of relationship issues. In addition, with the agreement of the school, counselling could include parents or other family members:

This enables the counsellor to address issues such as the parents' relationship with one another and the impact it is having on the child and/or their schooling or other family relationships as identified as appropriate to assist the young person. For over 2 years Relate has worked in schools in the North West providing counselling services to 81 children during this period.[36]

In January 2012, Relate received support from the Public Health Agency to provide relationship counselling services to families affected 'by hidden harm in relation to substance misuse in the Belfast and South Eastern Health and Social Care Trust areas'. Action MS (formerly the Multiple Sclerosis Society Northern Ireland) entered into a partnership with Relate to enable the organisation to provide relationship counselling for MS clients. This disease, of course, could impact on couple and family relationships; Relate provided services to families, couples, individuals and young people who were living with MS and experiencing relationship difficulties.

Towards the end of the 2012/13 financial year, the Belfast Health and Social Care Trust entered into a contractual arrangement with Relate to provide psychosexual counselling services to clients referred by the Trust.

In 2013 following the launch of phase two of Belfast City Council's Youth Engagement Project, Relate secured a tender award to deliver counselling support services to families and young people in four interface areas of Belfast. The project was developed in response to rising levels of community disorder, anti-social behaviour and violence at specific interface areas across Belfast. Relate partnered both statutory and community organisations in delivering a range of support services that have identified both need and gaps in provision. Young people and their families have the opportunity for tailored counselling support from Relate and mentoring and education support is provided by other community partners in the Youth Engagement Project. This programme is supported through the European Union Peace III Belfast Peace and Reconciliation Plan.

Also in 2013 Relate joined a consortium of eight organisations comprised of Action Mental Health, Praxis Care, Aware Defeat Depression, Mindwise, Cause, Cruse Bereavement Care and Nexus NI which successfully secured a tender award for a contract to deliver a range of services under a Big Lottery Fund's tender for the promotion of positive mental health in Northern Ireland. This consortium service has been branded 'Together For You' and is being delivered over a two and a half year period which commenced in the autumn of 2013.

In the autumn of 2013, following a procurement process, Relate also entered into a partnership with the Office of the First and Deputy First Minister (OFMDFM) to provide facilities and counselling support for Victims and Survivors of Historical Institutional Abuse.

Being a chief executive officer could be rather lonely at times. Gerald Clark felt sure that other CEOs with links to the Relate Federation should meet together regularly for the beneficial sharing of experiences. Quarterly 'Five Nations' meetings were arranged involving the CEOs of Relate Wales, Relate England, Relationships Scotland, Marriage Care England, Marriage Care Scotland and ACCORD.[37]

Before he retired in 2011, Gerald Clark had overseen the transformation of Relate NI, an undertaking skilfully and diplomatically continued by his successor, Dave Murphy. Such change would not have been possible without unpaid volunteers, those who made up the Board of Trustees.

Training

Relate NI was now providing its own training for all new counsellors in Northern Ireland. The organisation worked in partnership with several counselling organisations to provide placements to students undertaking a Professional Programme in Couple Counselling at the University of Ulster on the Jordanstown campus from 2009-2011. This course was designed to: develop counsellor skills and knowledge to enable them to work in a variety of different approaches to couple counselling; to learn the pragmatics of the different approaches; and to understand the processes involved in working therapeutically with issues such as abuse, domestic abuse, sexual relationships and separation. It also provided counsellors with an understanding and knowledge of relational issues for individuals and couples who may seek counselling and support.

During 2010-2011 Relate facilitated a number of Training Workshops for other agencies and professionals. In Maghaberry Prison Relate facilitated its 'Developing Healthy Relationships' programme which, in a series of workshops, explored issues such as: communication and self-esteem; conflict and assertiveness; stress and relationships; addiction and relationships; and maintaining healthy relationships. A similar programme was also provided to the Shepherd's View Young Parents' Project in Derry/Londonderry. This programme was adapted specifically to look at the issues impacting on young adults and at their experiences in becoming parents. Relate also responded to a request from the 'Towards Understanding and Healing Project' for training on communication and listening skills for its staff to assist with the project's work in relation to storytelling and the recording of stories.

Relate continued to offer Continuous Professional Development training opportunities to its own staff. In 2010-2011 these included training by Roger Bailey, consultant clinical psychologist, entitled 'Beyond the Name Game' to assist counsellors working with clients diagnosed with mental illness. As the referrals from the Health and Social Care Trusts continued to increase, training was undertaken with Relate's counsellors to reflect on the nature of these referrals and the support or assistance therapeutic relationship counselling could have on the 'presenting situations; whilst also developing the interface and expectations of counselling and statutory agencies'.

Training was also provided to counsellors not only on the impact of domestic violence on relationships but also to heighten their awareness of statutory responsibilities. Some of the new counsellors attended a workshop to develop assessment skills for the initial engagement stage with clients.

Between June 2011 and March 2012 seven counsellors undertook Relate's relationship counselling training to develop further their counselling skills and knowledge. This training consisted of five modules 'looking at the development of practice from working with one client to two, systemic approach, life and relationship stages, psychodynamic working with couples and the theme of sexual intimacy and functioning'. The student counsellors also had to undertake a 75-hour placement, 50 of those hours being with a couple in the counselling room. This was supported with individual formal monthly clinical supervision and attendance at a monthly supervision group.

Other counsellors undertook training to facilitate Relate's 'Safety in Relationship Awareness Raising Service' – a service for those clients who, in their relationships, encountered abusive attitudes and behaviour. The counsellors were trained in 2011-2012 to 'facilitate this educative-therapeutic' nine week programme with clients.[38]

Being a Trustee

Relate Northern Ireland in the new millennium was offering the public a thoroughly professional service, a service which was also regularly drawn upon by voluntary organisations, government agencies and arms-length bodies, charities, churches, schools and colleges. This required a fully-qualified paid staff: in 2010-11 the organisation had 26 employees (4 Senior Management Team, 2 Finance Team, 2 Administration Team, 9 Belfast Reception Team, and 9 Local Centre Reception Staff), 29 counsellors and 6 supervisors. And yet the organisation, despite its dependence on funding from public bodies, was a charity governed by a Board of Trustees. In short, the input of unpaid volunteers was still pivotal.

From the outset the Northern Ireland Marriage Guidance Council had attracted to it leading members of society and this did much to raise the organisation's profile and to ensure helpful publicity in the press and the broadcast media. Senior Protestant clergy were well to the fore in the early years. The Rev Dr Hedley Plunkett was Vice President of Relate NI during much of the 1990s and, while two past chief executives were ordained ministers, the organisation had long ceased to be regarded as a body run by members of just one side of the community.

Undoubtedly the great majority of those who came forward to give their time and expertise to Relate without financial reward were motivated by a conviction that society in Northern Ireland badly needed the services offered. They felt that their training and experience could be of value. Considerable dedication was certainly required by those who agreed to act as Honorary Treasurer. For example, David Clements, a chartered accountant who had retired from a senior position in the civil service, in the 1990s agreed to act as the first Honorary Treasurer of the Integrated Education Fund but then also in the same position for Relate NI. In addition, he served on the Board of Trustees in the new millennium.

Those with business and financial experience brought much-valued skills to

Relate, as well as raising the organisation's profile if they were at the apex of Northern Ireland society. One such was Sir Eric McDowell, a chartered accountant who held an impressive clutch of company directorships and became Chairman of Capita Management Consultants. As well as first joining the executive committee of Relate in 1981, he was a trustee of the Presbyterian Church in Ireland, a member of the Senate of Queen's University and a member of the Advisory Committee, Northern Ireland Investment Fund for Charities. Appointed Chairman of Relate in 1997, he was at the helm when the organisation became a charitable company limited by guarantee (exempted from using the word 'limited' in its name) and the executive committee became a Board of Trustees. Derick Woods recalled:

Joan Wilson and I were the first two trustees: we signed the document and others were invited by us to become trustees. I must say I felt once we became a company limited by guarantee we were more isolated from the counsellors and the people who did the work because they were no longer permitted to be on the executive. And, while the attempt was made to bring us together by inviting particular ones to come and talk about what they were doing, it's not the same thing as having two or three of them sitting together throughout the meeting adding their four-penny-worth on all sorts of topics.

When asked in 2006 whether or not he would recommend changes in Relate, Derick responded: 'No, other than getting executive people to know the counsellors'. Like others interviewed for this book, he had an enormous respect for Bruce Stewart, the founder of RelateTeen – 'he was a very, very fine fellow, he inspired people'. Derick Woods chaired the Family Mediation Service for several years. It started as 'a separate entity', funded by the Department of Health and Social Services for three years, and so a separate committee was set up – 'I was packed off to go to mediation'. The government was keen to refer people with difficulties to an organisation with trained and experienced counsellors. He had a high opinion of two Board of Trustees chairs who had considerable expertise in this area, John McKee and Jill Downing. 'I was going off the executive when Gerald was appointed' but Gerald Clark, the new CEO, whose children had been taught by Derick, successfully made this appeal: 'Don't desert me'. He delayed his departure once more to lend a hand when Relate had to get out of its Dublin Road premises.[39]

Bob Jordan took over as Chairman from Sir Eric while he was still Chairman of the governing body of the Belfast Institute for Further and Higher Education (he had overseen the amalgamation of the three further education colleges in the city). With his impressive CV as a business manager, in the Chamber of Commerce and as a person who served on public bodies, his experience was much appreciated by Gerald Clark. Chairman and CEO set about planning the root-and-branch changes needed to turn Relate NI around. Bob Jordan greatly admired Judge John McKee QC who took over the chair after him. John McKee had great expertise and experience in family law and on the family bench and it was during his tenure that the new contracts for counsellors (requiring a minimum of six hours a week and accreditation) were introduced.

Gerald Clark, preparing and putting through major structural changes in the organisation, clearly had the solid backing of his trustees. Eric McDowell, Bob Jordan and David Clements continued for many years more as trustees, and were joined by Derick Woods (associated longer than anyone else as an executive committee member) and – amongst many others – Patricia Donnelly (a clinical psychologist and a senior manager in the Belfast Health Trust), Jill Downing (a well-known solicitor specialising in family law) and Dr Alan Elliott (a retired senior civil servant).

Bob Jordan recalled that the trustees worked together very harmoniously – 'there was never any friction or flak'. Such unity of purpose was vital during a period of major change. For some trustees, Christian commitment was clearly an important factor in their decision to give so much of their time to Relate without financial reward. Both Bob Jordan and Derick Woods when interviewed were at pains to inform the author of the strength of their religious belief. Both men unhesitatingly felt they should strive 'to keep marriages together', but they had no difficulty in accepting other kinds of live-in relationships and the changing attitudes to relationships. Two previous chief executives, Roy Simpson and John Chambers, were ordained ministers and Gerald Clark was and remains a very active member of the Church of Ireland. Gerald Clark held strong Christian beliefs but no doubt he was aware that counsellors did not necessarily share them. Gerald Clark worked closely with ACCORD and collaborated with that organisation in partnership work. Patricia Donnelly thought that ACCORD was 'very helpful for those who wish to work within that belief system' and on Relate NI she observed: 'We have good evidence that we have a more universal and secular appeal…although very clearly the origins were very specifically Protestant'.[40]

Relate Northern Ireland was just one piece of an interlocking system of care even well before the onset of the new millennium. The Northern Ireland Marriage Guidance Council had subsisted on government and local authority grants, donations from clients in particular, grants from trusts, and money gathered in from collections, coffee mornings and the like. As the old millennium was drawing to a close it was more and more obvious that Relate NI was becoming a very different kind of organisation.

Led by Gerald Clark, the organisation established partnerships which not only helped to eliminate crisis management and reduce direct dependence on the public purse but also spread its expertise widely throughout the public and voluntary sector. Of course, Relate NI in turn benefited from the knowledge and experience of those in the organisations which had become partners. It made good sense, therefore, that representatives of those bodies should be encouraged to become involved in Relate as trustees.

The longest serving trustee was Dr Alan Elliott. He had left 'Inst' (Royal Belfast Academical Institution) in 1955 to study classics at Trinity College Dublin. Graduating with a good degree, he could have gone on to Cambridge to study for a PhD but instead he applied for the Northern Ireland civil service. Duly appointed, he began his career in the Ministry of Health and Local Government. There he stayed in the same ministry (which became the Department of Health and Social Services) for a total of thirty-seven years. 'Looking back, I would have liked more variation', he said later but it goes without saying that over this period Alan Elliott built up an unrivalled expertise in this area and an acquaintance with a great many people involved in this sector.

Alan's networking ensured that he had regular contact with all the main charities and voluntary organisations that made up the third sector. He became acquainted with nearly all the directors of these bodies and remembered with particular affection Dr Gerard Newe, 'the famous G B Newe', regional organiser and secretary to the Northern Ireland Council of Social Service since 1948. 'A very wise, interesting guy', Newe was to be the only Catholic in fifty-one years ever to serve in a Northern Ireland government: he was Minister of State in the Prime Minister's office, with a responsibility for promoting better community relations, in 1971-72. Relate was one of the organisations in regular contact with the health and social services department and this is how Alan came to know John Chambers.

In 1997 Relate NI prepared to celebrate its fiftieth anniversary. Alan was about to retire and was approached by John Chambers who persuaded him to become involved in Relate. At the same time his wife Olive Elliott agreed to join the committee formed to plan the fiftieth anniversary celebratory events and (while protesting 'I'm not a fund-raiser') became deeply involved. Alan Elliott began his long direct association with the organisation by agreeing to become President of Relate NI in 1997-98. Thereafter he became a trustee and remained on the board to the time of writing.

When still a young civil servant Alan Elliott had been involved in setting up training in areas which would be of direct interest to Relate. Eileen Younghusband (only daughter of Francis Younghusband, the famous explorer, mystic and leader of the British Tibet campaign of 1903-4) had in her Carnegie reports of 1947 and 1950 advocated 'generic' training – a set of core knowledge common to all social workers. She pioneered the teaching of a generic course that was to become the prototype of professional social work training in other universities. In 1955 she chaired a Ministry of Health working party on the provision of training for social workers. The outcome, the Younghusband Report established a Council for training in social work and a social work certificate. The Stormont government eventually concluded that this report should be applied in Northern Ireland. Eileen Younghusband was invited over to speak about her report at a conference in the Slieve Donard Hotel in Newcastle, Co. Down. She arrived wearing her hiking boots and declared: 'I hear this is great walking country – let's walk!' The party obediently followed her down the beach at a brisk pace. When the conference ended it was agreed to set up a social work course as recommended in her report. Alan Elliott had this responsibility. John Benn, the permanent secretary in the department of Education, recommended the newly-opened Rupert Stanley College of further education in east Belfast. And here began the first social work course following the Younghusband recommended approach. 'If truth be told it was at a rather low level', Alan Elliott recalled and later it was upgraded and transferred to the Ulster Polytechnic, later the University of Ulster.

Both during his time in the civil service and after his retirement Alan Elliott served on a large number of governing bodies – 'they vary quite a lot in my experience'. More than in most similar organisations, the trustees in Relate got involved in the day-to-day activities of the organisation, 'they got in the way of being really quite involved in the nitty gritty'. This, he felt, made the job of being a trustee much more interesting. When everything was going smoothly it was a matter of reading and approving papers submitted by the CEO to the board, then 'come a change, come a crisis…the Board of Trustees is the ultimate authority, in the driving seat' and this becomes particularly important when, for example Gerald Clark retired in 2011, a new CEO had to be appointed. In that case, the Chair, Jill Downing, went to a recruitment firm, Forde May, to draw up the criteria and the advertisement.

Alan Elliott, as the longest serving trustee, was in good position to comment on Relate NI's relationship with the national body (which in its literature simple described itself as 'Relate' or 'Relate: the relationship people'). Contact with the national organisation was maintained 'but increasingly at arms length'. Relate NI was a separate body with its own charitable status but also a paid-up member of the Relate Federation. Alan Elliott preferred to use the word 'affiliate' rather than 'member' – that distancing arose because 'Relate National would embark on some great new initiative which we didn't think fitted in with Northern Ireland's needs'. 'There were one or two stand-offs', he recalled. The national body's CEO and President crossed the Irish Sea 'set on making Northern Ireland toe the line, and we were saying, "Hold on a minute, this is a separate organisation" – we had to go and fend off takeovers from the national organisation'. Of course the national body ultimately authorises the use of the word 'Relate'. The distancing was to some extent caused by the expense of sending counsellors to Rugby for training. Increasingly, training and accreditation were provided by the University of Ulster and by Dublin City University, which greatly facilitated the provision of home-based placements.[41]

Relate NI 'broadened its perspective to reflect societal changes'

From its inception the Northern Ireland Marriage Guidance Council had included an exceptionally high proportion of women on its management committees. Admittedly, such women were usually from comfortable backgrounds, married to professional men, with time to give to voluntary organisations (unlike female teachers and other women in full-time employment) as their children approached adulthood. In the new millennium, however, the organisation saw the need to attract to its governing body representatives of trusts, agencies and other organisations with whom it was forging lasting partnerships. Some of these were captains of industry, mostly male, and also a number were professional and business women.

Patricia Donnelly joined Relate as a trustee in 2002. She for a time headed up the psychology department in the Royal Victoria Hospital and this, inevitably, meant that she often found herself working closely with Relate. Bruce Stewart had been a colleague and he went on to work for Relate where he pioneered the service for young people, RelateTeen. Patricia greatly admired him and what he was doing and, like so many others, was devastated by news of his death in 1993 – 'When I was approached to do anything for Relate, I always said "yes" because of Bruce'.

When Patricia joined Relate she undoubtedly brought valuable skills and experience to the organisation. She was then Director of Clinical Services in the Belfast Health & Social Care Trust, covering 'all of the services dealing with intensive care, theatres, sterile services, laboratories, microbiology, biochemistry, all imaging services, all pharmacy, dietetics, speech and language therapy, autopsy service, psychology'. She recalled that as a consultant clinical psychologist she already had 'a lot of input to Relate' through making referrals in particular. 'Because I came from the mental health sector, I had been involved in a lot of marital work, a lot of family work', she recalled. 'I was one of the few clinical people...other people had come from a business background, financial services and the legal profession'. This meant that, as a member of Relate's governing body, she could ask the professionals searching questions about their practice and be alert for fresh issues 'only starting to bubble up' in the national organisation. Business executives were not the only ones who could advise on how best to run Relate. Patricia Donnelly not only had an 'interest in good governance' but also was required in her own job to ensure 'that it happened'. 'I've balanced the books', she said and added that she was able to bring to Relate, concerning staff, the ability to deal with 'a few disciplinary and grievance matters – something I had to do in my own Trust'. And, indeed Relate NI, like almost all similar organisations, did have staff who on occasion invoked the grievance procedure. Grievance arose from a change of contract for counsellors over a two-year period which 'moved it on to a more professional footing which we were required to do anyway...Some people were not happy about that'. As Vice-Chairman of Relate NI 'I was dealing with hurt feelings' and it was imperative that she should 'try to find some resolution to it'.

Patricia Donnelly, asked to what extent Relate NI had changed in her time associated with the organisation, observed that 'I think it broadened its perspective to reflect societal changes'. After all, there were now much more common law partnerships, 'it's much more open'. She felt that work done by Relate 'around families has a much more systemic approach so it is not just focussing on the couple but on a wider working on individuals, working on relationship issues, rather than just partnership issues'. She believed that the development of some of the consultation and training services 'have really added enormous value and, more recently, the training and provision of services around domestic violence'. This required careful planning and risk assessment.

She spoke about the difficulties of becoming involved 'in a relationship where there's one or both partners behaving violently or aggressively or even abusively whether it is verbal or physical'. She continued:

It doesn't always feel safe because if it continues you're either condoning it or you failed to protect someone. You carry risk with it. A lot of professionals – never mind the non-statutory sector – wouldn't feel comfortable with doing it.

In such cases setting up the contract must be done with care and the organisation must ensure that there is always a third party to act as a kind of regulator.

Since her first contacts with Relate, Patricia Donnelly found that the organisation had become ever more professional. She thought that the services provided by Relate 'rival the statutory professional services in terms of training people and the provision they have'. 'It is not a volunteer service', she emphasised. It was not a case of, 'Oh, I'd like to work in marital relationships and do a bit of training and give people a few hours'. The demands made on those who are accepted for relationship counselling are very considerable – 'it's a tough act, not everyone can do it'. 'It's not a judgemental service now', she observed. In the Northern Ireland Marriage Guidance Council during the early years 'a lot more judgements were made about a relationship, about what people's roles were, about what was right and what was wrong'. She continued:

You work within whatever people are trying to achieve within the relationship, if it is a parting rather than a reconciliation, or whether it is conciliation to allow access. There are not the same judgements around that. I think the professionalism brings that detachment. So we are not bringing ourselves…

You can't always do what you've always done. You must always refresh yourself from a theoretical base. You must always look at "Where to next?" and be already training people in the "Where to next?" and diversify the product…I think if you are not continually evaluating and investing in training and development and looking ahead, then you do get out of touch and you wonder how you are not having the same impact or credibility.[42]

In 2011-12 Relate NI launched a public advertising campaign to recruit new board members. It elicited an exceptionally strong response and, as the Chair Jill Downing reported, 'we recruited a cohort of new Trustee Board members from a range of backgrounds and highly skilled in their respective fields of work'. It was particularly appropriate that two of those chosen as trustees, Julia Greer and Rosemary Dunlop, brought to the board the experience of having served as Relate counsellors for very many years .[43]

Planning for the future 'in these stringent economic times'

Relate Northern Ireland, a dozen years into the new millennium, was still recognisable as the organisation which had developed from the Northern Ireland Marriage Guidance Council founded sixty-five years before. In 2012, as in 1947, the organisation existed because it was 'all too aware of the impact that relationship difficulties, separation and divorce have on the health and wellbeing of the individuals involved and particularly upon children who suffer physically, mentally and emotionally as a direct result of the breakdown of their parents' relationships'. Present-day Relate, however, had broadened its reach to a degree which would have been incomprehensible to those who had first met in the Lord Mayor's parlour in Belfast in 1947. In particular it was enmeshed in the kaleidoscope of bodies which operated to ensure a civilised, humane and caring society:

Relate works with a range of statutory and voluntary organisations in a range of environments as part of a multi-disciplinary approach to contribute to the emotional health and wellbeing of families, children, young people and individuals where relationship issues and breakdown, alcohol and substance abuse, interaction with the criminal justice system and mental ill-health issues are presenting factors.

The organisation's services were now contributing significantly to the five Health Trusts' core business of keeping children safe.[44]

When Gerald Clark retired in 2011, Dave Murphy took over as Chief Executive. Commenting that in his first year in the post he had 'been struck by the quality and commitment of our Staff and Trustees to providing the best possible service to our clients', he outlined the latest additions to the services offered by Relate during 2011-12. Relate was 'working more closely than ever before with other organisations and exploring innovative and different ways to meet clients' needs'.

The year 2011-2012 marked another year of growth for Relate NI and Jill Downing, Chair of the Board of Trustees, in her message in the Annual Review of that year said that 'despite the general economic conditions, reductions in public spending, uncertainty over the future of the health and social care sector and external challenges faced by the voluntary and community sector in Northern Ireland'. She continued:

The past year has seen continued improvement in our ability to demonstrate the effectiveness of our work. This remains a high priority in these stringent economic times and is clearly contributing to our capacity to win new work from a range of statutory and voluntary agencies, which we are succeeding in doing.[45]

The statistics for that financial year showed that the organisation increased the number of appointments by approximately 10 per cent, from 9,316 in 2010-11 to 10,259 in 2011-12. Relate was able to extend its service delivery and opened an additional centre in Ballymena. This raised the number of local centres to nine, the others being Coleraine, Foyle, Cookstown, Irvinestown, Portadown, Downpatrick, Newry and Belfast. Of the 1,457 newly registered cases in that year 74 per cent were married, 12 per cent co-habiting, 8 per cent separated and 3 per cent civil partnerships. The remaining cases were widowed, divorced or not in a relationship. Seventy five per cent of clients were self-referred. The remaining 25 per cent were referred by Health and Social Care Trusts and other agencies Relate worked in partnership with: Probation Board NI; NI Prison Service; MS Society Northern Ireland; Public Health Agency; Church of Ireland; schools; and ACCESS.

Relate was able to keep a £35 per hour payment level in spite of financial pressures and, of course, clients could still request a reduced payment if their circumstances required it. Former Chairman, Derick Woods, had said in 2006 that he always insisted that those who did not contribute should not be penalised or turned away – 'if ever it got to the stage that people were turned away I would resign immediately'.[46] The organisation's original bespoke computerised appointments system was upgraded – not only was it time-saving but it also enabled the insertion of additional client data and means to produce presenting issues and outcome reports on the work Relate was delivering in the counselling room.

Relate NI's Strategic Plan for 2012-2015, launched by John Compton, Chief Executive of the Health and Social Care Board, followed an extensive consultative exercise with all the organisation's stakeholders. It focused on the pursuit of key strategic aims derived from Relate's Vision – 'a future in which healthy relationships form the heart of a thriving society' – and its Mission – 'to enhance emotional wellbeing in individuals, couples, families and communities by delivering counselling and therapeutic services'. The plan identified the key areas where Relate intended to focus its resources.

Consulting 'key stakeholders' included meetings with staff, counsellors and clinical supervisors, Trustee Board members, and an 'organisational wide consultation event' held in January 2012. Client evaluation feedback was incorporated into the planning process and key funders, government officials, health and social care professionals and partner agencies were surveyed in December 2011. Relate's 'operational context' had to be assessed. Naturally, the 'general economic downturn presents significant challenges'. However, it was concluded that Relate's delivery of a range of therapeutic interventions to children, young people and families could 'provide positive outcomes with longer term cost savings for Health and Social Care Trusts and improved outcomes in education, social care and youth justice systems'. The organisation welcomed the government's Strategy for the Development of Psychology Services (2010) which aimed to deliver interventions and services that were 'clinically effective, safe, cost effective, comprehensive, co-ordinated, user friendly and commissioned and delivered to a standard consistent with national and regionally agreed standards and guidelines'.

The operational context included the Northern Ireland Assembly's Programme for Government, the Review of Public Administration, the Comprehensive Spending Review (which 'will impact adversely on public spending') and – on an upbeat note – the Northern Ireland Executive's 'two new funding streams', the Social Investment Fund and the Social Protection Fund.

Challenges and opportunities required an examination of the latest statistical returns. Although the marriage rate had declined since a peak in the 1970s and divorce rates had been fluctuating in recent years, 'marriage and relationship breakdown is still very common'. In 2010, just over 4,500 children or stepchildren were affected by divorce; 2,700 children or stepchildren were aged under 18 at the time of the divorce and 1,800 children or stepchildren were aged 18 and over at the time of the divorce. A third of all children were born to unmarried parents in Northern Ireland in 2010. Eighteen per cent of the region's population was aged 60 or over in 2005; that figure was expected to rise to 22 per cent by 2015. Thirty-five per cent of Northern Ireland's population was under the age of 25. The conclusion here was that Relate's services would have to adapt to demographic changes 'by innovation and partnership working' and the propensity of younger people 'to utilise new technology to access services and conduct their business effectively challenges Relate to ensure that we are able to market and deliver our services in ways that are appropriate to younger people'.

Another factor to be taken into account was the presence of minority ethnic communities which were making 'a substantial contribution to Northern Ireland's economy, but continue to experience racial discrimination and employment related problems which impact on the emotional health and wellbeing of these communities'. Also levels of poverty 'are anticipated to rise' which 'has impacts on family stability, children's educational attainment, individual emotional and physical health and wellbeing'. This would result in an increasing number of people seeking help from Relate and 'require us to consider funding options for those who cannot pay for our services'. Relate needed to comply with the Charities Act and the Data Protection Act, and auditing, monitoring, inspection and regulation by statutory organisations would require 'a continuous focus on Relate's governance, operational and risk management arrangements'.

The Strategic Plan then set out six 'high level strategic aims':

1. Service Delivery: to continue to deliver excellent services to our clients
2. Service Development: to develop services which enhance the emotional wellbeing of individuals, couples, families and communities
3. Resources: to support and develop Relate's systems and resources
4. Governance: to ensure that Relate develops governance and structures in line with legal requirements and good practice
5. Partnerships: to develop partnerships which are strategically and mutually beneficial for Relate's clients
6. Profile: to develop Relate's public profile

These were supported by fifteen 'key strategic objectives'. For example, two of three objectives under the heading of Service Delivery were to:

Undertake a feasibility study on appropriate accreditation frameworks relevant to Relate and achieve the identified accreditation framework(s).

Support and ensure staff are appropriately accredited and have access to relevant training and development opportunities to enable them to deliver a professional benchmarked service.

The plan concluded with assurances that Relate would continue to deliver Value for Money services 'by being effective, economic and efficient in deploying its resources', that it would 'align its service provision with Regional and Local Health Commissioning Plans', that it would 'focus on meeting relevant objectives of central government policy and strategic objectives' and 'support its own plan by annual operational plans presented in a balanced scorecard which will set...targets against which Relate's Trustee Board will monitor progress on a quarterly basis'.[47]

'feeling stronger, more focused and excited about the future'

A total of 393 clients completed self-assessment evaluation forms at the end of counselling in the year 2011-2012. More than one answer could be given to the question, 'Why did you initially contact Relate?': 71 per cent 'to help communication'; 64 per cent 'to preserve relationship'; 57 per cent 'to understand partner better'; 47 per cent 'to understand self better'; 48 per cent 'to find ways of coping'; 43 per cent 'to be offered advice'; 36 per cent 'to understand relationships'; and 11 per cent 'to obtain help with separation'. 71 per cent wished they had come to Relate sooner. Asked, 'has your overall wellbeing improved after counselling at Relate?' 84 per cent responded 'emotional', 62 per cent 'mental', 25 per cent 'physical' and 6 per cent 'other'. Five per cent decided that they would not recommend Relate to others, leaving 95 per cent who would recommend it. As for the counselling provided, 52 per cent described it as 'excellent', 42 per cent as 'good' and 6 per cent as 'fair'.[48]

Positive comments included the following:

I started Relate at a very difficult time in my life. I found my counsellor to be kind, caring and supportive. I feel like she really cared. I am thankful to my counsellor and to Relate for helping me reach a better place in my life.

I just want to personally thank my counsellor for all his work with me. I am leaving counselling feeling stronger, more focused and excited about the future – something I haven't been able to say for a very long time. A very heartfelt thank you.

I was unsure at first but after my first meeting I understood the process and the benefits of Relate. I am now in a better place and would like to thank all those involved.

Sessions have helped me cope with an intensely difficult situation by maintaining a consistent focus weekly which I knew was allowing me to voice my anxieties and fears.[49]

A week before Christmas 2012 the *Irish News* included a supplement entitled *Family and Parenting*. The leading feature was the outcome of an interview with the distinguished Professor of Organisational Psychology and Health, Professor Cary Cooper, author of over a hundred books (a great many of them on the subject of stress) and President of Relate National. The article began: 'Christmas is a time for families to reconnect and come together, but…If you're divorced and share custody of the children, or have a step-family and two sets of in-laws, navigating the arrangements for the festive celebrations can pose an emotional minefield'. 'Having wed twice himself,' it continued, 'with two children from each marriage, Prof Cooper has first-hand experience of tackling complicated family arrangements – but he is confident that steps can be taken to keep stress to a minimum'. He told the *Irish News* reporter:

A characteristic of the modern family – traditional or otherwise – is they lead a very diverse life and only come together for a longish period of time over Christmas and family holidays. At Christmas, you're having to reintegrate with, say, your teenage kids, who during a normal week you're just doing tactical behaviour with: "Who's picking you up?", "Did you do your homework?", "You're not listening very much;

you're not talking very much". Now, you're dumped in a box for 10 days, and that process of reintegrating is stressful because you're having to tolerate everybody else, whereas before you could just do your own thing.

For step-families, still in the early phase, adjusting to the new dynamics could take time, 'and members may barely know each other, let alone like each other'. The Professor recommended 'steps you can take to keep festive feuds low and festive fun high, and planning ahead is a good place to start.' If this planning involved interacting with an ex-partner 'with whom you're not on the best of terms', he was adamant in advising that calling was safer than texting or emailing – 'In an email, you just make one mistake and use a particular word and you could get into real trouble'. He also suggested enlisting the aid of grandparents.

Professor Cooper continued at some length, giving advice: 'ask the kids to set the table, and mothers-in-law to chop the vegetables'; get everyone involved in family games; the whole family should agree on a maximum price per present to prevent difficult discrepancies; and be supportive if 'your step children want to phone other relatives at various points during the day'.

Relate, indeed, was given extensive coverage in that issue of the *Irish News*. Dave Murphy, the Chief Executive of Relate NI, was also asked for his advice. 'We hear stories of how parents put their conflicts to one side and get together just for Christmas Day so that the children can open their presents and be "a family" for a short time', he began but quickly added that the reality was that for a lot of parents the pretence of being a family 'just for Christmas' was too much to ask. 'Wounds can be deep and the painful re-enactment of what was or what might have been is often simply avoided'. Dave Murphy continued:

- Think of the children first – Taking it in turns is often a reasonable arrangement. However, children might have their own preferences. For example, they may always want to have Christmas in one place and celebrate Christmas on another day in their other parent's home. Try talking to them to get a feel for what they want and don't put all the pressure on them to choose…
- Consider any travel arrangements and have some alternatives up your sleeve…Involve the children where possible and do listen to their worries and concerns…
- Presents – if the children are old enough to make a Christmas wish list it's ideal to share this with the non-resident parent. Try not to compete for who buys the best present – it is so hard to keep this up and children usually see right through it. Avoid promises that can't be kept…

The newspaper asked several Relate clients to say how they had developed new Christmas traditions to accommodate two Christmas celebrations. One explained:

I have always wanted my son to spend Christmas with my new wife and our children but his mother says he never wants to leave her at Christmas…I have tried hard to change this but now I realise that neither of us have a claim on him just because it's Christmas.[50]

The fact that this Christmas supplement, 'Family and Planning', gave Dave Murphy and Cary Cooper a central role in providing advice – in a newspaper which until recently had rarely referred to Relate's activities – demonstrated how thoroughly embedded the organisation had become in Northern Ireland society.

Anniversary Conference – 'The opportunity not only to look back but also more importantly to look forward'

November 2012 marked the 65th anniversary of Relate Northern Ireland, an anniversary celebrated by holding a clinical conference in Antrim, chaired by Lynda Bryans formerly of UTV, entitled 'Relationships and Families – Hope for the Future'. The conference was addressed by the Minister for Health, Social Services and Public Safety, Edwin Poots, MLA and Jill Downing, the Chair of the Board of Trustees, opened the conference, saying:

While reaching the age of 65 used to mark retirement age and receipt of the State Retirement pension, as we know now, retirement age is being extended all the time!! In fact the appropriate gift for a 65th anniversary is a blue sapphire which I am told is five times harder than glass and is therefore very durable and resilient, characteristics which I am sure you will agree are appropriate to Relate's longevity in Northern Ireland!

She continued by observing that, while Relate may be resilient, 'developing our clients' resilience has been a key feature of our counselling services for the past sixty-five years. Our 65th anniversary provides us with the opportunity not only to look back but also more importantly to look forward'. While the organisation was set up initially to address relationship and marriage issues in a post-war environment, it thereafter reflected 'tumultuous societal changes'. Its counselling services had to evolve, develop and diversify to:

reflect increasing rates of breakdown of couple and family relationships, increasing divorce rates, the development of blended families, sexual and intimacy issues, the impact of domestic abuse, services for children and young people, the impact of addiction issues on families, those interacting with the health and social care and criminal justice systems and more recently the impact of the current economic difficulties on relationships.

In preparation for the future, as we have seen, Relate recruited a cohort of new Trustee Board members from a wide range of backgrounds and highly skilled in their respective fields of work. This, it was felt, strengthened the organisation's governance arrangements. At the same time – after an extensive consultation exercise with both internal and external stakeholders – Relate launched its three-year Strategic Plan. This aimed to build on the organisation's strengths and to develop its services while recognising 'the significant challenges that lie before us'.

The three-year strategy paper outlined Relate's aims to focus and align its services with strategies and commissioning plans 'to invest in early intervention and family support services to achieve better outcomes for children and their families'. This was to make an important contribution to the five Health and Social Care Trusts' remit to keep children safe. Jill Downing also explained that Relate aimed to align its services with the six 'high level outcomes' contained in the regional strategy published by the Office of the First Minister and Deputy First Minister, 'Our Children and Young People: Our Pledge: A 10 Year Strategy for Children and Young People in Northern Ireland'. She also emphasised the pivotal role of partnership:

Relate currently collaborates with an range of statutory, voluntary and community organisations to improve outcomes for families and children and we firmly believe that working in partnership provides a more holistic approach to achieving better outcomes for our clients.[51]

Addressing the conference, the Minister, Edwin Poots, MLA said:

Relate has changed and grown over 65 years because it has recognised the changes in society, and developed its range of services to help families of all shapes and sizes, when they need support.

Speaking at the 65th Anniversary dinner that same evening, the Minister, reflecting on the current landscape in health and social care said:

This is a time of great opportunity for organisations such as Relate. The Third Sector has consistently shown that it is able to quickly adapt to new and changing demands, to develop new or alternative services and ensure that the needs of Northern Ireland's population are met in the future.... I'm confident that you can continue to innovate to meet new demands, maintaining the positive impact that Relate's services role have in people's lives.

Launch of Annual Review

The following week, on 22 November 2012, as part of the organisation's 65th anniversary celebrations, Relate launched its Annual Review 2011/12 at the Belfast Metropolitan Arts Centre (The MAC) and called for increased access to psychological therapies at a time when Northern Ireland was still in the grip of recession.

Dave Murphy, Chief Executive of Relate speaking at the event said:

We know that people across Northern Ireland are finding it tough right now. Whenever we ask our counsellors what the biggest issues that relationships are facing, money worries, debt, family difficulties and lack of time together are always at the top of the list. We hope that by demonstrating the benefits of relationship counselling we can increase access to psychological therapies and earlier intervention services which are supported by additional resources from government and statutory health and social care agencies.

The Annual Review was launched by Sue Ramsey, MLA, Chairperson of the Northern Ireland Assembly's Health, Social Services and Public Safety Committee who remarked that Relate is assisting parents provide stable family environments which are so important for children's development and even if reconciliation is not possible Relate works with parents to reduce the stress and upset for all involved. She went on to say:

My Committee values the work carried out by counselling organisations such as Relate and the importance of people with relationship, emotional and mental health difficulties being able to access professional talking therapy services in a timely and cost effective manner. Access to such services, particularly on an early intervention basis, can also be more cost effective than prescribing medication to resolve these issues.

A Newer Counsellor's View of the Future

Jill Downing's speeches at both the 65th anniversary conference and dinner, a distillation of the Board of Trustees' view of Relate's current position and of its plans for the future, was very much a formal and public laying out of the organisation's wares. In a more informal setting, in an interview in November 2013, Elaine McCormick, a counsellor with most of her career still ahead of her, reflected on Relate Northern Ireland's role in the second decade of the twenty-first century and on areas for the future development of the organisation's services she would like to see taken forward.

Elaine's first thought was that Relate could penetrate the corporate world much more than it has done so far – in other words, that its services could be made more available, not just in the health trusts and in the public sector but also in the private sector, in large businesses in particular. 'Regardless of how strong you think your relationship is', she said, 'if you are in any kind of long-term relationship – and you are honest – it can be challenging at times'. In short, contented workers make much more productive employees. 'There's room for relationship work in big corporate organisations', she continued:

Employees there are just normal husbands, wives, partners…If you've got a healthy mind and you are in a good place emotionally, it just has a knock-on effect in all your relationships be it at home, at work, or driving down the road. If you are driving down the road and you are in a bad place and somebody suddenly pulls out in front of you, you are more likely to get out and knock his block off, if you are already angry about something else.

If employees are given the opportunity to talk problems through with a Relate counsellor, either alone or together as a couple, then all can benefit. For example, Elaine conducts counselling sessions on Wednesdays in an office tucked away in the corner of a business centre in Ballymena. She feels that the availability of Relate's services could be given a higher profile here in the business centre, in the shopping centre and generally round the town. 'The name's already there; people know what it is; and if I say I work for Relate they know what that is'. Elaine also feels that Relate's services could be marketed more strongly in schools and colleges to make younger people aware of what can be done for them.

'I absolutely love the work', Elaine declared more than once. She would like to be employed full-time as a counsellor by Relate, but at present that opportunity is not there.

Elaine had just been on a training course on how technology is likely to advance between now and the year 2020. The experience strengthened her view that a major challenge for Relate in the years to come is the impact of social media, that is, Facebook and the internet – 'this is a big one'. 'This is a big, big one because people are now presenting a perfect outward profile on Facebook: "Here I am; this is my family; these are my friends; I'm doing this; I'm doing that", but the reality can be quite different'. Connections are made with people they have never met. 'This is great for the opportunist', she said, 'so it's dangerous'. 'Of course the new technology has brought great benefits with it', she observed, 'Facebook has brought a lot of people together'. Chuckling she added: 'I suppose it's a great way of having affairs which are all the time happening', commenting that the statistic is that one in four in marriages or long-term relationships are having affairs, 'but I think it would be higher than that'. 'If you are at home on a Tuesday evening and your husband is out and you get a message on your laptop from an old flame on Facebook and you start typing away and it goes all downhill from there'. She continued:

I've had clients who have come for counselling having met and rekindled their romance on the internet – having gone to school together and dated when they were sixteen – and having left their spouses and got together. Then they come to counselling because they can't cope with the whole thing because it's not reality.

But, Elaine reflected, is electronic communication 'just another way of going to the pub and meeting people'? She had discovered that even texting on mobile phones could lead to unexpected aggravation. Arguments conducted by texting 'seem to lose reality'. A comment can be spoken in a tone that identifies it as a joke but when it is written down it can assume a more menacing character. Elaine gave an example of a couple sitting on the same settee communicating with each other solely by texting, the dialogue becoming steadily more abrasive, chipping away destructively at the relationship.

The dynamics of a relationship can be changed completely by a change in circumstances. Elaine McCormick encountered this frequently amongst couples in their thirties, married for a while and then the relationship has to adapt to parenthood. Another time of crisis, she finds, is when grown-up children leave home, leaving the roles of the parents not as rigidly defined as they had been. But the most striking change she has noticed in recent years, profoundly affecting relationships, is the recession. Redundancy alters the whole perception of yourself, because 'you were identified by your role in work and you got a buzz going to work' and, having lost your job, 'you're just plodding along, filling your day – it's back to the man in the car with underlying anger having an effect on everyone around you'.

Elaine noticed the impact in particular on those who seemed to be doing especially well before the world financial crash. 'I've had clients who had been worth a million on paper, with a hundred and more properties, and then had banks chasing them day and night – imagine the pressure that puts on a relationship'. 'If you've never had it then you never miss it; but these people were affluent, or seen as affluent, with a couple of children, spending lots of money – now they were feeling the pinch'. Since Elaine does a good deal of regular relationship counselling in Ballymena, she was able to observe at close quarters the impact of the collapse in 2012 of Patton Construction, a well-respected firm in business for a hundred years. She encountered couples where at the same time both husband and wife had lost their jobs in the firm. Speaking in November 2013, Elaine expected that the full impact of this high-profile collapse would not be felt for another six months, especially on those employed in the many small businesses which had been dependent on Patton Construction for regular orders. Those used to being taken out for a nice dinner had to adapt quickly to a lifestyle change, staying in instead to eat spaghetti Bolognese at home with a cheap bottle of wine. Many rather suddenly had to count every penny. How were they going to find £100 to take four children to the pantomime?

Relate Northern Ireland charges £35 a session. As a result of the economic downturn, Elaine McCormick has noticed a sharp increase in the number of clients seeking bursaries to cover the cost.

In this interview, without being prompted, Elaine McCormick observed repeatedly how much she loved her work as a relationship counsellor. This view was based not just on the interaction with clients but also on her respect for the organisation, its ethos and her colleagues. She observed about Relate Northern Ireland:

It's very professional; the processes are very well thought out; the training is excellent; I so appreciate the way the other counsellors are very supportive and very helpful; it's got a sensible approach and I do feel that if I put an opinion forward it will be listened to, if not acted upon – certainly you get the chance to say what things could be improved or maybe would work better, and what isn't working so well; it's very trustworthy and you are protected in a way.

To explain her last comment she emphasised the crucial importance of supervision. If Elaine was struggling with a client or a piece of work, her supervisor Marjorie Houston 'would be very helpful mentoring me and advising me'. Counsellors have a group session with each other for an hour and a half every month and if Elaine was wrestling with a particular issue other counsellors would prove themselves most helpful, for example, by photocopying relevant new material and leaving it in her pigeonhole. Each counsellor also has an hour-and-a-half one-to-one session with a supervisor every month. 'That's really, really helpful to the work especially if I am personally struggling with anything – it's pretty rigorous and intense, and I know that by the time my supervision's coming up I really need it'.

Elaine has availed of most of the training offered to her which has included courses on conducting sessions with perpetrators of domestic violence and on the impact of alcohol abuse and other addictions on relationships. She is also continually adding to her qualifications, including (at the time of writing) a Level 6 course in counselling supervision at the Northern Regional College in Ballymena, the fees for which she pays herself.

She finds that the experience she has acquired in relationship counselling has been of great help in her employment, travelling across Ulster to sell office equipment. It also rubs off beneficially on her own family dynamics – much appreciated by her husband and two daughters. Acknowledging 'my own demanding nature' she said she had learned at Relate 'about taking responsibility for yourself and your own actions'. Relationship counselling is at the heart of what Relate does. Often those coming to couple counselling have already 'moved on in their heads…it's not that we can wave a wand'. But perhaps it can be useful to obtain confirmation that the relationship was already over. Those coming for counselling must be there of their own free will, not 'just to tick a box'; otherwise, their time and the time of counsellors is wasted. However, many counsellors remember the sessions where people coming in the doors got the help they were desperately seeking. Elaine McCormick, when asked 'what has surprised you most about the work you do with clients?' responded:

I suppose what has been most surprising is how nearly you can get into the clients' shoes with them. It can a very, very close relationship…some of the things you hear are absolutely heart-breaking, traumatic…I am really honoured that people put enough faith in me to disclose information that they have maybe never told anybody before… that can be quite emotional, emotional for me as a counsellor as well as the clients.[52]

Conclusion

Clearly, the organisation now called Relate NI has made giant strides since its formation as the Northern Ireland Marriage Guidance Council in 1947, some sixty-five years ago. From its early steps in the fifties, financed on a shoestring, and growing in years of hope in the sixties, it had to cope through the traumatic years of the troubles, and extended its scope substantially in the eighties from marriage guidance to professional counselling on relationships of all kinds as the newly named Relate NI.

Recent years have seen further adaptations in response to changing circumstances, working in partnership with public and private sector partners to achieve better relationships between people in a rapidly changing environment, against the background of severe economic recession and new means of social exchange through technology and new social media.

The appointment of a new Chief Executive, the recruitment of a new cohort of Trustees, and the launch of the latest three-year Strategic Plan are clear indications that Relate NI is still successfully adapting to change, and looking forward with confidence to meeting the challenges of the future.

Notes

1   Relate NI Annual Report, 1997-98 and 1998-99
2   Interview with Bob Jordan, April 2008
3   Relate NI Annual Report, 1998-99
4   Interview with Gerald Clark, 9 May 2013
5   Interview with Julia Greer, 14 August 2013
6   Interview with Julia Greer, 14 August 2013
7   Interview with Gerald Clark, 9 May 2013
8   Interviews with Bob Jordan and Patricia Donnelly
9   Graham Brownlow, 'Business and Labour since 1945' in Liam Kennedy & Philip Ollerenshaw (eds), *Ulster Since 1600: Politics, Economy, and Society*, Oxford, 2013, pp. 298-300
10   Interview with Gerald Clark, 9 May 2013
11   Relate NI Annual Report, 1998-99
12   Interview with Julia Greer, 14 August 2013
13   Relate NI Annual Report, 1998-99, pp. 3-4
14   Interview with Gerald Clark, 9 May 2013
15   Relate NI News Release, 26 May 2005
16   Interview with Gerald Clark, 9 May 2013
17   Relate NI Annual Report, 1994-95
18   Interview with Rosemary Dunlop, 21 July 2012
19   Interview with Julia Greer, 14 August 2013
20   Relate NI Annual Report, 1994-95, p. 2
21   Interview with Patricia Donnelly, 2 March 2009
22   Relate NI Annual Report, 1994-95, p. 3
23   Interview with Patricia Donnelly, 2 March 2009
24   Relate NI Annual Report, 1994-95, p. 6
25   Relate NI Annual Report, 2002-3
26   Relate NI Annual Report, 1993-94, 1994-95, 2002-3, and 2010-11
27   Relate NI Annual Report, 2010-11
28   Relate NI Annual Report, 1999/2000
29   Interview with Gerald Clark, 9 May 2013
30   Relate NI Annual Report, 2005-6
31   Relate NI Annual Report, 2010-11
32   Interview with Gerald Clark, 9 May 2013
33   Relate NI Annual Report, 2005-6
34   Relate NI Annual Report, 2010-11
35   Relate NI Annual Reports, 2010-11 and 2011-12, and interview with Gerald Clark, 9 May 2013
36   Relate NI Annual Reports, 2010-11 and 2011-12
37   Interview with Gerald Clark, 9 May 2013
38   Relate NI Annual Reviews, 2010-11 and 2011-12
39   Interview with Derick Woods, 9 March 2009
40   Interviews with Gerald Clark, Bob Jordan, Derick Woods and Patricia Donnelly
41   Interview with Alan Elliott, 4 December 2012
42   Interview with Patricia Donnelly, 2 March 2009
43   Relate NI Annual Review, 2011-12; interview with Rosemary Dunlop, 21 July 2012; interview with Julia Greer, 14 August 2013
44   Relate NI Strategic Plan, 2012-2015, Introduction
45   Relate NI Annual Review, 2011-12, Chair's Message
46   Interview with Derick Woods, 9 March 2009
47   Relate NI Strategic Plan 2012-2015
48   Relate NI Annual Review, 2011-12
49   Relate NI Annual Review, 2011-2012
50   *Irish News*, 18 December 2012
51   Jill Downing's welcome speech to the 65th Anniversary Conference, November 2012
52   Interview with Elaine McCormick, 25 November 2013

relate
Northern Ireland